Ageing and Employment Policies: United States 2018

WORKING BETTER WITH AGE AND FIGHTING UNEQUAL AGEING

OECD
BETTER POLICIES FOR BETTER LIVES

Please cite this publication as:
OECD (2018), *Ageing and Employment Policies: United States 2018: Working Better with Age and Fighting Unequal Ageing*, OECD Publishing, Paris.
http://dx.doi.org/10.1787/9789264190115-en

ISBN 978-92-64-19009-2 (print)
ISBN 978-92-64-19011-5 (PDF)

Series: Ageing and Employment Policies
ISSN 1990-102X (print)
ISSN 1990-1011 (online)

Photo credits: Cover © iStockphoto.com/MirekP.

Corrigenda to OECD publications may be found on line at: *www.oecd.org/about/publishing/corrigenda.htm.*

Foreword

Given rapid population ageing, providing older people with better work incentives and choices is tremendously important to promote economic growth and to ensure the sustainability of public social expenditures. Therefore, in 2011 the OECD Employment, Labour and Social Affairs Committee decided to carry out a new series of policy reviews entitled *Working Better with Age* to encourage greater labour market participation at an older age, through the fostering of employability, job mobility and labour demand. It builds upon previous work that the OECD has conducted in this area in the Ageing and Employment Policies series, summarised in the Organisation's major cross-country report *Live Longer, Work Longer*, published in 2006.

In parallel to population ageing, inequality is also on the rise in many countries, growing from one generation to the next and old-age inequality will almost certainly increase among future retirees with higher risks of poverty among them. The OECD has stepped up its research efforts to identify ways of preventing this unequal ageing, recognising that a lower level of inequality is both an end in itself and a way of increasing countries' resilience to the consequences of demographic change. As a part of the OECD's inclusive growth agenda, the report *Preventing Ageing Unequally* published in October 2017 documents how disadvantages in education, employment and health lead to deeply entrenched inequalities. Effective and well-tailored policy action is needed to achieve greater inclusiveness in later life while making sure that pension spending does not become an unsustainable financial burden for society.

This report points to areas where changes or new reforms are needed in the United States to improve work incentives and employment opportunities at an older age as well as to promote more equal outcomes across older workers.

The report benefited greatly from discussions with experts, officials, employer federations, academics and businesses during an OECD mission to the United States in early 2017, including a kick-off seminar, and from comments to various drafts provided by several authorities and stakeholders.

This report is published under the responsibility of the Secretary-General of the OECD.

Acknowledgements

This report was prepared by two divisions of the Directorate of Employment, Labour and Social Affairs (ELS): the Skills and Employability (SAE) Division (Daniel Alonso Soto, Dana Blumin, Luke Haywood, Duncan MacDonald, Monica Meza-Essid, Veerle Miranda, Anne Saint-Martin and Anne Sonnet (Team leader)) and the Social Policy Division (SPD) (Hervé Boulhol (Team leader), Manuel Flores, Natalie Lagorce, Marius Lüske and Andrew Reilly). Editorial assistance was provided by Marlène Mohier and Lucy Hulett (ELS) as well as from Kate Lancaster (Public Affairs and Communications Directorate).

The report was prepared under the general supervision of Gabriela Ramos, OECD Chief of Staff and Sherpa to the G20. We are very grateful to Stefano Scarpetta (ELS Director), Mark Pearson (ELS Deputy Director), Monika Queisser (SPD Head) and Mark Keese (SAE Head) for their useful comments on various versions of the report.

We thankfully acknowledge the many suggestions provided by colleagues from AARP and the U.S. Department of Labor.

This report is published with the financial assistance of AARP. The views expressed in this report should not be taken to reflect the official position of AARP.

Table of contents

Acronyms and abbreviations **9**

Executive summary **13**

Chapter 1. Pathways out of the labour market for older workers in the United States **17**

Introduction 18
Old-age poverty risk in the United States and internationally 18
Main drivers of early retirement in the United States and other OECD countries 26
Direction for policy 44
Notes 51
References 52

Chapter 2. Supporting employers to retain and hire older workers in the United States **55**

Introduction 56
US labour market for older workers in an international perspective 56
Skills and productivity of older workers 63
Labour costs of older workers 81
Public policies and practices in firms towards older workers 85
Directions for policy 92
Notes 94
References 96
Annex 2.A. The labour market situation of older workers in the United States 101
Older workers most frequent occupations and industries 103

Chapter 3. Promoting the employability of United States workers throughout their working lives **105**

Introduction 106
From old to new skills: the importance of training 106
Employment programmes and older jobseekers 116
Working conditions 130
Flexible retirement 135
Directions for Policy 139
Notes 141
References 142

Tables

Table 3.1. Retirees have higher skills than the older unemployed but lower skills than the older employed 111
Table 3.2. Participation in adult education and training by age group, United States and OECD, 2012 115
Table 3.3. Few older workers served by WIA services 125

Table 3.4. Far fewer older workers than in younger age groups receive training provided by WIA programmes 125
Annex Table 2.A.1. Older workers scoreboard, 2006 and 2016, United States, OECD and High 5 and Low 5 countries 102
Annex Table 2.A.2. Older workers (aged 55 and over) versus prime-age workers (aged 25-54) in the United States by selected job and workplace characteristics, 2016 and 2006 104

Figures

Figure 1.1. Poverty is very widespread in the United States, especially among the over 75s 19
Figure 1.2. Inequality in the United States is higher and has been increasing faster between generations than in the OECD 20
Figure 1.3. Inequality in the United States is high among the population 65 and over 20
Figure 1.4. In the United States wealth is distributed more unevenly across age groups than in most other countries 21
Figure 1.5. Pension replacement rates are low in the United States 22
Figure 1.6. If voluntary pensions were more widespread old-age income would be less of a problem 24
Figure 1.7. Labour market exit ages are unevenly distributed in most countries 27
Figure 1.8. High-educated people tend to leave the labour market later 28
Figure 1.9. Many low-educated people enter retirement from inactivity or unemployment 29
Figure 1.10. Older workers are not equally represented across sectors 30
Figure 1.11. Many workers retire at age 62 in the United States 31
Figure 1.12. Health is an important retirement driver among men 35
Figure 1.13. Healthy women have a higher chance of remaining employed 36
Figure 1.14. Many older people with care responsibilities do not work 37
Figure 1.15. The relationship between caregiving and working differs across educational groups 38
Figure 1.16. Defined benefit pension plans provide less incentive to retire early than in the past 40
Figure 1.17. Combining pensions and work is uncommon in many OECD countries 41
Figure 1.18. In the United States working hours decline only slightly with age 43
Figure 1.19. High-educated people reduce their working hours more with age than the low-educated in most countries 44
Figure 2.1. The Great Recession coincided with large fall in hiring of older US workers 57
Figure 2.2. High employment rates of older US people but little change in recent years compared to other OECD countries, except after 65 58
Figure 2.3. US workers retire across a wider age range than workers in other large OECD countries 59
Figure 2.4. Large disparities in employment rates by education and disability status in the United States 61
Figure 2.5. Germany and the United States have greater wage dispersion for older workers 62
Figure 2.6. Federal employment protection law is very limited in the United States 63
Figure 2.7. Age differences in literacy are small in the United States 64
Figure 2.8. Age differences in numeracy are small in the United States 65
Figure 2.9. Older US workers with same education are no less literate than young 66
Figure 2.10. Older workers' lower numeracy skills also driven by lower educational outcomes 66
Figure 2.11. Differences in participation are not driving age differences in literacy and numeracy proficiency 68
Figure 2.12. Differences in reading, writing and numeracy tasks performed at work 70
Figure 2.13. In the United States, skill use of older workers declines less than in other countries, due to smaller educational differences across generations 71

Figure 2.14. Older workers use skills less because they have lower skill levels, but are over-proportionally found in occupations that use their skills efficiently 72
Figure 2.15. Worker age profiles differ across countries and occupations 74
Figure 2.16. Older workers more likely to supervise colleagues, have higher task discretion, use planning skills and influencing others more often 75
Figure 2.17. Older workers only see a small reduction in physical effort 76
Figure 2.18. Use of ICT at work 77
Figure 2.19. Modest age differences in ICT use except for 60-65 year olds 78
Figure 2.20. Population ageing is associated with the introduction of robots 79
Figure 2.21. Population ageing is not associated with lower growth rates 80
Figure 2.22. Moderate variation in average earnings over the life cycle 82
Figure 2.23. The United States has low levels of non-wage labour costs when employer health care is not included 83
Figure 3.1. Older workers of tomorrow will be better educated, except for men in Germany and the United States 107
Figure 3.2. Small skills gap by age in the United States but poor skills performance of future older workers 108
Figure 3.3. US older adults are among the most proficient in the use of ICT but US young adults among the least 109
Figure 3.4. US adults participate in education and training more than most OECD countries, but large discrepancies exist by employment status 114
Figure 3.5. Compared with other OECD countries, very little is spent on active labour market programmes and training 123
Figure 3.6. Above-average working conditions among older workers in the United States but far from reaching job quality levels in top OECD countries 132
Figure 3.7. Low prevalence of part-time work among older workers in the United States, 2016 137

Acronyms and abbreviations

AARP	American Association of Retired Persons
ADA	Americans with Disabilities Act
ADEA	Age Discrimination in Employment Act
AET	Adult education and training
AJC	American Job Centre
ALMP	Active Labour Market Programme
ATAA	Alternative Trade Adjustment Assistance
BLS	Bureau of Labor Statistics
CIPD	Chartered Institute of Personnel and Development
CTE	Career and Technical Education
CPS	Current Population Survey
DC	Defined Contribution
DEI	Disability Employment Initiative
DOL	Department of Labor
EEOC	Equal Employment Opportunity Commission
ELSA	English Longitudinal Study of Ageing
ETA	Employment and Training Administration
EPL	Employment Protection Legislation
ER	Employment Rate
ES	Employment Services
EU	European Union
EU-OSHA	European Agency for Safety and Health at Work
FTE	Full-Time Equivalent
FY	Fiscal Year
GDP	Gross Domestic Product
HRS	Health and Retirement Study
ICT	Information and Communications Tools
INQA	Initiative New Quality of Work

ISCO	International Standard Classification of Occupations
NAIRU	Non-Accelerating Inflation Rate of Unemployment
NGO	Non-Governmental Organisation
NRA	Normal Retirement Age
OAA	Older American Act
ODEP	Office of Disability Employment Policy
OECD	Organisation for Economic Co-operation and Development
OPM	Office of Personnel Management
OSH	Occupational Safety and Health
OSHA	Occupational Safety and Health Administration
PIAAC	Programme for the International Assessment of Adult Competencies
RFOA	Reasonable Factors Other than Age
RTAA	Reemployment Trade Adjustment Assistance
SCSEP	Senior Community Service Employment Program
SEWN	Strategic Early Warning Network
SHARE	Survey of Health and Retirement in Europe
SHRM	Society for Human Resource Management
SIPP	Survey of Income and Program Participation
SME	Small and Medium-sized Enterprises
TAA	Trade Adjustment Assistance
TAP	Technical Assistance Program
TIOW	Targeted Initiative for Older Workers
TRA	Trade Readjustment Allowance
TRIP	Transition-To-Retirement Pension
UI	Unemployment Insurance
USD	US dollars
VET	Vocational Education and Training
WIA	Workforce Investment Act
WIASRD	WIA State Annual Reports and Summaries
WIOA	Workforce Innovation and Opportunities Act

OECD country ISO codes

Country	Code	Country	Code
Australia	AUS	Korea	KOR
Austria	AUT	Latvia	LVA
Belgium	BEL	Luxembourg	LUX
Canada	CAN	Mexico	MEX
Chile	CHL	Netherlands	NLD
Czech Republic	CZE	New Zealand	NZL
Denmark	DNK	Norway	NOR
Estonia	EST	Poland	POL
Finland	FIN	Portugal	PRT
France	FRA	Slovak Republic	SVK
Germany	DEU	Slovenia	SVN
Greece	GRC	Spain	ESP
Hungary	HUN	Sweden	SWE
Iceland	ISL	Switzerland	CHE
Ireland	IRL	Turkey	TUR
Israel	ISR	United Kingdom	GBR
Italy	ITA	United States	USA
Japan	JPN		

Executive summary

In the United States, employment rates at older ages are comparatively high at 62% among 55-64 year-olds against 59% on average in OECD countries in 2016. However, there are large disparities across population groups. Early retirement remains a widespread phenomenon, especially among workers from vulnerable socio-economic backgrounds. Preventing old-age disparities in terms of employment outcomes and retirement income from widening is crucial. Poverty among older persons in the United States is already a challenge today, as more than 20% of those over 65 have incomes under the relative poverty line – defined as half of median disposable household income – compared to less than 13% on average in the OECD. Social Security and Supplemental Security Income provisions are set at low levels compared to other countries. Effective and well-tailored policy action is needed to achieve greater inclusiveness at old age. Further efforts should promote broader access to employment opportunities and foster longer and better working lives.

Promoting longer careers for all socio-economic groups is one way of reducing old-age poverty without putting additional strain on public finances. In the United States, like in many other OECD countries, life expectancy, working lives and the pathways out of the labour market vary substantially across socio-economic groups. Low-educated people tend to stop working earlier than their high-educated peers and they are far more likely to face long periods of unemployment or disability prior to retirement. In addition, poor health as a barrier to extended careers is more widespread among low-educated people.

The following actions can promote longer careers among all socio-economic groups and reduce old-age poverty:

- *Link the early and normal retirement ages to life expectancy, while considering distributional effects of possibly widening inequality in life expectancy.* Linking pension ages to life expectancy is becoming more common amongst OECD countries as a way to maintain the level of retirement income in a financially sustainable way. Financial sustainability is an important issue in the United States as well. When changes in life expectancy increase inequality across socio-economic groups such automatic links can be problematic. They may have regressive effects, which should be taken into account in order to design inclusive policies.
- *Provide easily understandable information, with a special focus on groups with poor financial literacy, on the impact of anticipating or postponing retirement on pension entitlements to promote well-informed choices between work and retirement.*
- *Increase the Supplemental Security Income level to help reduce the high levels of poverty amongst the older age groups.* Poverty levels for the over 75s, at more than twice those of the working-age population, need to be reduced. Increasing the means-tested component of the pension system is one way of addressing this

issue. The level of the old-age safety net is equal to 17% of the average gross wage compared to 22% on average in the OECD. Bringing the level to the OECD average would therefore imply a raise of 29%.

- *Increase occupational pension coverage among current workers, for instance through auto-enrolment in pension plans.* Around half of workers are not covered by any private pension as a supplement to social security. Introducing auto-enrolment would increase the number of covered workers, as shown in New Zealand and the United Kingdom, thereby increasing future pension entitlements.
- *Design specific training programmes targeting low-skilled workers.* These programmes should, among other things, facilitate job change in mid-career and at an older age. While continued training is needed to ensure upskilling, especially in times of quick technological change, many low-educated workers only have limited access to training opportunities. Specific training programmes targeting low-educated workers should be offered to ensure that training is accessible to workers from all educational groups.
- *Increase opportunities for more flexibility in work arrangements and retirement entry, e.g. teleworking, part-time work and combining work and pensions.* Flexible work arrangements provide workers with more choice and more opportunities to shape the last years of their working careers and retirement entry according to their wishes.
- *Improve health among all workers,* including older workers, through preventive measures and better access to health care services.

With relatively little employment protection and no mandatory retirement age, US firms' willingness to hire and retain older workers is key to ensuring older workers have access to and retain good jobs. Employers' attitudes are central. While the United States has pioneered anti-age discrimination, coverage has not been extended to all workers so far. The skill-set of older workers in the United States is relatively good, both with respect to younger workers and older workers in other large OECD countries. While older workers perform less well on information-processing tasks, they have interpersonal skills that are called upon to plan, supervise, and influence others. This highlights the importance of mobility across tasks, jobs and occupations. Occupational mobility is higher in the United States than in other large OECD countries but changes to health insurance rules (such as repealing the Affordable Care Act) risk creating barriers to job mobility of older workers. Non-wage costs continue to create a disincentive to hire older workers, especially the higher costs for health insurance of older workers.

The following actions could support firms in hiring and retaining older workers:

- *Expand the federal age-based anti-discrimination law to cover all workers in all firms.* Protection under the Age Discrimination in Employment Act (ADEA) should be extended to people of any age rather than to just those aged 40 and over. The exemption of smaller companies should also be reconsidered. The 2000 EU directive concerning age discrimination extends protection to people of all ages and in all firms. It ought to be considered whether to extend the coverage of the ADEA to cases where discrimination is based on more than one characteristic (e.g. both age and gender).

- *Make anti-discrimination legislation more easily enforceable for workers.* Compared to other OECD countries with greater employment protection legislation, the role of anti-discrimination legislation is greater in the United States. Removing barriers to legal expertise and counsel are thus important for all workers to benefit from the same protection.
- *Continue and expand the Disability Employment Initiative (DEI).* Conditional on a positive evaluation of the DEI, this pilot programme should be rolled out also in currently non-participating US states.
- *Eliminate the Medicare as a second-payer rule.* Extending the advantage of public health-care to employed individuals would reduce labour costs for older workers. While Medicare expenses would increase, additional revenues from higher income taxes may be generated at a similar magnitude as a result of increased work incentives for older workers.
- *Avoid job lock for workers with pre-existing health conditions.* Avoid changes to rules governing health insurance that may discourage workers with pre-existing health conditions from changing jobs.
- *Support the business case for promoting longer and better working lives.* The outreach and educational activities of the Equal Employment Opportunity Commission should be intensified. Key stakeholders in the United States, including NGOs, should identify firms' best policies to retain, retrain, and recruit older workers and learn from good practices implemented in other OECD countries.
- *Encourage research on firms' decisions of employing older workers.* There is little research on determinants of labour demand for older workers. Making linked employer-employee data available on a federal scale would enable more focused research.

In addition to strengthened economic incentives and age-friendly employer practices, employability and willingness to stay on are prerequisites for longer working lives. The employability of older workers depends importantly on three key factors: up-to-date skills; ready access to employment services; and good working conditions. Older adults in the United States are relatively highly educated, skilled and among the most frequent participants in training in the OECD. However, the United States faces large disparities among older adults in education, access to training and quality employment services as well as in working conditions.

The following measures can improve the employability of older workers:

- *Take concerted action to boost basic skills of workers throughout their working lives and tackle inequalities accumulated by those with poor basic skills.* Without action, the United States will fall further behind other countries which could harm the prospects of future generations of older workers as well as reinforce the persistence of inequalities at an older age.
- *Improve access to employment and training programmes for older jobseekers and the quality of services received.* It is not clear whether the federally-funded employment programmes help older jobseekers to find jobs. The evaluation of the Senior Community Service Employment Program (SCSEP) was a first step. Further impact evaluation of employment and training programmes on employment outcomes of older jobseekers is needed.

- *Enhance opportunities for phased retirement.* Phased retirement is uncommon in the United States. Low-paid workers planning to phase into retirement confront financial obstacles. Moreover, existing regulations may discourage employers from implementing phased retirement programmes. More research is needed to help guide policy choices. As a first step, the problems encountered in deploying the federal phased retirement programme should be analysed. In addition, lessons can be learned from flexible retirement options in other OECD countries.
- *Encourage and assist employers to enhance working conditions throughout working lives.* Employers should be encouraged to set up websites with information on best practices and tools to assess their own performance as age-friendly employers. The European Healthy Workplaces campaigns and the Healthy Workplaces Good Practice Awards can serve as an example.
- *Design and implement experience-rating programmes* that effectively motivate employers to improve safety and expand the experience rating of workers' compensation insurance to smaller firms. In the absence of such an expansion, the Occupational Safety and Health Administration (OSHA) should target its enforcement efforts toward smaller firms.

Chapter 1.

Pathways out of the labour market for older workers in the United States

Poverty rates are very high in the United States compared to other OECD countries, especially among older people. Supporting longer careers for all socio-economic groups is one way of reducing old-age poverty without putting additional strain on the fiscal sustainability of pension systems. In the United States, like in many other OECD countries, working lives and the pathways out of the labour market vary substantially across socio-economic groups, however. Low-educated people tend to stop working earlier than their high-educated peers and they are far more likely to face periods of unemployment or disability prior to retirement. In addition, bad health as a barrier to extended careers is more widespread among low-educated people. Tackling the main drivers of early retirement involves eliminating disincentives to work in the pension system, preventing health problems among all workers, including among older workers, and increasing the flexibility of labour market exits through well-tailored policy intervention.

The statistical data for Israel are supplied by and under the responsibility of the relevant Israeli authorities. The use of such data by the OECD is without prejudice to the status of the Golan Heights, East Jerusalem and Israeli settlements in the West Bank under the terms of international law.

Introduction

The financial sustainability of pension systems has become a major concern in OECD countries. Population ageing is gathering momentum and progressing at a fast pace in many countries, and the share of retirees in the population is steadily growing. The United States is not exempt from this trend, yet the changes are taking place more slowly than in other OECD countries. The so-called old-age dependency ratio - defined as the number of people aged 65 and over for every 100 people of working age - in the United States is currently below the OECD average (25 against 28) and it is expected to increase less strongly over the next decades, by 60% by 2050 against 90% in OECD countries (OECD, 2017[1]).

While life expectancy at the age of 65 has substantially increased since the 1970s in the OECD, the average effective age of labour market exit (or effective age of retirement) plummeted by about 5.5 years between 1970 and the early 2000s. Only recently have effective labour market exit ages started to rise again – in many countries at least partly as the result of pension reforms. In the United States, the rising normal retirement age, higher average educational attainment among older workers and changing family patterns are factors that contributed to the trend reversal. Yet, effective labour market exit ages across the OECD are still considerably lower today than 45 years ago, adding to the financial pressure on pension systems.

This chapter examines the pathways that are available and commonly used to exit the labour market within the United States and in other OECD countries. A comparison and discussion of the main retirement drivers between the United States and a set of European countries is also provided. Conclusions are then given at the end of the chapter. Initially, however, the chapter begins by setting the scene of the current situation of older age groups within the United States in comparison to other OECD countries, to help put the main content of the chapter into context.

Old-age poverty risk in the United States and internationally

Older people in the United States are more strongly exposed to poverty risks than their peers in most other OECD countries, particularly for those aged over 75, as their poverty rate is 26% in the United States compared to 14% in the OECD (Figure 1.1). Poverty rates have increased over time amongst the working age population, particularly for those younger than age 50, whilst people over 65 have seen a steady decline since the mid-1980s. Even so, people over 75 are still the group with the highest overall poverty risk and are far more likely to have incomes under the poverty line than younger age groups.

Figure 1.1. Poverty is very widespread in the United States, especially among the over 75s

Poverty rates by age group, United States

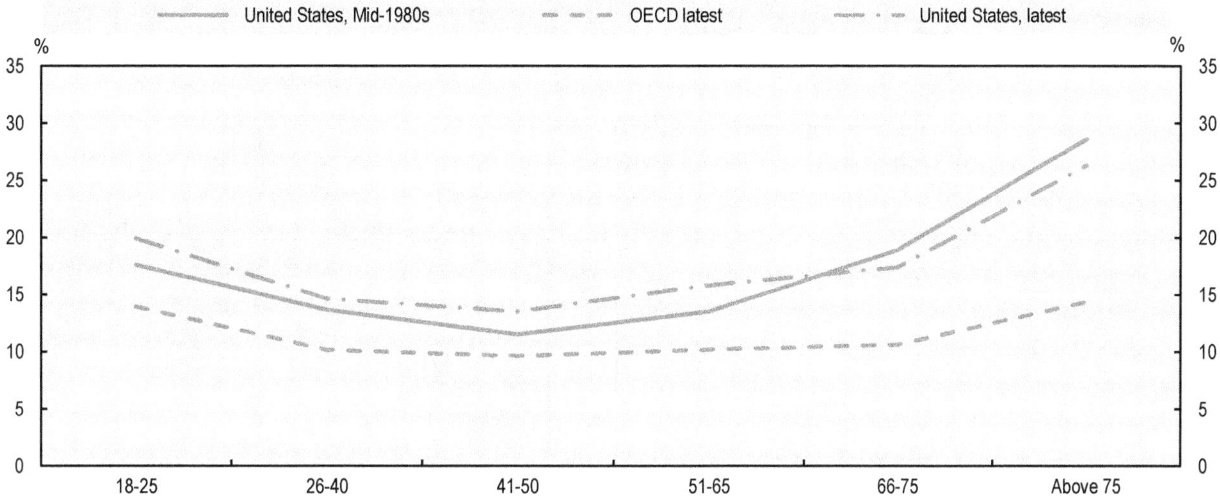

Source: *OECD Income Distribution Database*, www.oecd.org/social/income-distribution-database.htm.

StatLink http://dx.doi.org/10.1787/888933643540

One of the reasons for the poverty problem is that inequality in the United States is high and has been increasing from one generation to the next at a faster pace than on average across OECD countries (Figure 1.2). Gini coefficients by age and birth decade show that income inequality decreases slightly in early adulthood, for people in their 20s, as young adults enter the labour market; it then increases during working life and finally decreases after the retirement age. This pattern has been common across generations in the United States (Panel A) and in the OECD (Panel B). Strikingly, income inequality at the same age has been shifting up from one generation to the next in the United States. In the OECD, such an increase could also be observed for about two-thirds of countries (OECD, 2017[2]) but it has been less pronounced than in the United States. Younger generations – born in the 1970s or later – tend to have similar levels of age-specific income inequality at early stages of their working life.

Figure 1.2. Inequality in the United States is higher and has been increasing faster between generations than in the OECD

Gini coefficients by five-year age groups and birth decade

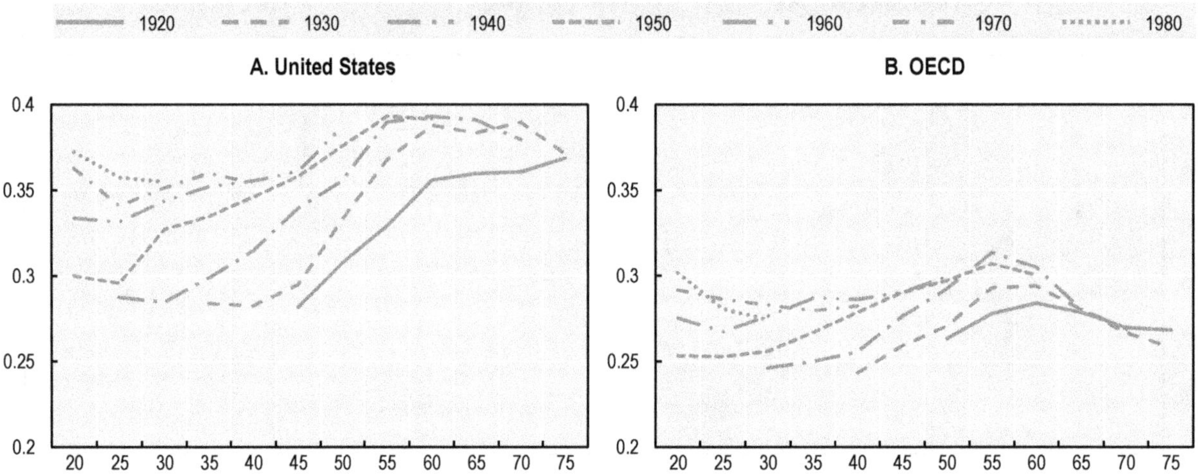

Source: OECD calculations based on the *Luxembourg Income Study Database*, http://www.lisdatacenter.org/our-data/lis-database/.

StatLink http://dx.doi.org/10.1787/888933643559

Also among the 65+ inequality levels are high in the United States compared to other OECD countries (Figure 1.3). The Gini coefficient in the United States (0.40) is almost twice as large as the one in Norway (0.22), one of the least unequal countries in the OECD. If the trend of rising inequality across generations continues this may also affect older people future retirees in the United States will become even more unequal than current retirees.

Figure 1.3. Inequality in the United States is high among the population 65 and over

Gini coefficient for the population aged 65 and older, 2014 or latest available[a]

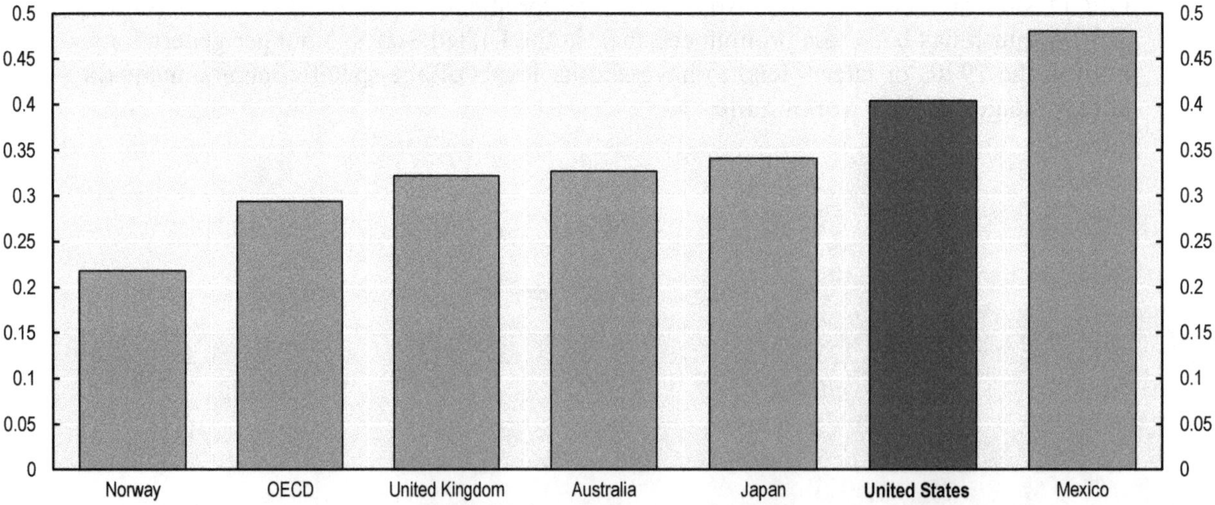

a) 2012 for Norway and 2013 for Japan, Mexico and the United Kingdom.
Source: *OECD Income Distribution Database*, www.oecd.org/social/income-distribution-database.htm.

StatLink http://dx.doi.org/10.1787/888933643578

Wealth, as a complement to income, also affects households' capacity to deal with negative economic shocks. It is a critical factor for the accumulation of inequality over the life course, given that wealth inequality is typically much larger than income inequality (Murtin and Mira d'Ercole, 2015[3]). Due to substantial data limitations, a thorough analysis of wealth disparities across cohorts is unfortunately not possible. Available data, however, do allow comparing average wealth across age groups – who thus belong to different cohorts – for a recent period for 19 OECD countries.

At a given point in time, older individuals are wealthier than their younger peers. On average across 19 OECD countries, wealth in 2010 was 4.4 times higher among the 55-64 year-olds, where the wealth level peaked, than among the 16-34 year-olds (Figure 1.4). The age-wealth relationship was similar in a number of developed countries, including Australia, Canada and the United Kingdom. The United States showed a steeper age pattern in wealth than the average. For instance, the peak was reached at later ages (65-74) and the ratio between older and younger age groups was substantially higher (14.1). The increase across age suggests that, in addition to receiving bequests and *intervivo* transfers, households use a substantial part of their income to build up wealth during their working life, hence replicating patterns of income inequality in the wealth distribution. During retirement, average wealth declines due to the loss of labour earnings in old age, uninsured expenditures (e.g. health and long-term care costs) and due to monetary transfers to children and other relatives. In the United States, wealth among the 75+ was still about 40% higher than among the total population in 2010.[1]

Figure 1.4. In the United States wealth is distributed more unevenly across age groups than in most other countries

Mean household net wealth in different age groups relative to population average, 2010 or latest available

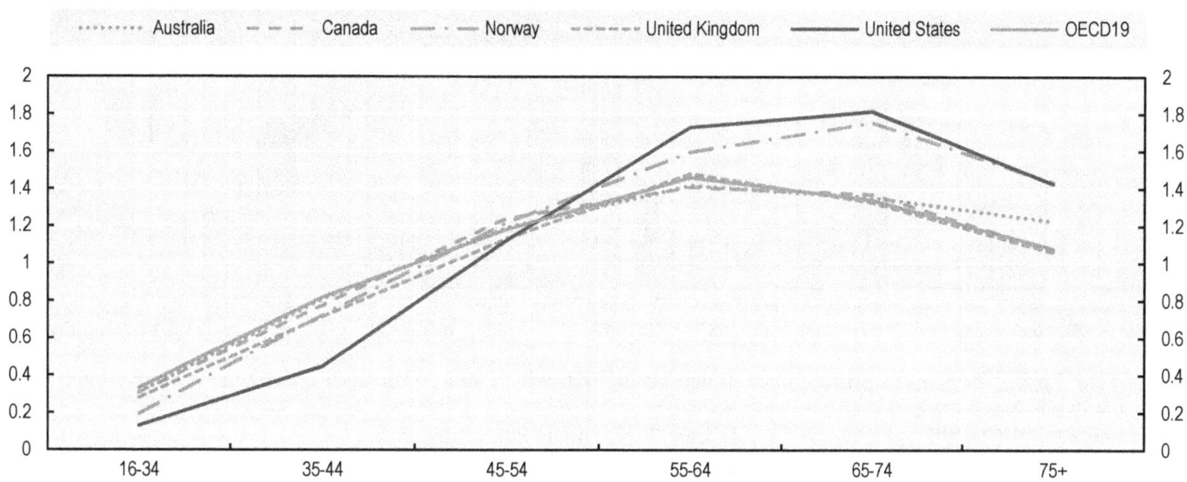

Note: OECD19 is an unweighted average of the 19 OECD countries with available data. Data refer to 2010 for the 13 European countries and the United States, to 2011 for Chile, to 2012 for Australia, Canada and the United Kingdom and 2013 for Korea.

Source: *OECD Wealth Distribution Database* http://stats.oecd.org/Index.aspx?DataSetCode=WEALTH.

StatLink http://dx.doi.org/10.1787/888933643597

A key component of the financial situation amongst the older age groups is their pension entitlement, whether from mandatory or voluntary schemes. The pension system in the United States has three components, each of which plays a different role (Box 1.1).

One explanation of the high relative poverty – defined as 50% of median household disposable income - and inequality levels in the United States can be found in the pension promise from the mandatory Social Security and Supplemental Security Income schemes. Even with a full career from age 20 to retirement age, based on OECD pension models, the gross replacement rate at the low earnings levels (50% of average earnings) will be under 50% of previous earnings in the United States, which is very low in international comparison (OECD, 2017[1])). That is, retirees with low past earnings in the United States, even after a 47-year career, will have a pension lower than one-quarter of average earnings, generating a high risk of poverty. Although these are projections for future retirees, they are also relevant to today's retirees in the United States as there has been minimal reform to the pension system over the last few decades.

These low pension replacement rates in the United States are not just confined to low income earners, but are extended across higher earnings levels unless retirees dispose of additional non-mandatory pension components. The United States ranks as a country with one of the lowest replacement rates from mandatory schemes across the OECD (Figure 1.5).

Figure 1.5. Pension replacement rates are low in the United States

Future net replacement rates for full career workers as a proportion of earnings for selected OECD countries

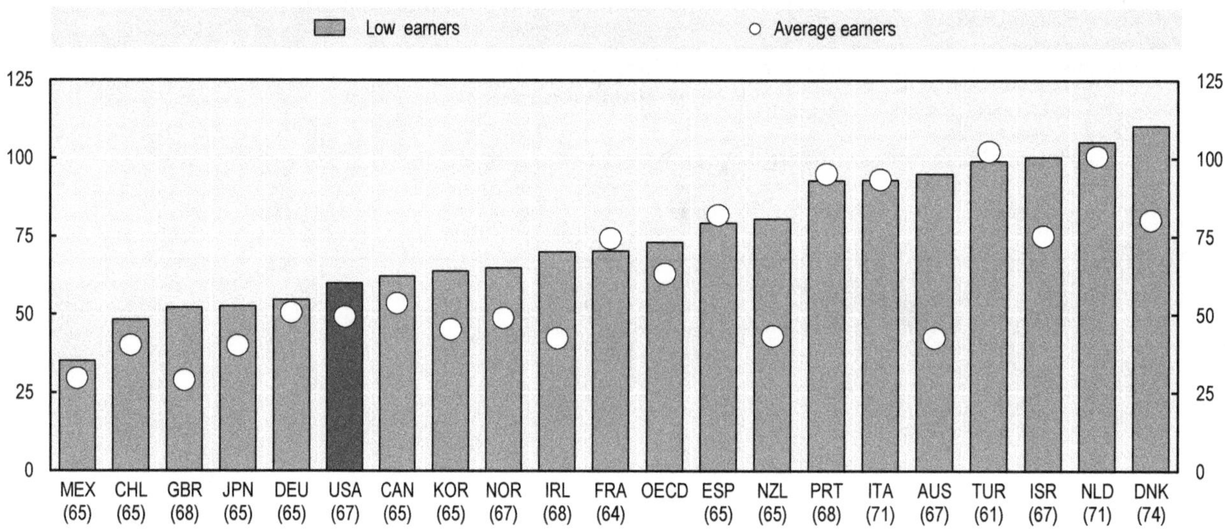

Note: Labour market entry is assumed at age 20 in 2016 with a full career until the normal retirement age (shown in brackets).

Source: (OECD, 2017[1]), *Pensions at a Glance 2017*, OECD Publishing, Paris.

StatLink http://dx.doi.org/10.1787/888933643616

Box 1.1. Pension system in the United States

The pension system contains three separate components: Social Security, Supplemental Security Income and private pensions.

The normal retirement age (NRA) – the age at which eligible for full Social Security benefits - is currently 66 years and four months for workers aged 62 in 2018, and will increase to 67 years for workers aged 62 in 2022. It is possible to retire early at age 62, subject to an actuarial reduction. For each year of retirement before the normal age, the benefit is reduced by 6.67%. However, after three years, the reduction falls to 5%. This applies to retirees with a NRA of over 65. Initial receipt of the pension can be deferred until after NRA, and credit is given for deferment up to age 70. The actuarial increment is 8% for each year deferred.

The earnings-related **Social Security** pension benefit requires a minimum of 10 years of contributions to be eligible. The formula for calculating the benefit is progressive with the first USD 896 a month of relevant earnings attracting a 90% replacement rate. The band of earnings between USD 896 and USD 5 399 a month is replaced at 32% with earnings up to USD 10 725 replaced at 15%.

Earlier years' earnings are revalued up to the year in which the recipient reaches age 60 in line with growth in economy-wide average earnings. The basic benefit is computed for payment at age 62 years. Thereafter, the basic benefit is adjusted in line with price increases. The benefit is based on the career average earnings for the 35 highest years of earnings, after revaluing, including years with zero earnings if needed to total 35 years. Pensions in payment are adjusted in line with price increases.

It is possible to combine work and pension receipt subject to an earnings test. For beneficiaries who are receiving benefits in a year before the year they reach their NRA, the pension is reduced by 50% of earnings in excess of USD 17 040. Benefits are reduced by USD 1 for every USD 3 of earnings above USD 45 360 in the year the insured reaches the full retirement age. Beginning the month the insured reaches the full retirement age, there is no earnings test.

There is a means-tested benefit for the elderly, known as **Supplemental Security Income**. Individuals aged 65 or older without an eligible spouse can be eligible for up to USD 9 000 a year depending on assets and other income. The maximum benefit rate for cases where both members of a couple are eligible is USD 13 500 (50% higher than the rate for singles). These benefit rates are equivalent to around 17% and 26% of the estimated national average wage index for 2016, respectively. Individual states and the District of Columbia can supplement the federally determined minimum. The maximum benefit is indexed to price increases.

The final component is **private pensions** which are entirely voluntary with no obligation for employees or employers to make contributions. In the United States, 47% of workers are covered by such a scheme (OECD, 2015[41]). These are primarily defined contribution plans for new employees, with an assumed contribution rate of 9%.

The results shown in Figure 1.5 are based solely on the mandatory pension schemes that exist for private sector workers, but a number of countries, including the United States, have highly developed private savings schemes in the form of voluntary pensions. The rules for these schemes clearly differ between countries, in terms of whether they are auto-enrolment, such as in New Zealand or the United Kingdom or purely voluntary, such as Germany and Ireland, whether incentives are offered to contribute and indeed the level of contribution.

Within the OECD there are eight countries that have funded private pension schemes with over 40% of those aged 15-64 covered: Belgium, Canada, Germany, Ireland, Japan, New Zealand, the United Kingdom and the United States. In two countries, Canada and Japan, a defined benefit scheme has been modelled, with the other six countries having a defined contribution scheme, with contribution rates varying between 4% and 10%. The impact on net replacement rates of including these schemes differs across countries (Figure 1.6).

Figure 1.6. If voluntary pensions were more widespread old-age income would be less of a problem

Future net replacement rates for full career workers from mandatory and voluntary pensions

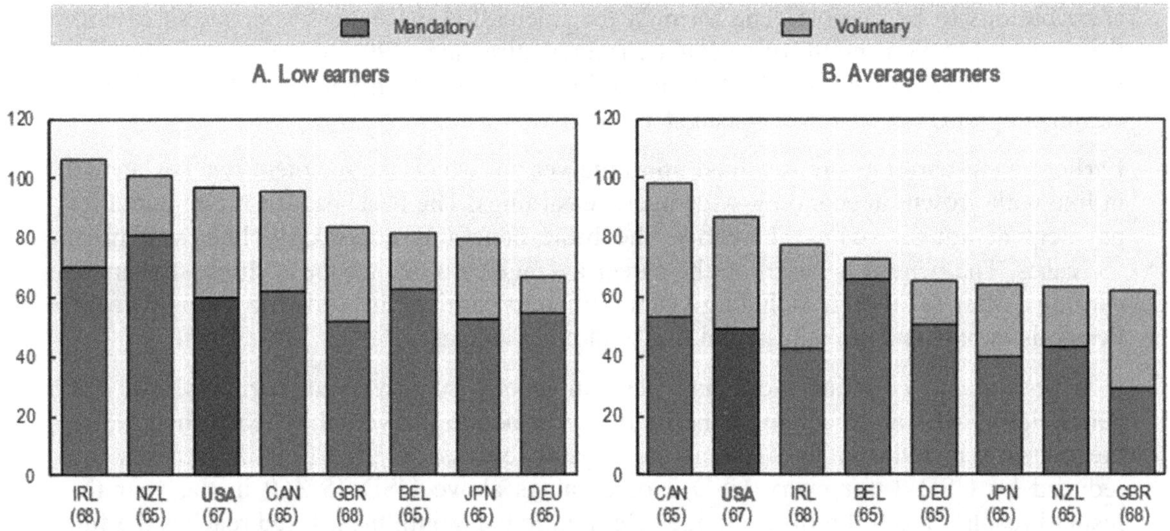

Source: OECD (2017), *Pensions at a Glance 2017*, OECD Publishing, Paris.

StatLink http://dx.doi.org/10.1787/888933643635

For average earners the replacement rate for the voluntary schemes in Canada, Ireland and the United States is only slightly less than that from the mandatory component and it is larger in the United Kingdom. In these four countries full career workers would in fact approximately double their pensions if they contributed to the voluntary scheme throughout their working lives. For low earners the impact is slightly lower, at around a 50% increase in Canada and Ireland, 60% in the United Kingdom and 70% in the United States. Therefore if low earners were able to contribute to the voluntary scheme for a full career in the United States old-age poverty would no longer be an issue for them.

These replacement rates represent the best case scenario when everyone has a full career with full contribution periods to both the mandatory social security pension and to a voluntary private pension. However, for this to be the case the coverage rate would have to be close to 100%. This is certainly not the case for the United States as only 47% of workers are covered. By comparison the auto-enrolment scheme in New Zealand covers 75% of those aged 15 to 64, with the voluntary scheme in Germany also covering over 70%.

While the level of coverage from voluntary pensions is relatively high in international comparison, differences in the coverage level by age and income are huge. Poterba (2014[5]) reports that only 13% of the lower half of the income distribution receives (occupational and personal) private pensions in the United States compared to over 50% of the upper half. Also only 20% of younger employees, aged 20-24, are contributing, compared to 70% of those aged 55-64 (Antolín, 2008[6]). Although coverage tends to increase with age in all OECD countries, it generally falls back for those aged 55-64. Uniquely in the United States the upward trajectory continues to the older worker age group.

According to Dushi et al. (2017[7]) defined contribution coverage levels barely increased between 2006 and 2012, going from 49% of full-time wage and salary workers aged 25-59 in 2006 to 52% in 2012. Starting from only 14% and 26%, coverage improved most for those at the lowest earnings levels, going up by 3.5 and 4.5 percentage points for the 1st and 2nd income deciles, respectively. Despite these increases the level of coverage for the bottom two deciles remains well below the levels for all other income deciles, the top decile earners are the best covered at a rate of 82%.

The differences in voluntary pension coverage levels by age group and income level imply disparities across ethnic groups. The proportion of White employees covered by an occupational pension is higher than that of African Americans and Asians, and much higher than that of the Latino population (Rhee, 2013[8]). Although these statistics do not control for other characteristics correlated with ethnicity, such as education and income, amongst the 25-64 year-old employees only 38% of those classified as Latino have an employer offering a sponsored retirement plan. By contrast 54% of African Americans or Asians and 62% of White employees have such an employer.

This difference is even more significant when limited to private sector employees with African Americans and Asians being 15% and 13%, respectively, less likely than Whites to have access to an employer sponsored retirement plan. For Latinos this discrepancy trebles to being 42% less likely than White employees to be offered such a scheme. However, the level of take-up is relatively consistent across the ethnic subgroups, ranging between 78% and 87%, suggesting that if employers of Latino workers in particular were to offer a retirement plan then there would be less disparity in coverage levels.

These coverage differences are not a recent phenomenon, and they translate into ethnic differences in accumulated pension savings for those approaching retirement. For heads of household aged 55-64, the total pension assets are, on average, three times as high if the head is White compared to non-White, with the African American head subgroup being less than one-sixth that of a White head household (Rhee, 2013[8]). When looking at median figures, White households are four times that of non-White households for the 55-64 age groups, at USD 120 000 and USD 30 000, respectively.

In sum, long-term inequality, variable voluntary pension coverage and low replacement rates from mandatory pensions all contribute to the old-age poverty problem in the United States. Pension entitlements dictate the level of poverty as they are often the main source of income after retirement. The level of these pensions directly depends on workers' career paths during their working life and the age at which they exit the labour market. The following section focuses on labour market patterns among older workers, recognising that employment outcomes and poverty at older ages are narrowly intertwined.

Main drivers of early retirement in the United States and other OECD countries

Extending working lives beyond their current levels could considerably alleviate the financial pressure on pension systems and obviate restrictive measures, such as benefit cuts, that bear the risk of increasing old-age poverty. Life expectancy at birth increased by almost 3.5 years across OECD countries between 2000 and 2015 and much of these increases have led to additional lifetime spent in good health, i.e. without disability. (OECD, 2017[2]). Providing incentives for people to spend some of these additional healthy life years in work is a frequently formulated policy objective because employment rates fall much more steeply with age than can be explained by health factors (OECD, 2017[2]).

Average life expectancies and *average* labour market exit ages hide substantial disparities across population subgroups, however. While some workers are able to work until older ages, others are not. These differences need to be taken into account in order to design effective, inclusive and politically sustainable policy measures to support longer working lives.

Labour market exit patterns in the United States and internationally

In the United States, average effective labour market exit ages are higher than in many other OECD countries (Figure 1.7), exceeding 66 years for men (Panel A) and 65 years for women (Panel B) in 2016. While these already high levels may leave only limited scope for further working life extensions on average, labour market exit ages are unevenly distributed. Both late labour market withdrawals and early exits are common. Even the number of workers who leave the labour market before age 62, when Social Security benefits become available, is far from negligible. Targeted policy measures have the potential to reduce the share of workers who exit the labour market too early to secure sufficient incomes at older ages.

Employment rates among 65-69 year-olds are higher in the United States (31% in 2016) than in most other OECD countries (25% on average), indicating that many people work beyond normal retirement age. Only seven OECD countries, including Iceland, Japan and Korea, report higher employment rates in this age-group than the United States. In most OECD countries, especially in Europe, employment rates among 65-69 year-olds are substantially lower; in the European Union only 15% of men in this age group work. While further employment increases at older ages are possible, the international experience on how to achieve high employment rates among 65-69 year-olds is very limited.

Figure 1.7. Labour market exit ages are unevenly distributed in most countries

Lowest tercile, mean and highest tercile of effective labour market exit ages, 2016

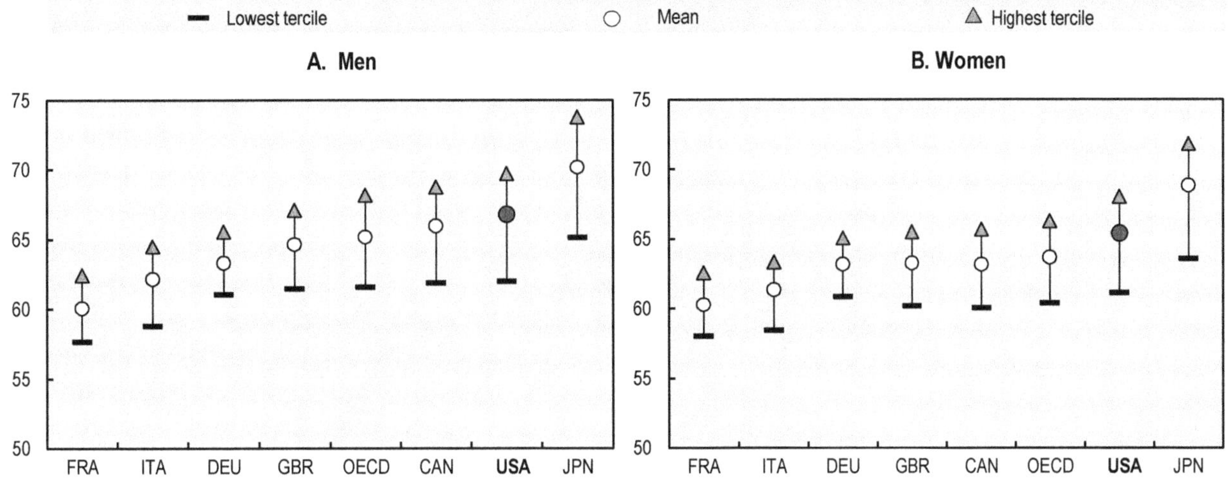

Note: The OECD average does not include Australia, Estonia, Finland, Hungary, Iceland, Norway and Sweden.
Source: OECD estimates based on Labour Force Statistics.

StatLink http://dx.doi.org/10.1787/888933643654

Socio-economic and gender differences

Withdrawing early from the labour market usually reduces pension rights and entails a financial penalty. As a consequence, low-wage workers who retire early face higher risks of old-age poverty. Workers' socio-economic backgrounds are key drivers of their labour force participation at older ages (Figure 1.8). While highly-educated people leave the labour market late in the United States – their average age of effective labour market withdrawal exceeds 68.5 years for men and 66 years for women – other educational groups exit several years earlier. Especially women in the lowest education category often leave the labour market years before reaching full retirement age. Similar patterns can be found in many other OECD countries.

Understanding under which circumstances and why workers from different socio-economic backgrounds leave the labour market is instrumental to ensuring that longer careers and adequate pension levels are accessible to everyone. Several factors can help explain why highly educated workers retire later in most countries. On average, the high-educated invest more time and resources in building up their human capital and start working later than their lower-educated peers; as a result, they often benefit from better working conditions and have spent shorter periods in employment than low-educated workers of the same age, who typically started their working lives very early. It is physically easier for high-educated workers with good job conditions and shorter career histories to stay on their jobs, which is one of the reasons why they retire later.

In addition, highly educated people tend to earn higher wages and forgo larger sums than their low-educated peers when they retire early and stop receiving their salaries. In some cases, low-income workers earn wages that are only slightly above old-age safety net provisions and the financial incentives to work are reduced. On average across OECD countries, pension replacement rates are higher for low- than for high-income earners, implying that high-income earners forgo more money when they retire not only in absolute but also in relative terms.

Figure 1.8. High-educated people tend to leave the labour market later

Average effective age of labour market withdrawal in OECD countries, by educational attainment, 2016

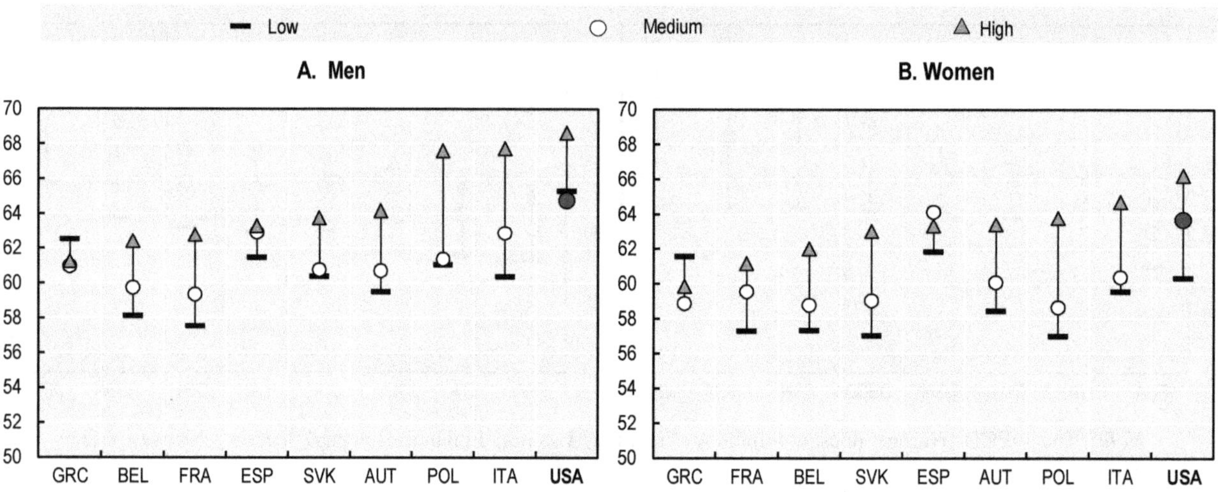

Note: Levels of educational attainment are defined in accordance with the International Standard Classification of Education (ISCED): low education (ISCED 0–2), medium education (ISCED 3–4), and high education (ISCED 5–6).

Source: OECD estimates. Labour market exit age data are based on the results of national labour force surveys and the European Union Labour Force Survey.

StatLink http://dx.doi.org/10.1787/888933643673

On the labour demand side, employers are typically more inclined to retain high-educated older workers with very specialised job skills who are difficult to replace (see Chapter 2). More training opportunities are available to high-educated older workers than to their low-educated peers, exacerbating job prospect disparities (see Chapter 3).

There are exceptions to this typical education gap, however. In Greece, low-educated men and women leave the labour market later than their peers with higher educational attainment. This unusual pattern may be driven by the fact that low-educated population groups tend to have low income levels and may not be able to afford retirement at younger ages.

In addition to employment patterns, the typical exit paths out of the labour market differ across socio-economic groups (Figure 1.9). The vast majority of men with high educational attainment transits directly from employment to retirement in both the United States (about 80%) and European countries (about 85%). Among the low-educated, the share is lower, at about 50%. Alternative pathways into retirement, e.g. unemployment and spells of inactivity due to sickness, are much more common among the low-educated.

Gender differences are striking. Many women self-define as inactive for reasons other than health – sometimes because they take care of household chores – prior to retirement, while the corresponding share among men is low. Especially among low-educated women inactivity is widespread, much more than among their high-educated peers. Overall, the share of low-educated women who report a period of inactivity just before retirement, either due to sickness or other reasons, exceeds 60% both in the United States and European countries.

Figure 1.9. Many low-educated people enter retirement from inactivity or unemployment

Last labour force status before retirement by education level and gender in the United States and European countries, 2014/2015

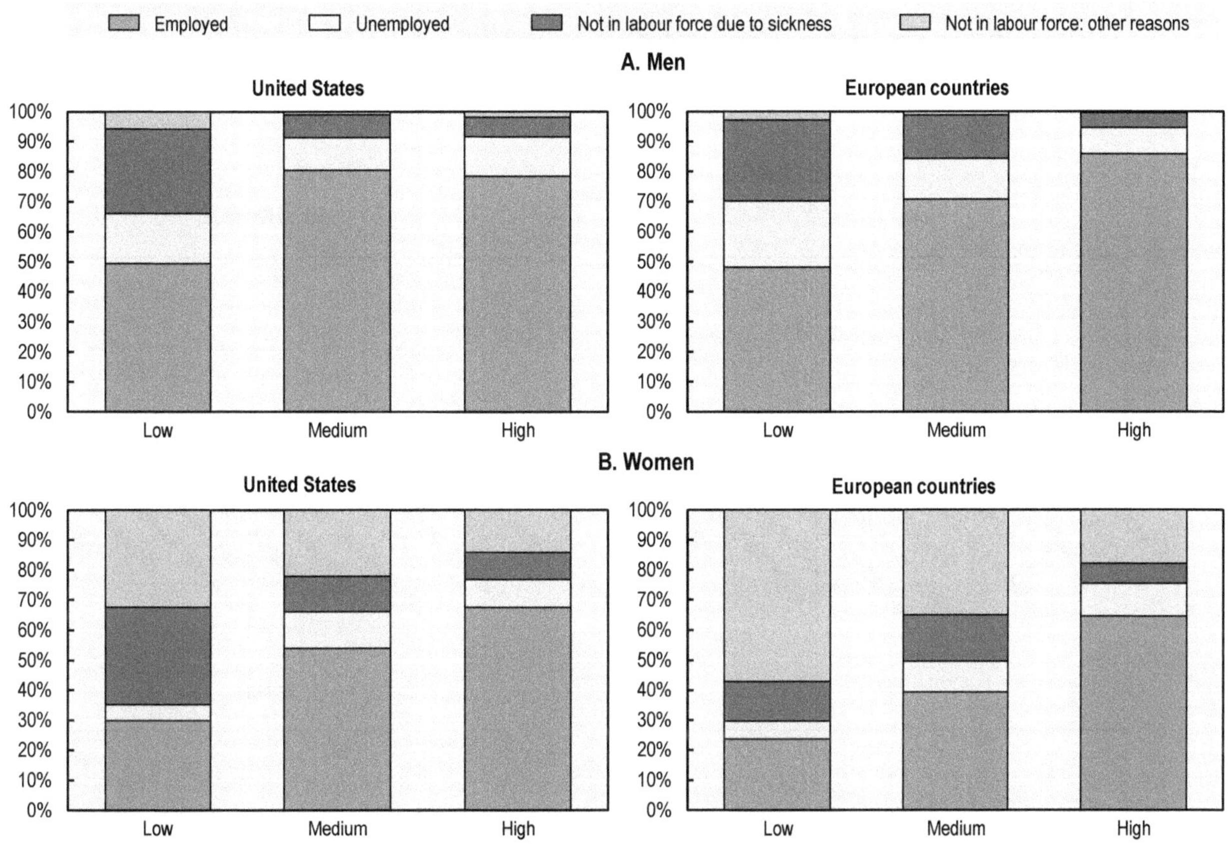

Note: The pathways are not age-specific. The European countries covered are Austria, Belgium, the Czech Republic, Denmark, Estonia, France, Germany, Israel, Italy, Luxembourg, Slovenia, Spain, Sweden and Switzerland. Levels of educational attainment are defined in accordance with the International Standard Classification of Education (ISCED): low education (ISCED 0–2), medium education (ISCED 3–4), and high education (ISCED 5–6).

Source: OECD calculations based on micro-level data from the English Longitudinal Study of Ageing (ELSA), the Health and Retirement Study (HRS) and the Survey of Health and Retirement in Europe (SHARE).

StatLink http://dx.doi.org/10.1787/888933643692

Sectoral differences

The length of working careers is far from uniform across sectors. While just over 5% of workers in "leisure and hospitality" jobs are between 60 and 69 years old in the United States, this share exceeds 15% in "agriculture". In many sectors, the share of workers drops sharply between ages 50-59 and 60-69. This is the case, for instance, in "manufacturing", "transportation and utilities", and in "financial activities", suggesting that early retirement may be common in these professions. In some cases, job changes from one sector to another may also be at play. Internationally, older workers do not specialise in the same sectors. In Poland, the share of 60-69 year-olds in "leisure and hospitality" is higher than in most other sectors, contrasting with the situation in the United States. Overall, the share of workers between 60 and 69 among all workers is higher in the United States than on average in 14 European OECD countries in all sectors except "leisure and hospitality". In "financial activities", the difference is particularly striking, with 11% of workers being 60-69 year-olds in the United States against less than 4% in European OECD countries.

Figure 1.10. Older workers are not equally represented across sectors

Share of workers aged 50-59 and 60-69 in different sectors, 2015

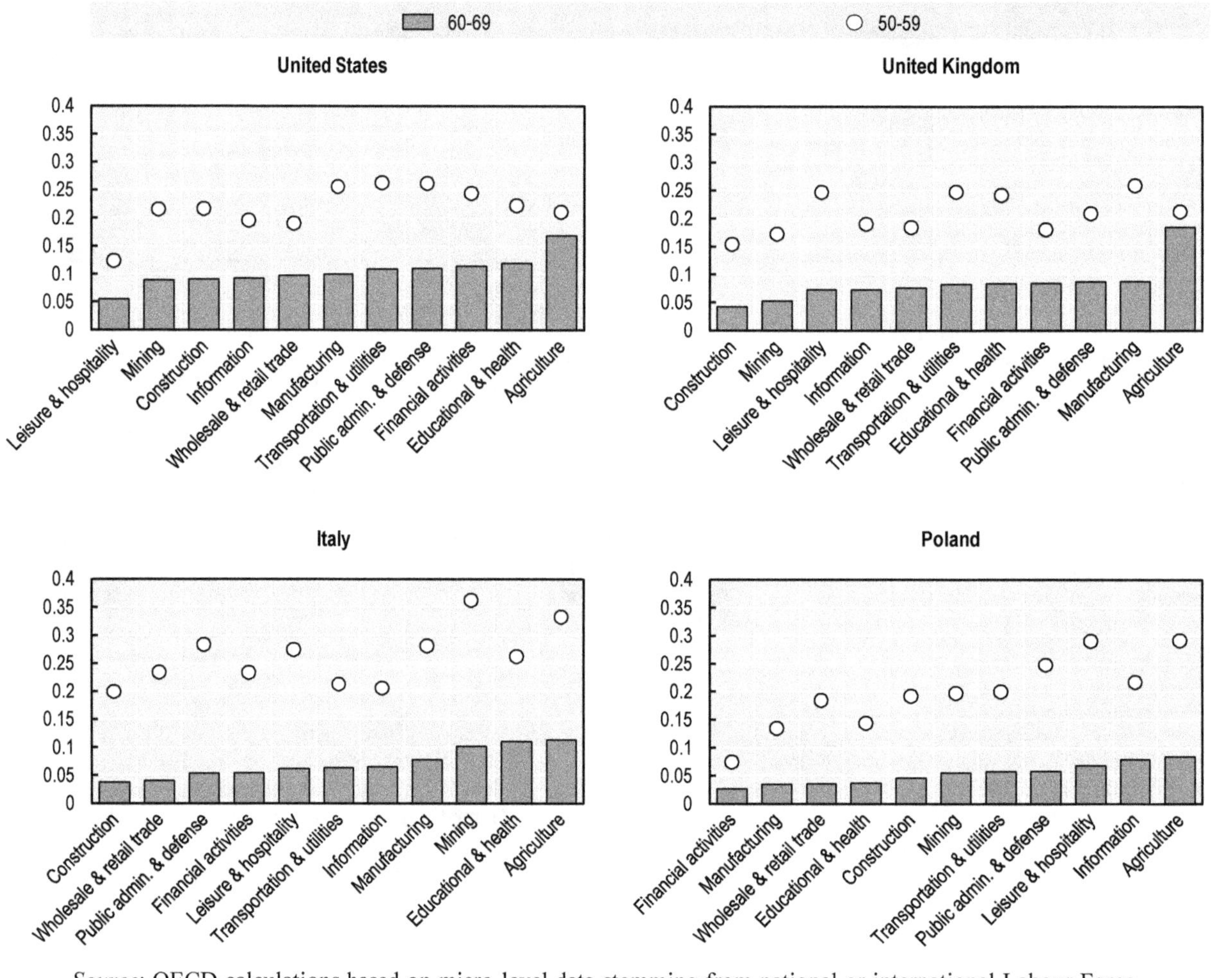

Source: OECD calculations based on micro-level data stemming from national or international Labour Force Surveys.

StatLink http://dx.doi.org/10.1787/888933643711

Determinants of early retirement

This section aims to identify the factors that lead to the large disparities in employment rates at older ages and retirement patterns across the population. Employment is the outcome of labour demand and labour supply and the numerous factors that impact on them. Only when sufficient labour supply and sound labour demand come together can employment rates among older workers increase.

Importance of retirement system characteristics

A country's institutional setting influences labour supply at older ages, for instance through its social security entitlements and labour market regulation. According to economic research, much of the increase in labour force participation among older adults in the United States between the late 1980s and the early 2000s can be explained by the increase in the Social Security full retirement age and higher rewards for claiming pension benefits after the full retirement age.[2] In the past, delaying benefits beyond the full retirement age increased pension rights only slightly; this bonus has been gradually strengthened and today deferred benefits increase by no less than 8% for each year up to age 70.

The OECD carried out an econometric analysis using data from the Health and Retirement Study (HRS) to estimate age-specific retirement rates in the United States (Figure 1.11). The results reflect retirement patterns for the time period 1992-today for different socio-economic groups. They suggest that many workers – in particular men with low and medium educational attainment – retire at the age of 62, when Social Security benefits first become available to them. The drop in labour force participation at age 62 is very large among these population groups. Among women, reaching age 62 does not single out as a retirement driver as clearly as among men, which is at least in part due to the fact that alternative pathways out of the labour market are much more common among women than among men (Figure 1.9). Even so, both male and female employment decreases rapidly between the early retirement age and the full retirement age, underscoring how strongly pension parameters influence retirement patterns.

Figure 1.11. Many workers retire at age 62 in the United States

Age-specific probability that a worker, who was employed at age 55, still works at a given age, United States, 1992-present

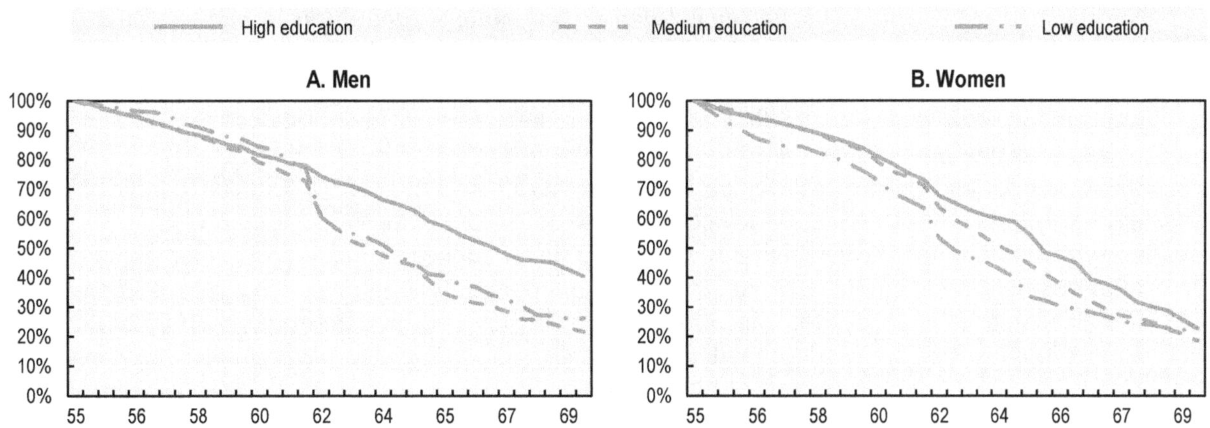

Note: The estimates refer to people who worked at the age of 55 and reflect their probability of still being employed at a given age. For technical reasons, only people with a direct work-retirement transition are considered. The way to read the graphs is as follows: Among high- and low-educated men in the United States who were employed at age 55, correspondingly, about 75% and 60% are still employed at age 62 (Panel A).

Source: Estimates based on survey data from the Health and Retirement Study, all waves (1992-present).

StatLink http://dx.doi.org/10.1787/888933643730

Health

Old age brings a greater risk of chronic or acute health problems. And poor or deteriorating health is a frequent reason for early labour market exit[3]. Older workers with low socio-economic backgrounds leave the market earlier than their high-educated peers (Figure 1.8) and are on average in worse health (OECD, 2017[2]). The OECD analysed a sample of people who worked at age 55 to single out the importance of health for their future labour force status, disentangling the health effect from other potential employment and retirement drivers. Health is captured as a summary measure of many different health indicators, including severe diseases, such as cancer and functional limitations. This technique allows ranking the sample in terms of "health quartiles" (Box 1.2).

A bad health status lowers the probability of remaining employed and increases the chances of retiring, becoming unemployed and becoming disabled. This general result holds both in the United States and Europe for the low-educated and the high-educated (Figure 1.12 and Figure 1.13). In Europe, the high-educated in good health are the population group with the highest probability of remaining employed and the lowest probability of becoming unemployed or disabled, although the latter two probabilities are overall fairly small. In the United States, education matters less when workers are in good health: Both healthy high-educated and healthy low-educated people have a high probability of being employed and a low probability of retiring, or becoming unemployed or disabled.

While employment levels after age 55 are higher in the United States than in Europe, health-related gaps within education groups tend to be larger in the United States. Among men, the percentage point difference between the healthy and the unhealthy in the probability of staying employed is about 12-13 percentage points in Europe, against 16 percentage points in the United States.

Similarly, there is a large health-related gap of becoming retired. Men in bad health are 6 percentage points more likely than their healthy peers to retire at a given age in Europe. In the United States, the difference is even larger, at 12 percentage points. One possible explanation for the higher health effect on retirement in the United States may be that access to disability benefits is more easily granted in some European countries than in the United States and people can rely on these benefits instead of retiring. Education-related gaps within health categories turn out to be smaller in the United States than in Europe, however. While in Europe high-educated men in good health are 4 percentage points more likely to be employed and 4 percentage points less likely to be retired than low-educated in good health, education-related employment and retirement differences among healthy men are small in the United States.

Box 1.2. Modelling employment and retirement drivers

The empirical analysis of the retirement decision in this section uses longitudinal data from two surveys: The Health and Retirement Study (HRS), with twelve waves that cover the period 1992-2014, and the Survey of Health, Ageing and Retirement in Europe (SHARE), with five waves that cover 2004-2015. HRS contains data on the United States whereas SHARE includes 15 European countries – Austria, Belgium, the Czech Republic, Denmark, Estonia, France, Germany, Greece, Italy, the Netherlands, Poland, Slovenia, Spain, Sweden and Switzerland – and Israel. An important advantage of using these surveys is that they are well comparable. They include, for instance, similar questions to measure health problems, labour market outcomes and certain job characteristics. Nonetheless, some caution is warranted as cultural and linguistic differences may bias responses (Chan et al., 2012[9]; Kapteyn, Smith and Soest, 2007[10]).

Two different methodologies are implemented to model retirement and employment drivers. First, survival analysis is used to estimate age-specific retirement rates. As this technique requires long panels it is implemented for the United States only (Figure 1.11). It starts with a sample of people who worked when they were 55 years old. For technical reasons, only workers who transited directly from work into retirement are considered and workers following other pathways out of the labour market are excluded. The curves in Figure 1.11 report the non-parametric Kaplan-Meier estimators of the "retirement survival curve", i.e. of the share of people who, at a given age, have not retired yet. Defining w_t as the number of workers who at age t are not retired yet and r_t as the number of former workers who are already in retirement, the estimated "retirement survival curve" S at age t is calculated as $\hat{S}(t) = \prod_{i=55}^{t} \frac{w_i - r_i}{w_i}$.

The second methodology disentangles the effect of health on retirement patterns from other retirement drivers (Figure 1.12 Figure 1.13). This analysis relies on data from SHARE and HRS and includes 55-to-70 year-olds who were working when they were first observed in the survey. The longer workers are observed, the older they get and the more likely they are to retire at some point. To take account of this fact and make results based on HRS and SHARE comparable, the sample is restricted to individuals with two to five observations only. Five labour force outcomes are considered: Workers can either continue working (W), become retired (R), become unemployed (U), become disabled (D) or move into the group of other inactive (OI), which are mostly homemakers. More precisely, the dependent variable, y^*_{itj}, represents the latent propensity for each individual i at time t to be in labour force status j, where $j = W, R, U, D, OI$. The following equation is used to estimate the effects of various independent variables on the propensities y^*_{itj}:

$$\forall j \in (W, R, U, D, OI): y^*_{itj} = \alpha_{ij} + \boldsymbol{X}'_i \beta_j + \boldsymbol{Z}'_{it} \gamma_j + \epsilon_{itj} \quad (1)$$

where

- $\boldsymbol{X}_i$ is a vector of individual characteristics that do not change over time, including dummy variables for educational attainment defined according to the International Standard Classification of Education (ISCED) (low education (ISCED 0–2), medium education (ISCED 3–4), and high education (ISCED 5–6)), a measure for working on a physically demanding job defined when the person is first observed and variables indicating the country of residence (only for the regressions using SHARE data),

Box 1.2. Modelling employment and retirement drivers *(Cont.)*

- $\boldsymbol{Z}_{it}$ is a vector of time-varying characteristics, including a measure of health (the quartiles from a health index that is obtained from an auxiliary health regression as in e.g. Disney et al. (2006[11])), a dummy variable for having a retired spouse, a dummy variable for being married, a dummy variable for caring for one's parents at least one hour per week, the number of parents that are alive, household size, the distance to the normal retirement age in years (which depends on an individual's age, country, year, year of birth, gender, marital status and the number of children), and the unemployment-rate gap defined at the country-year level as the deviation of the unemployment rate from the Non-Accelerating Inflation Rate of Unemployment (NAIRU), which is included to capture cyclical time effects,
- β_j and γ_j are the corresponding parameter vectors to matrices $\boldsymbol{X}_i$ and $\boldsymbol{Z}_{it}$ that have to be estimated,
- α_{ij} is a random individual-specific effect, that may be correlated with the independent variables in the specifications that take possibly correlated individual unobserved effects into account (see below),
- ε_{itj} is an error term, which is independent and identically distributed across all outcomes j.

Equation 1 is estimated as a multinomial logit model. Despite the rich set of independent variables that are included in the analysis, there could still be omitted variables that drive the association between the independent and the dependent variables. For instance, personality traits, such as openness to experience, conscientiousness or preferences for leisure, could drive the correlations between health and labour force status. To address this issue, equation 1 is also estimated as a fixed effects multinomial logit model, allowing for correlated unobserved individual time-constant effects (i.e., the α_{ij} terms can be correlated with the independent variables).* Because this model uses only individuals who switch labour force status, it is implemented on the full HRS data set including all twelve waves. A similar model was tested for Europe but could not be fit, most likely due to the much shorter panel in the SHARE data set. This model estimates, by definition, only the effects of characteristics that vary over time (included in $\boldsymbol{Z}_{it}$). The results confirm that even after accounting for possible time-constant confounding factors that are not measured in the data, health remains an important driver of early labour market exit in the United States, especially for men. Below, only the results from Equation 1 are discussed, as these allow for a comparison between the United States and Europe.

*: The Stata module *femlogit* (Pforr, 2014[12]) is used to estimate this fixed effects multinomial logit model.

Figure 1.12. Health is an important retirement driver among men

Probability of transiting into five labour force states for men in the United States and Europe; sample of individuals aged 55-69 who were initially working

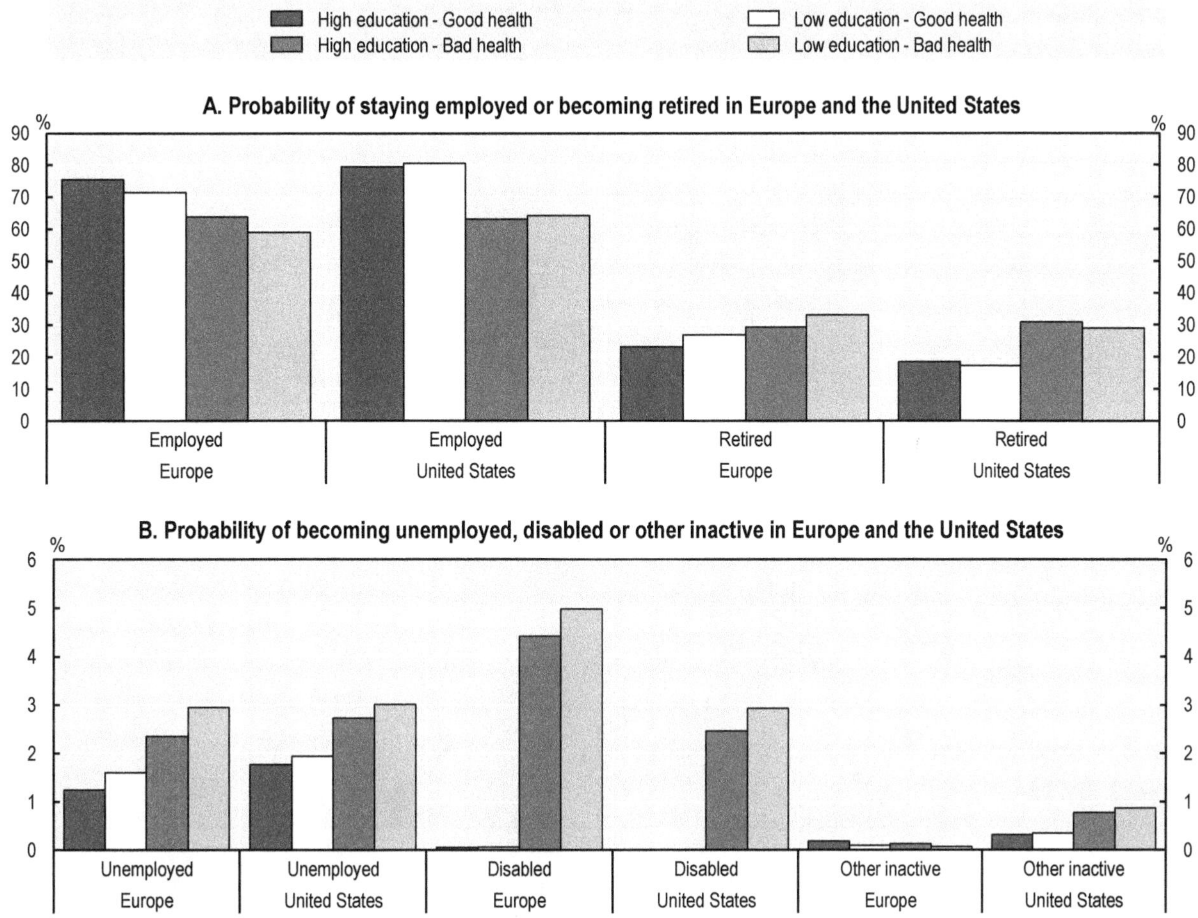

Note: The predicted probabilities are computed after estimating Equation 1 as a multinomial logit model (see Box 1.2) setting education level at either high (ISCED 5–6) or low (ISCED 0–2) and health status at either good or bad health, but using otherwise respondents' actual characteristics.

Source: OECD calculations based on the Survey of Health, Ageing and Retirement in Europe (SHARE, all five longitudinal waves) and the Health and Retirement Study (HRS, first five waves of each respondent).

StatLink http://dx.doi.org/10.1787/888933643749

Predicted employment probabilities among women in the sample are similar to men's both in the United States and Europe (Figure 1.13). Gender differences are small because the sample is restricted to people who were still working at the age of 55, which excludes some individuals, especially women.

While health is among the factors that matter for the timing of retirement and bad health is an important driver of early labour market exit, health alone cannot explain the sharp drop in employment rates for the people in their late 50s and early 60s. Other factors, such as the availability of early pension benefits and potentially shrinking labour demand at older ages, sometimes due to age discrimination, also contribute to the decline in employment as people get older. If health was the only barrier to longer working lives, employment rates among older adults could be considerably higher (OECD, 2017[2]).

Figure 1.13. Healthy women have a higher chance of remaining employed

Probability of transiting into five labour force states for women, United States and Europe; sample of individuals aged 55-69 who were initially working

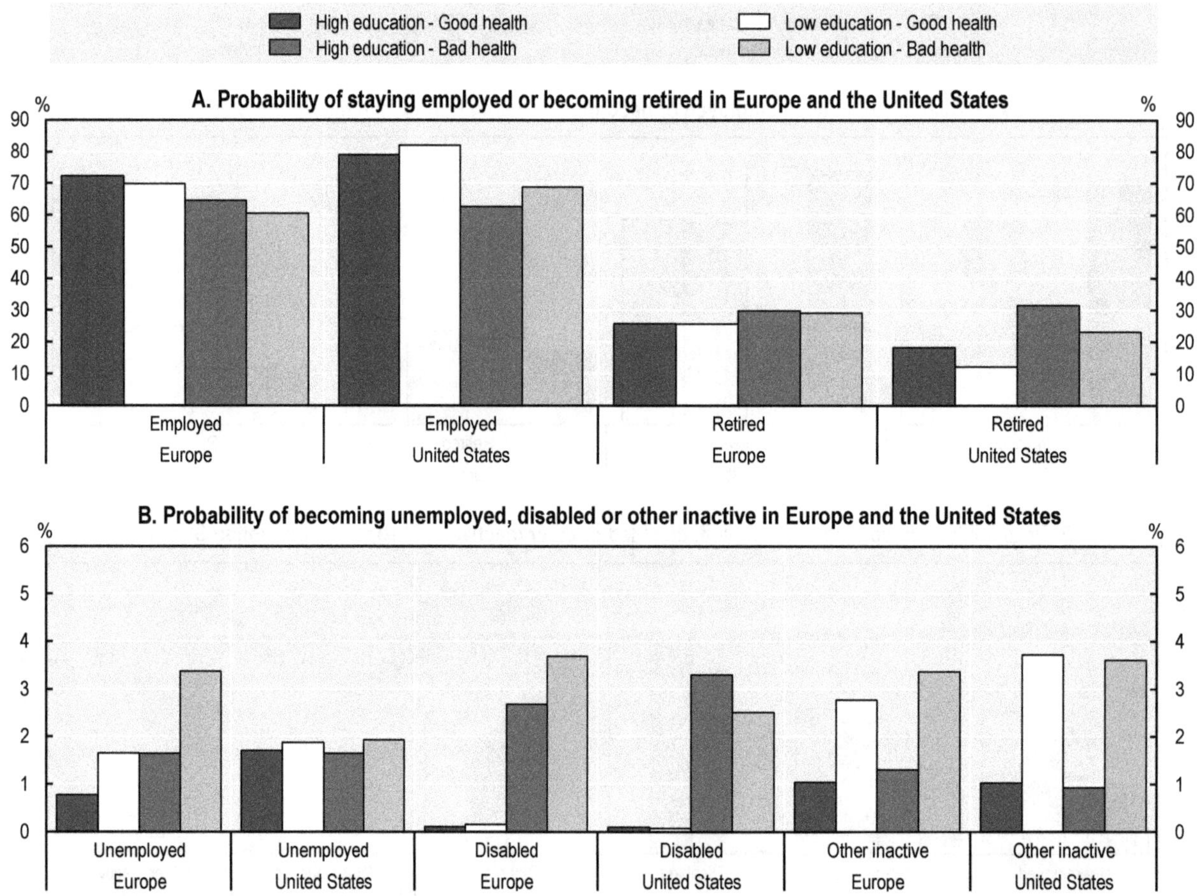

Note: The predicted probabilities are computed after estimating Equation 1 as a multinomial logit model (see Box 1.2) setting education level at either high (ISCED 5–6) or low (ISCED 0–2) and health status at either good or bad health, but using otherwise respondents' actual characteristics.

Source: OECD calculations based on the Survey of Health, Ageing and Retirement in Europe (SHARE, all five longitudinal waves) and the Health and Retirement Study (HRS, first five waves of each respondent).

StatLink http://dx.doi.org/10.1787/888933643768

Other determinants of the retirement decision

In addition to socio-economic characteristics, retirement system parameters and health, other factors also affect the timing of retirement.

Difficult *working conditions* drive early retirement. Working conditions can be difficult because the job is physically very demanding, very stressful or because of complicated personal relationships within teams. Bad working conditions are particularly common among workers from low socio-economic background and push some of them out of employment, hence reinforcing labour market disparities among older adults. The empirical model of the retirement decision (see Box 1.2) includes a measure for working on a physically demanding job. Among male workers aged 55 and over in the United States, having a physically demanding job increases the probability of retiring over a given time frame by 7%, and the risk of becoming unemployed by 15% among their female peers.

Caregiving responsibilities prevent some older workers from extending their working lives and pull them into retirement, especially in the case of women. In the United States, 16% of 60-64 year-old women and 9% of men who do not work take on care activities for their parent(s) at least one hour per week, compared to 13% and 5% among working women and men of the same age (Figure 1.14). In Europe, 20% of non-working 60-64 year-old women and 13% of men fulfil care activities. For both sexes in the United States and for women in Europe, caring for a parent is more common among older individuals and, within the same age group, among those who do not work (for people with at least one living parent). Moreover, in the United States, part-time workers aged 65-69 are more likely to care for their parent(s) than full-time workers and those not working. Overall, part-time workers are slightly more likely to care for their parents than full-time workers among men, but this does not hold among women.

Figure 1.14. Many older people with care responsibilities do not work

Share of people with care responsibilities for a parent, by age and working-states, United States and Europe

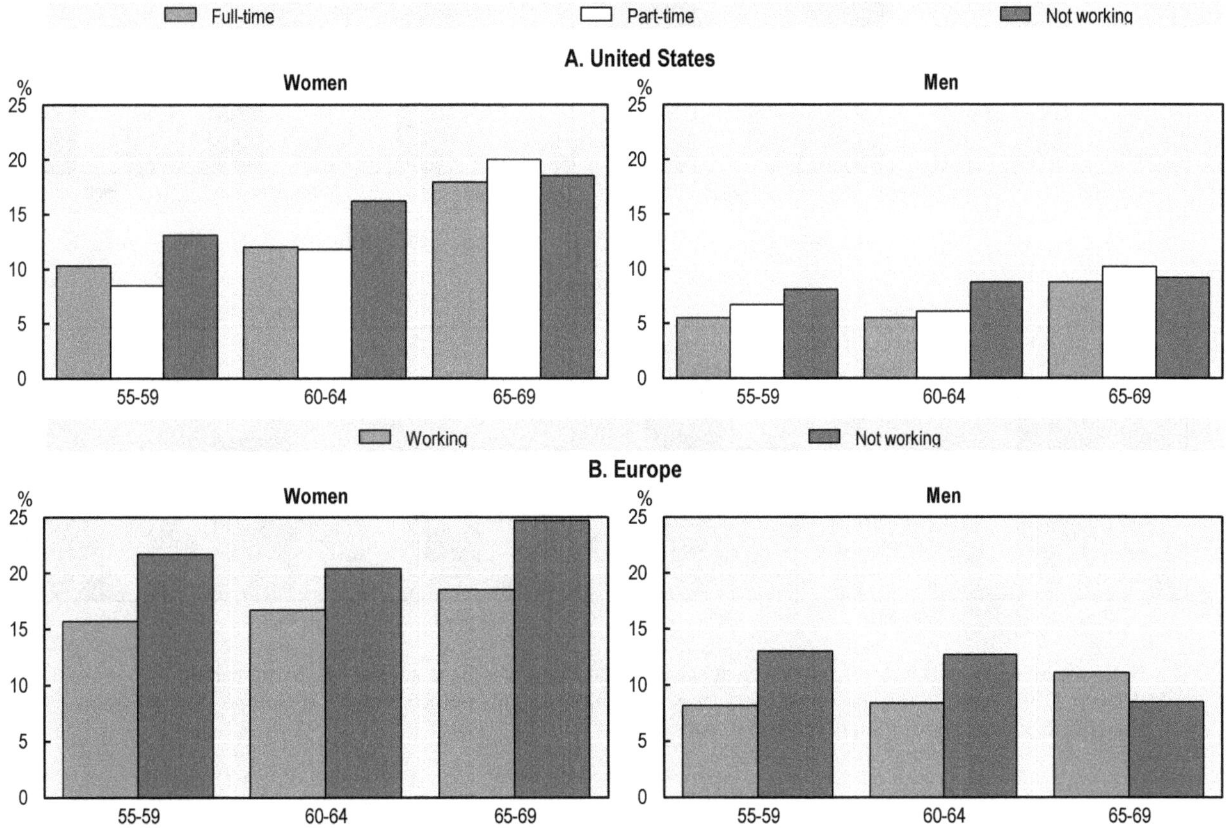

Note: Only individuals who were working at age 55 and who have at least one living parent. The way to read the graphs is as follows. Among 60-64 year-old women in the United States, for example, about 17% of those not working have care responsibilities for a parent, while they are only 13% among those who work full-time or part-time (Panel A, left).

Source: OECD estimates based on the Survey of Health, Ageing and Retirement in Europe (SHARE) and the Health and Retirement Study (HRS), all waves.

StatLink http://dx.doi.org/10.1787/888933643787

Among women, the low-educated are more likely to care for a parent than their peers with higher educational attainment while the opposite is the case among men (Figure 1.15). Within all education groups, people who do not work are more likely to care for their parent(s) and in both the United States and Europe non-working high-educated women take on care responsibilities for their parent(s) more frequently.[4]

Figure 1.15. The relationship between caregiving and working differs across educational groups

Share of 55-69 year-olds who care for a parent by age and educational attainment, United States and Europe

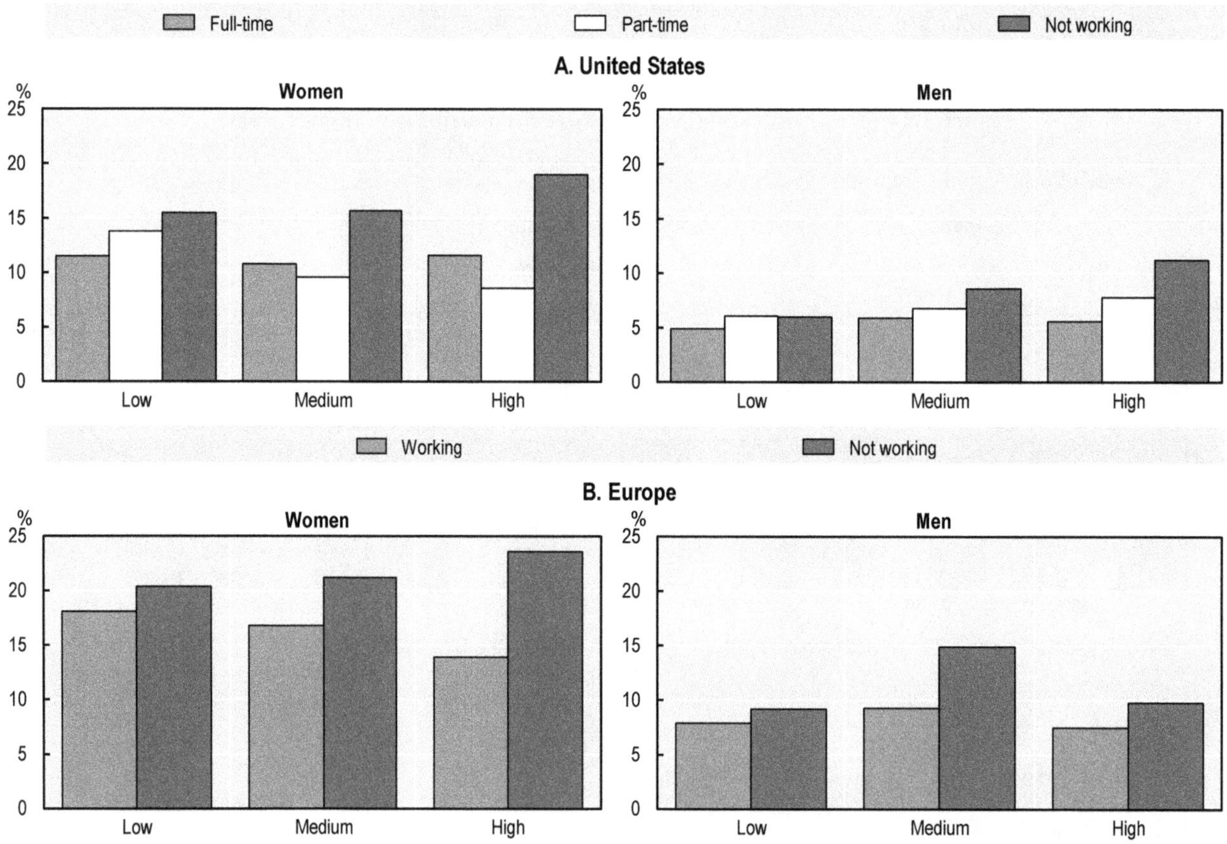

Note: Only individuals who were working at age 55 or later and who have at least one living parent.
Source: OECD calculations based on the Survey of Health, Ageing and Retirement in Europe (SHARE) and the Health and Retirement Study (HRS), all waves.

StatLink http://dx.doi.org/10.1787/888933643806

Macroeconomic conditions and trends over time can have a substantial impact on labour demand. The Great Recession, for instance, posed serious challenges to employment among workers of all ages. In recent years, many workers have delayed retirement or re-entered the workforce in response to the financial losses they endured during the Great Recession. To account for such time trends, the empirical model of retirement drivers (Equation 1 in Box 1.2) includes cyclical unemployment (the unemployment-rate gap) as an explanatory factor, i.e., the deviation of the unemployment rate from the Non-Accelerating Inflation Rate of Unemployment (NAIRU). Cyclical unemployment, by definition, increases during economic downturns and decreases during economic booms, even if structural unemployment (NAIRU) is unchanged. For workers aged 55 and over in the United States, a 1 percentage point increase in cyclical unemployment (the unemployment-rate gap) increases their probability to become unemployed by about 9% compared to staying employed, while it decreases their probability of becoming retired by about 16%. Among female workers, it also decreases the probability of becoming disabled or moving into the group of other inactive by about 30% compared to staying employed.

In the past, mandatory retirement at a prescribed age was not uncommon in the United States. In such cases, the incentives to stop working altogether were considerable: People who wanted to continue to work had to sign a new contract or find a new employer, which often involved a wage loss. In 1986, Congress amended the Age Discrimination in Employment Act, prohibiting mandatory retirement regulation for most professions. Except for some particular job families, such as air traffic controllers, mandatory retirement was phased out over the following years and is less common today.

The effect of *private pensions* on retirement behaviour can be very strong, also without mandatory retirement rules. Workers who remain employed after having reached the age of pension eligibility and do not claim their retirement benefits reduce the total discounted value of their pensions -pension wealth, i.e. the expected net present value of their pensions – if benefits are not adjusted upwards in an actuarially neutral way. In many cases, defined benefit plans do not increase benefits for delayed retirement, thereby making longer careers less attractive.

Over the last years, the financial disincentives to work have decreased in private pension plans. The Health and Retirement Study (HRS) provides estimates of the value of workers' employer-related defined benefit plans, depending on the age at which workers retire. The OECD used these estimates to compare financial incentives in defined benefit plans in the United States over time (Figure 1.16). Workers whose employment began a long time ago often face decreasing net present values of their total defined benefit pensions if they do not claim benefits at age 62 but continue employment until 65. This disincentive to work is a lot less common among workers with shorter tenure. Workers who started their last job only a few years ago are much more likely to face sizable penalties if they retire at age 62. In addition, there is a notable trend among employers to offer defined contribution plans rather than defined benefit plans. Defined contribution plans usually do not generate financial incentives to retire early. As there has been a general shift from defined-benefit to defined-contribution in private pension schemes worldwide (see OECD (2016[13])), disincentives to work from occupational pensions are likely to become less of a concern in the future.

Figure 1.16. Defined benefit pension plans provide less incentive to retire early than in the past

Value of defined benefit pension if worker retires at 62 relative to value if he/she retires at 65, by year in which employment spell began, United States

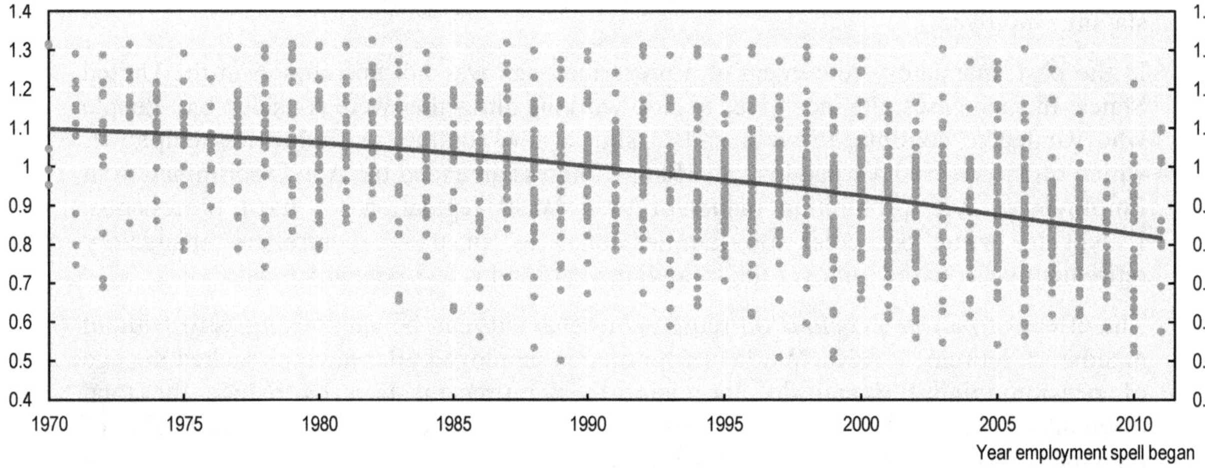

Note: The graph shows how much the defined benefit occupational pension is worth if benefits are claimed at age 62 versus age 65. More precisely, it compares the present value of all expected future pension benefits, depending on the age at which payments start. 100% stands for actuarial neutrality (excluding contributions), 110% means that the value of all expected benefits is 10% higher if payments start at age 62 rather than 65. The fitted line is based on non-parametric scatter-plot smoothing, the so-called lowess smoother with bandwidth=0.8. The results rely on HRS estimates of net present values of pension plan entitlements.
Source: Unweighted calculations based on the Health and Retirement Study's (HRS) estimates on net present values of defined benefit pensions.

StatLink http://dx.doi.org/10.1787/888933643825

The working status of workers' spouses can also impact retirement patterns. Married workers often exit employment at about the same time as their spouses, suggesting that interactions within couples are at play. Preference for shared leisure time may be one of the main reasons behind joint retirement of couples[5]. Having a retired spouse has been shown to increase the chances of retiring for both men and women. In the United States, one-fourth of the increase in labour force participation between 1994 and 2005 among 55-64 year-old married men is attributed to an increase in their wives' labour force participation; this share is even higher in the United Kingdom (one-third) and Canada (one-half) (Schirle, 2008[14]). Blau and Goodstein (2010[15]) study a longer time period (1980s to first half of the 2000s) and find that the rise in labour force participation of married women explains about 16% of the increase in older married men's labour force participation, which is just below the effect of better educational attainment (18%). The empirical model of the retirement decision in Equation 1 (Box 1.2) controls for having a retired spouse. Both male and female workers are more likely to retire when their spouse is already retired.

Towards a more flexible retirement system?

In many countries, the retirement decision remains a binary choice: retire or continue working full time. In addition, the timing of retirement is often rigid. In some cases, mandatory retirement rules give employers the option to terminate contracts of older workers at a certain age. Moreover, working after the retirement age can be financially unattractive, for example because combining work and pension can be subject to earnings limits beyond which pensions are reduced. Such limits are in place in Australia, Denmark, Greece, Israel, Japan, Korea and Spain. Retirement is not always a rigid process, however, and flexible retirement options are sometimes available (OECD, 2017[1]).

A flexible retirement process can take different forms. In its most common use, the term "flexible retirement" refers to drawing a pension benefit – full or partial – while continuing in paid work, often with reduced working hours. This mechanism is also called "gradual", "partial" or – specifically in the case of reduced working hours – "phased" retirement. Flexible retirement can also refer to systems in which the timing of retirement is not fixed but workers can choose when they want to retire. Allowing people to draw a pension before or after the official pension age introduces flexibility in the form of early or deferred retirement. Some countries have implemented age ranges for retirement, e.g. workers can freely choose when to retire within the boundaries of these age corridors.

Opinion surveys confirm that many workers consider the option to enter retirement flexibly as positive: Almost two-thirds of EU citizens say it appeals more to them to combine a part-time job and a partial pension than to fully retire. Retirement planning and retirement wishes differ across countries, however: a 2015 survey found that in Japan, 43% of the survey respondents wanted to continue working past retirement, whereas in France only 15% were considering this option (Aegon Center for Longevity and Retirement, 2015[16])).

Intentions and actual behaviour do not always coincide, and flexible retirement is still uncommon in many OECD countries. In most European countries for which data is available, less than 5% of people aged 60-69 combine work and pensions (Figure 1.17). However, in some other countries, including the United States and Estonia, more than 15% of people in this age group work and receive a pension at the same time. The way retirement systems are constructed, how high pension levels at different ages are and the gains from working longer are also important factors that shape workers' desire for flexibility.

Figure 1.17. Combining pensions and work is uncommon in many OECD countries

Share of 60-69 year-olds who combine work and retirement benefits, 2014/2015

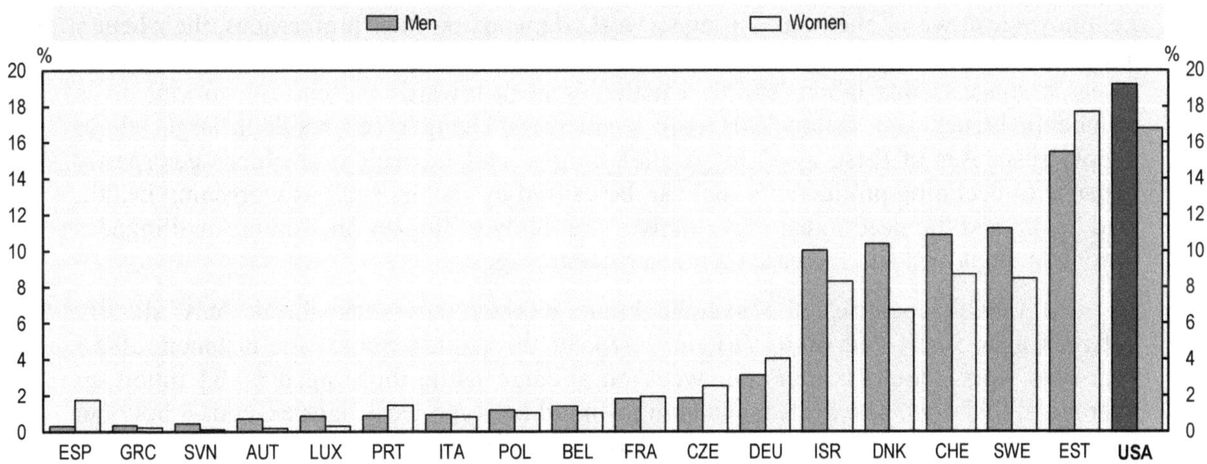

Source: OECD calculations based on the Health and Retirement Study (HRS) and the Survey of Health, Ageing and Retirement in Europe (SHARE).

StatLink http://dx.doi.org/10.1787/888933643844

In the United States, and even more so in many other OECD countries, employment rates fall sharply for the people in their 50s and 60s. Weekly hours of work per worker, by contrast, decline only gradually in most countries (Figure 1.18). This pattern demonstrates that the main changes in labour supply occur on the *extensive* margin and not on the *intensive* margin – most older adults stop working altogether and do not simply reduce their working hours when they get older. In the United States, employment decreases are particularly marked between age 62 and 65 (Figure 1.11), coinciding with the ages at which financial disincentives to work set in. Not only are workers able to draw Social Security benefits from age 62 onwards, they also become eligible for Medicare when they turn 65. The drop in employment rates also corresponds to an age range at which wages tend to decline[6].

For the older workers in the United States that are covered by private defined benefit pension schemes the pension levels in such plans are sometimes a function of a worker's last salary. In this case, a decline in working hours, and thus in earnings, can impinge negatively on pension benefits. Conversely, in the United Kingdom, most defined benefit pensions are calculated on a full-time equivalent basis. Moving from full-time to part-time at the end of their careers will not reduce workers' pension benefits in the United Kingdom unless the hourly wage decreases.

Smoothing the transition from work to retirement requires – on top of modifying pensions rules – both employers and employees to become more flexible in terms of retirement patterns. Some workers are able and willing to work until older ages, even beyond the retirement age, while others are not. In jobs without phased retirement arrangements workers face a binary decision: either they retire fully or they remain employed full time. Many employees who would have been able and willing to perform part-time work withdraw fully from the labour force as a result. Policy debate has evolved in several countries discussing whether phased retirement schemes can contribute to keeping people in the labour market until older ages.

Phased retirement may extend working lives, especially if it targets older workers who would otherwise leave the labour market. Conversely, if workers use phased retirement schemes to reduce their working hours as early as possible instead of staying employed full time, introducing phased retirement may reduce total hours worked. Recent research suggests that the second effect might dominate. The level of workers' reservation wages, i.e. the wage at which they are willing to work, depends on their preferences, their health and other factors, including fixed costs such as train tickets for commuters. Empirical research suggests that labour supply elasticities peak towards the end of working lives (Blundell, French and Tetlow, 2016$_{[17]}$); small wage changes can result in large labour supply responses at these ages. In parallel, wages tend to decline at older ages, partly because of declining productivity that can be caused by factors such as worsening health. Bad health and the need to care for relatives are likely to impact on workers' willingness to remain employed and increase their reservation wages.

In most OECD countries, the average hours worked per week shrink only slightly between ages 50-54 and 60-64 (Figure 1.18). In the United States, for instance, 50-54 year-olds work about 41 hours per week on average while those aged 60-64 report an average of 39 hours. The decrease in hours worked between these ages exceeds 4 hours in two OECD countries in the sample only: Austria and Finland.

After the age of 65, average hours worked per week decline much faster. In the United States, however, the difference between ages 60-64 (39 hours) and 65-69 (35 hours) is comparatively small, indicating that those older workers who remain employed work long hours on average. In many other countries, workers over 65 work less, suggesting that they withdraw from the labour market more gradually. In Austria and the Netherlands, 65-69 year-old workers work around 22 hours per week and in Luxembourg just under 25 hours.

Figure 1.18. In the United States working hours decline only slightly with age

Average hours worked per week, 2015

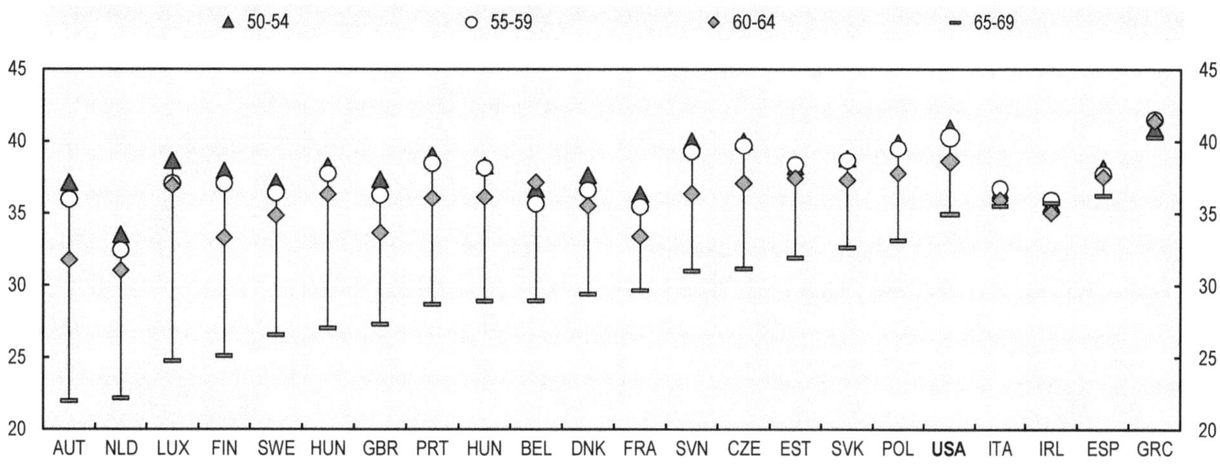

Source: OECD calculations based on Labour Force Surveys.

StatLink http://dx.doi.org/10.1787/888933643863

How flexibly workers leave the labour market differs across socio-economic groups. In the majority of OECD countries, high-educated prime-age individuals work longer hours than their low-educated peers, often much longer such as in France and in Austria (Figure 1.19, Panel A). Conversely, at older ages, there are numerous countries in which low-educated 65-69 year-olds work longer hours than their highly educated co-workers of the same age (Figure 1.19, Panel B). High-educated workers, who start from a higher level of weekly hours worked, reduce their working hours more markedly at older ages than low-educated people. This finding may indicate that low-educated people are less often in jobs that can be adapted to phased-retirement programmes. The situation is different in the United States. Educational disparities in terms of hours worked are actually a bit larger among older workers than among prime-age workers, suggesting that high-educated people do not exit employment more flexibly than their low-educated peers.

Figure 1.19. High-educated people reduce their working hours more with age than the low-educated in most countries

Average hours worked per week by education, 2015

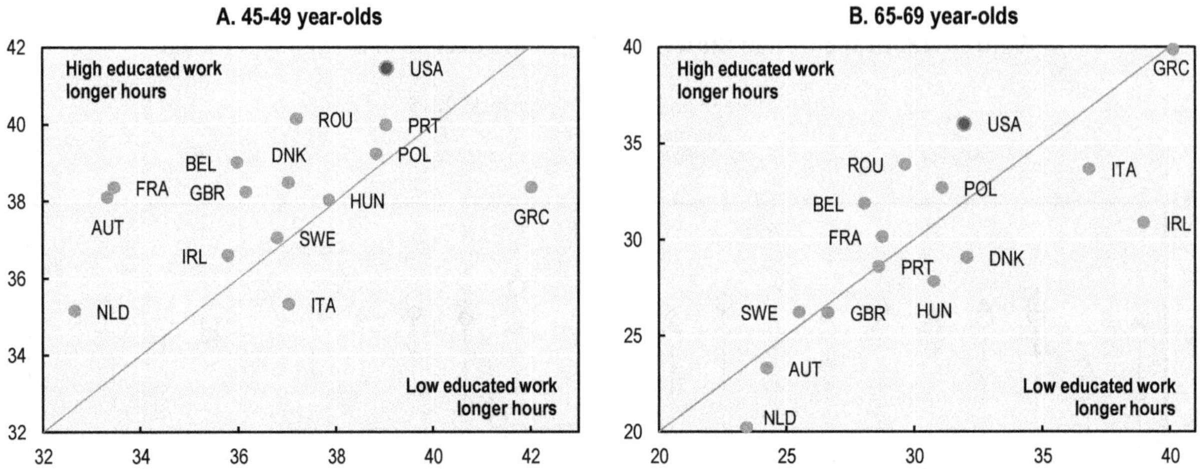

Source: OECD calculations based on Labour Force Surveys.

StatLink http://dx.doi.org/10.1787/888933643882

Direction for policy

The in-depth analysis above of the impact of education, health, retirement system parameters and other factors affecting employment aims to help identify effective and inclusive policy intervention to support better retirement conditions and longer careers among workers of all socio-economic backgrounds.

Increasing statutory and early retirement ages

Retirement ages are key determinants of individuals' retirement behaviour as this chapter and other research have shown.[7] This is the case even though retirement age increases cannot be expected to increase effective retirement ages by the same amount. The United States has one of the highest normal retirement ages (NRA) across OECD countries (OECD, 2017[1]). It is 66 for people born between 1943 and 1954 and will increase to 67 for people born in 1960 or later. Across OECD countries, the average NRA was equal to 64.3 years for men and 63.7 years for women in 2016 and will increase to 65.8 years for men and 65.5 years for women by around 2060.

Early retirement in the United States is possible from age 62, subject to an actuarial reduction, and under the current rules this option will remain available for a person entering the labour market today (see Box 1.1). According to current legislation, early retirement will remain available in the majority of OECD countries, usually between ages 60 to 63.

Linking normal and early retirement ages to gains in life expectancy, gains in healthy life expectancy or alternative demographic indicators can help to ensure that the number of retirees cannot grow disproportionally compared to the size of the workforce, thereby limiting the burden on younger generations. It is important, however, to acknowledge that some occupations are physically much more demanding than others, especially at older ages. In such cases, facilitating job changes to less arduous sectors and establishing phased retirement entry can alleviate the problem.

Maintaining current retirement ages in the long term will be challenging as the average age of the population continues to increase and retirees form an ever greater share. Although pension systems are designed to provide an income upon retirement they are not normally constructed to eliminate labour market differences across socioeconomic groups. Even for full-career workers, around half of wage inequality in the United States is transferred to pension inequality at retirement, against about two-thirds on average in the OECD (OECD, 2017[2]). The lower transmission of lifetime earnings into pension inequality in the United States comes mainly from the stronger progressive pattern of Social Security benefits. Moreover, as only the best 35 years of earnings are considered in calculating pension benefits, longer periods of unemployment, for example, which may more commonly affect lower earners, will not affect their replacement rates. However, on top there is retirement income inequality generated by differences in private savings accumulated during the working years.

The well-documented inequalities in life expectancy mean that increasing retirement ages as a response to longer lives may have undesirable distributional effects. While low-income earners receive greater pension replacement rates than high-income earners due to redistributive features built into the Social Security system, they also have a lower life expectancy. Pension arrangements do not take life expectancy disparities into consideration and low earners generally receive benefits over shorter periods than high earners, lowering their total pension benefits, that is, their pension wealth. Goldman and Orszag (2014[18]) showed that life expectancy gaps between income levels have a large impact on the progressivity of Social Security in the United States.

(OECD, 2017[2]) estimates that a life-expectancy difference of three years at age 65 between low- and high-earners – which is an order of magnitude that is in line with the gap between the high- and low-educated on average in the OECD as well as in the United States – further reduces their pension wealth by about 13%.[8]

As a result, apparently distribution-neutral schemes, such as a pure defined contribution pension, are in fact regressive. These estimates are relatively large and encourage policy makers to consider adjusting pension parameters to limit the impact of socio-economic differences in life expectancy on pension benefits (OECD, 2017[2]). Such inequalities can be addressed through first-tier pensions and redistributive components embedded in benefit and/or contribution rules.

A further issue relates to the distributive consequences of increasing the retirement age in line with life expectancy gains. If the effective retirement age were raised across the board, the increase would eat relatively more deeply into low earners' average remaining life expectancy due to socio-economic mortality differences. All other things being equal, low earners' accumulated pension entitlements would fall relative to those of high-income earners as retirement age increases would affect them more strongly given their shorter life expectancy. The relative fall would, however, remain moderate. If the retirement age were to be increased by three years between 2015 and 2060, the pension wealth of low earners relative to that of high earners would fall by a cross-country average of 1.2% (OECD, 2017[2]).[9]

However, if gains in life expectancy are not evenly distributed and favour higher-income groups, hence further exacerbating inequality in life expectancy, a higher retirement age would raise equity concerns. There is conflicting evidence about trends in life-expectancy inequality (OECD, 2017[2]). However, in some countries, such as Denmark and the United States, it has risen.

Leaving health aside, one of the main reasons why a higher retirement age might affect more disadvantaged groups relates to the shortage of employment opportunities as they near retirement. It is a serious issue. However, this does not imply that increasing the retirement age is the wrong policy. Low-earning workers' struggling to find work in their later years throws into relief the importance of labour market policies that foster a more inclusive older labour participation (Chapters 2 and 3 in this report). After all, shortcomings in the labour market are the root cause of these difficulties.

Moreover, it is important to assess whether individuals who retire early are well-informed and financially literate enough to understand the financial long-term consequences of their choice. The fact that claiming Social Security as early as possible is so widespread, especially among workers with low educational attainment, casts doubt on whether workers fully anticipate the monetary impact of their decisions and the costs of their future needs, for instance in terms of healthcare expenditure. In some cases, people who leave the labour market as early as possible incur old-age poverty risk, contributing to the high poverty levels among the over 75s in the United States. Adjusting early retirement ages or requiring a sufficient level of retirement income for early labour market exits can be ways of preventing financial distress at older ages.

Optimising occupational pensions

Occupational pensions are more common in the United States than in many other OECD countries. Recent analyses suggest that entitlements from private pensions are roughly as high as Social Security wealth in the United States. However, occupational pensions should not provide disincentives to work at older ages. Actuarially neutral adjustments for early and late retirement in employer-sponsored defined benefit plans are one way of making sure that early retirement is not more attractive than working longer. Today, recent defined benefit schemes typically include a penalty for early withdrawal, but sometimes fail to grant higher benefits when workers delay their benefit receipt beyond retirement age. This may create strong incentives to retire no later than the retirement age when working longer lowers the total value of all pension payments - the expected net present value of the pensions – as the pension is withdrawn over a shorter period.

Conversely, incentives to retire early are usually small or absent in defined contribution schemes. As more and more employers offer DC instead of DB schemes, the impact of occupation pensions on labour market exit ages will most likely diminish.

Only 31% of workers in the lowest income decile are even offered a DC scheme, compared to 76% in the highest decile. The take-up rate is 40% of those in the lowest decile compared to 81% in the top decile (National Compensation Survey, 2017). Therefore offering low paid workers a better option of saving through a DC scheme, perhaps through auto-enrolment, can increase coverage levels substantially. While offering every worker a private pension would increase the level of coverage, just providing the offer is not sufficient. Low-income earners may not be able to contribute a sufficient proportion of their salary to generate sufficient funds for a reasonable replacement rate.

For a guaranteed annual payment upon retirement purchasing an annuity is one available option, but these are not widely offered by employers. On average, only around one in ten Americans purchase a life-long annuity (TIAA, 2016[19]), with 68% saying they have no plans to purchase them in the future. Both of these figures contradict the fact that 49% declared their retirement goal as being able "To provide guaranteed money every month to cover your living costs in retirement". There is therefore an issue of understanding the value and purpose of annuity products; 66% of Americans are unfamiliar with annuities.

Beyond saving constraints experienced by some individuals, insufficient financial literacy raises obstacles for some workers to seize the opportunities offered by tax subsidies typically embedded in pension schemes, including voluntary pensions. According to the 2016 National Capability Study by the Financial Industry Regulatory Authority, nearly two-thirds of Americans could not pass a basic financial literacy test, and the pass rate has fallen by 5 percentage points between 2009 and 2015, despite society's greater awareness of financial matters during the financial crisis.

A low level of financial literacy is common among OECD countries (OECD (2016[20]).[10] It is important to start financial literacy early, ideally in school so that once reaching adulthood more people will be able to achieve a minimum level of financial knowledge. Moreover, women should be better targeted as they typically fare lower in financial literacy scores while being more likely to need to rely on financial products for longer due to greater life expectancy.

Increasing the value of mandatory pension components

A fundamental issue is that the level of benefit received from the mandatory earnings-related pension is low in the United States in comparison to other countries. Full-career average earners can expect to receive a future gross pension of around 38% of their last earnings at retirement, nearly 15 percentage points below the OECD average. In the United States both employees and employers each contribute 6.2% of earnings for pensions, compared to around 8% for employees and 15% for employers on average in the OECD. A higher mandatory contribution rate to pensions is the key parameter to improve pension prospects in the United States.

The level of the Supplemental Security Income is relatively low, under 17% of gross average earnings. This is around 55% of the relative poverty threshold (defined as 50% of median disposable incomes). As of July 2017, around 4.4% of those aged 65 and over are receiving the Supplemental Security Income, either on its own or with some Social Security. Fundamental reforms to this component could be expensive if the aim is to eliminate poverty entirely, but increases could partially alleviate the burden of old-age poverty. The level of the safety net is ultimately a political decision. Relative to average earnings, the level of SSI is among the lowest in the OECD, while poverty rates, in particular for the elderly, are among the highest. This strengthens the case for increasing basic protection for the most vulnerable older individuals.

Survivors' pensions are designed to primarily protect the spouses and children of retirees who die before or during retirement. These were often the only source of income for those remaining family members, and therefore an essential element to help alleviate poverty. However, the choice to subscribe, or not, to the joint-and-survivor life option for private pensions in the United States substantially changes the risk that surviving spouse falls into poverty (Orlova, Rutledge and Wu, 2015[21]). A great majority of couples prefer to opt out from the survivor pension to get a higher pension at the time of retirement. Hence, the joint-and-survivor life option should be automatic and reflected in either higher contributions or lower benefits. Maintaining standards of living after the death of an earlier spouse – at least when the survivor is older than a given, high enough age – should remain an objective of social policies.

Lowering the cost of the survivors' component may happen naturally in the United States as the next generation of female retirees will have longer working careers than their predecessors. However, legislation may be required to ensure that costs are reduced for benefits that may not actually be needed based on the value of their own entitlements.

Finding the right answers to health limitations

Bad health as an obstacle to longer working lives can present itself in the form of many different medical conditions. Different health problems require different policy responses. Especially in the case of arduous manual occupations, physical health problems are a common barrier to longer working lives. Ensuring that workers with physical impairments can find a less strenuous job would limit the problem. A flexible labour market and special training programmes are necessary to redirect workers with years of experience in arduous physical jobs to less strenuous employment, for which a very different set of skills is needed. Supporting training programmes throughout the career, including for older workers, to sharpen their skills in their current or a less strenuous sector is one way for policy to step in.

Even without persistent serious health limitations, health deteriorations can reduce labour market participation. Workers who perceive themselves as less healthy than before may expect to die earlier, value their leisure time more or perceive work tasks as more strenuous than before. As a result, they may reduce their working hours or quit employment entirely even though they are physically still able to carry out the same workload as previously. Financial incentives encouraging employment and flexible working conditions such as teleworking and flexible retirement entry can reduce the labour force loss in these situations.

From a policy perspective it is important to distinguish situations in which early retirement due to bad health is inevitable because a person is not able to work at all any more, i.e. severe disability, from situations in which people with minor disabilities are still able to work and want to continue working. In the second case, adequate policy measures (see below) can increase the number of older workers who keep working despite their health problems. In addition to measures aiming at preventing health problems policy makers can use tools to alleviate the impact health conditions have on employment rates.

Changes in health insurance provision

The provision of health insurance in European countries is mostly universal and therefore its impact on individuals' retirement patterns is limited. In many European countries, access to health care services and the age of retirement are only very loosely or not at all connected. This is not the case in the United States, where health insurance is often provided by the employer, at least until individuals turn 65 and become eligible for the Medicare system. Prior to age 65, the provision of health insurance is an important factor that keeps workers from retiring; this situation is sometimes referred to as "job lock". When employer-sponsored health insurance plans provide better coverage than Medicare, these incentives remain even at older ages (see more in Chapter 2).

Transforming disability into ability

The generosity of disability insurance can affect how health shocks affect the labour supply of older workers. High disability benefits may encourage labour market exit after an acute health shock if they cover a large part of the income loss from not working. While a high insurance coverage is desirable in the case of severely disabled people, it can create undesirable labour market incentives for workers with minor health problems. Conversely, in-job protection regulation contributes to retaining disabled workers in their jobs.

Too many workers leave the labour market permanently due to health problems or disability, and too few people with reduced work capacity manage to remain in employment. Disability benefit take-up has become a one-way street. People almost never leave disability benefits for a job; and if they leave the disability benefit scheme before retiring, they are far more likely to move on to another benefit (Wise, 2012[22]). This is why policy objectives have been shifting in most OECD countries from merely paying benefits to people with disability towards helping them stay in their job or return to work. Policy should continue on this path.

Keeping workers in their jobs requires different policies than bringing inactive people back to work. For a better job retention of workers, the main focus should be on the sickness absence phase. To promote hiring of inactive individuals, employer subsidies and similar measures play a crucial role. There is an inherent dilemma: strengthened retention requirements and financial incentives for employers can quickly turn into an obstacle for hiring jobseekers. In fact, most policies for persons with disabilities, including mandatory employment quotas and anti-discrimination legislation, are subject to this trade-off. While employment quotas and anti-discrimination legislation can a priori both reduce inflow into the group of disability beneficiaries and increase its outflow, empirical evidence suggests that among people with a disability, those in work gain and those without a job find it even more difficult to access the labour market - the net employment effect is often negative (DeLeire, 2000[23]; Humer, Wuellrich and Zweimüller, 2007[24]). This is why such policies should be complemented with mechanisms to stimulate labour demand of jobseekers with disabilities like wage subsidies to compensate for their lower productivity and subsidies for workplace adaptation of such workers (OECD, 2010[25]). This would also contribute to reducing the number of persons with disabilities with no or low attachment to the labour market, thereby improving their human capital and preventing their social exclusion.

Based on these considerations, the following actions could support longer careers not only among the well-educated, but among all socio-economic groups:

- Link the early and normal retirement ages to life expectancy, while considering distributional effects of possibly widening inequality in life expectancy.
- Provide easily understandable information, with a special focus on groups with poor financial literacy, on the impact of anticipating or postponing retirement on pension entitlements to promote well-informed choices between work and retirement.
- Increase the Supplemental Security Income level to help reduce the high levels of poverty amongst the older age groups.
- Increase occupational pension coverage among current workers, for instance through auto-enrolment in pension plans.

- Design specific training programmes targeting low-skilled workers. These programmes should, among other things, facilitate job change in mid-career and at an older age.
- Increase opportunities for more flexibility in work arrangements and retirement entry, e.g. teleworking, part-time work and combining work and pensions.
- Improve health among all workers, including older workers, through preventive measures and better access to health care services.

Notes

1. Among the 19 OECD countries, the United States is also the most unequal in terms of wealth, with 10% of its population holding 76% of total net wealth. This share is equals 50% in Norway.
2. Blau and Goodstein (2010[15]) find for the United States that the increases in the Social Security full retirement age and Delayed Credit Retirement can explain between 25% and 50% of the increase in labour force participation between the late 1980s and the first half of the 2000s.
3. See for example Disney et al., (2006[11]); Trevisan and Zantomio, (2015[26]).
4. Additional comparisons between Nordic, Southern, Eastern and Western European countries (which are not shown in this report) indicate small differences in caring percentages within genders among workers, while larger differences are apparent among those not working. The gap in caring activities between those not working and working is smallest in Southern European countries among women and in both Eastern and Southern European countries among men.
5. See Blundell, French and Tetlow (2016[17]).
6. See Blundell, French and Tetlow (2016[17]).
7. See Duval (2003), for example.
8. The range is from over 10% in Greece to nearly 17% in Latvia due to differences in average life expectancy and pension parameters.
9. Moreover, if the same argument – that is lower life expectancy for low earners – is applied to retirement ages that would be kept constant in a context with similar life expectancy gains for everyone, then the total pension benefits of low-income pensioners would increase relatively more. An increase in the retirement age together with longer life expectancy would restore neutrality.
10. OECD (2016[20]) shows that across the 30 participating countries, of which the United States is not one, the average score is 13.2 out of 21, in response to questions covering knowledge, behaviour and attitudes.

References

Aegon Center for Longevity and Retirement (2015), *The New Flexible Retirement*, Aegon Center for Longevity and Retirement, https://www.aegonseguros.es/siteassets/media/estudiosypublicaciones/3_oleada-flexible_retirement.pdf/ (accessed on 31 October 2017). [16]

Antolín, P. (2008), "Coverage of Funded Pension Plans", *OECD Working Papers on Insurance and Private Pensions*, No. 19, OECD Publishing, Paris, http://dx.doi.org/10.1787/241142156207. [6]

Blau, D. and R. Goodstein (2010), *Can Social Security Explain Trends in Labor Force Participation of Older Men in the United States?*, University of Wisconsin Press, http://dx.doi.org/10.2307/25703459. [15]

Blundell, R., E. French and G. Tetlow (2016), "Retirement Incentives and Labor Supply", in *Handbook of the Economics of Population Ageing*, Elsevier B.V., Amsterdam, http://dx.doi.org/10.1016/bs.hespa.2016.10.001. [17]

Chan, K. et al. (2012), "Measurement Equivalence in ADL and IADL Difficulty Across International Surveys of Aging: Findings From the HRS, SHARE, and ELSA", *The Journals of Gerontology Series B: Psychological Sciences and Social Sciences*, Vol. 67B/1, pp. 121-132, http://dx.doi.org/10.1093/geronb/gbr133. [9]

DeLeire, T. (2000), "The Wage and Employment Effects of the Americans with Disabilities Act", *The Journal of Human Resources*, Vol. 35/4, p. 693, http://dx.doi.org/10.2307/146368. [23]

Disney, R., C. Emmerson and M. Wakefield (2006), "Ill health and retirement in Britain: A panel data-based analysis", *Journal of Health Economics*, Vol. 25/4, pp. 621-649, http://dx.doi.org/10.1016/j.jhealeco.2005.05.004. [11]

Dushi, I., H. Iams and C. Tamborini (2017), *Contributory Retirement Saving Plans: Differences across Earnings Groups and Implications for Retirement Security*, https://papers.ssrn.com/sol3/papers.cfm?abstract_id=2964540 (accessed on 20 October 2017). [7]

Goldman, D. and P. Orszag (2014), "The Growing Gap in Life Expectancy: Using the Future Elderly Model to Estimate Implications for Social Security and Medicare.", *The American Economic Review*, Vol. 104/5, pp. 230-233, http://dx.doi.org/10.1257/aer.104.5.230. [18]

Humer, B., J. Wuellrich and J. Zweimüller (2007), "Integrating Severely Disabled Individuals into the Labour Market: The Austrian Case", *IZA Discussion Papers*, https://ideas.repec.org/p/iza/izadps/dp2649.html (accessed on 20 October 2017). [24]

Kapteyn, A., J. Smith and A. Soest (2007), *Vignettes and Self-Reports of Work Disability in the United States and the Netherlands*, American Economic Association, http://dx.doi.org/10.2307/30034404. [10]

Murtin, F. and M. Mira d'Ercole (2015), "Household Wealth Inequality across OECD Countries: New OECD Evidence", *OECD Statistics Brief*, Vol. No. 21, https://www.oecd.org/std/household-wealth-inequality-across-OECD-countries-OECDSB21.pdf (accessed on 31 October 2017). [3]

OECD/INFE (2016), *OECD/INFE International Survey of Adult Financial Literacy Competencies*, http://www.oecd.org/daf/fin/financial-education/OECD-INFE-International-Survey-of-Adult-FInancial-Literacy-Competencies.pdf (accessed on 20 October 2017). [20]

OECD (2010), *Sickness, Disability and Work: Breaking the Barriers: A Synthesis of Findings across OECD Countries*, OECD Publishing, Paris, http://dx.doi.org/10.1787/9789264088856-en. [25]

OECD (2015), *Pensions at a Glance 2015: OECD and G20 indicators*, OECD Publishing, Paris, http://dx.doi.org/10.1787/pension_glance-2015-en. [4]

OECD (2016), *OECD Pensions Outlook 2016*, OECD Publishing, Paris, http://dx.doi.org/10.1787/pens_outlook-2016-en. [13]

OECD (2017), *Preventing Ageing Unequally*, OECD Publishing, Paris, http://dx.doi.org/10.1787/9789264279087-en. [2]

OECD (2017), *Pensions at a Glance 2017: OECD and G20 Indicators*, OECD Publishing, Paris, http://dx.doi.org/10.1787/pension_glance-2017-en. [1]

Orlova, N., M. Rutledge and A. Wu (2015), "The Transition from Defined Benefit to Defined Contribution Pensions: Does It Influence Elderly Poverty?", Center for Retirement Research at Boston College, http://crr.bc.edu (accessed on 20 October 2017). [21]

Pforr, K. (2014), "Femlogit-implementation of the Multinomial Logit Model with Fixed Effects", *The Stata Journal*, Vol. 14/4, pp. 847-862. [12]

Poterba, J. (2014), *Retirement Security in an Aging Society*, National Bureau of Economic Research, Cambridge, MA, http://dx.doi.org/10.3386/w19930. [5]

Rhee, N. (2013), *Race and Retirement Insecurity in the United States*, National Institute on Retirement Security, http://www.nirsonline.org/storage/nirs/documents/Race%20and%20Retirement%20Insecurity/race_and_retirement_insecurity_final.pdf (accessed on 20 October 2017). [8]

Schirle, T. (2008), "Why Have the Labor Force Participation Rates of Older Men Increased since the Mid-1990s?", *Journal of Labor Economics*, Vol. 26/4, pp. 549-594, http://dx.doi.org/10.1086/589457. [14]

TIAA (2016), *TIAA 2016 Lifetime Income Survey*, TIAA, https://www.tiaa.org/public/pdf/C33638_Lifetime_Income_ExecSummary.pdf (accessed on 20 October 2017). [19]

Trevisan, E. and F. Zantomio (2015), "The Impact of Acute Health Shocks on the Labour Supply of Older Workers: Evidence from Sixteen European Countries", *SSRN Electronic Journal*, http://dx.doi.org/10.2139/ssrn.2655715. [26]

Wise, D. (2012), *Social Security Programs and Retirement around the World*, University of Chicago Press, http://dx.doi.org/10.7208/chicago/9780226921952.001.0001. [22]

Chapter 2.

Supporting employers to retain and hire older workers in the United States

With relatively little employment protection and no mandatory retirement age, US firms' willingness to hire and retain older workers is key to ensuring older workers have access to good jobs. Employers' attitudes are central. While the United States has pioneered anti-age discrimination, coverage has not been extended to all workers so far. The skill-set of older workers in the United States is relatively good, both with respect to younger workers and older workers in other large OECD countries. While older workers perform less well on information-processing tasks, they have interpersonal skills that are called upon to plan, supervise, and influence others. This highlights the importance of mobility across tasks, jobs and occupations. Occupational mobility is higher in the United States than in other large OECD countries but changes to health insurance rules (such as repealing the Affordable Care Act) risk creating barriers to job mobility of older workers. Non-wage costs continue to create a disincentive to hire older workers, especially the higher costs for health insurance of older workers.

The statistical data for Israel are supplied by and under the responsibility of the relevant Israeli authorities. The use of such data by the OECD is without prejudice to the status of the Golan Heights, East Jerusalem and Israeli settlements in the West Bank under the terms of international law.

Introduction

Employers play a key role in generating better labour market outcomes for older people. While many older people are working, there is still scope to improve the number and quality of the job opportunities that are available to them. In the United States, the employment rate of people aged 55 and over is higher than the OECD average but this gap has narrowed over time. Whereas the proportion of older people who are working has risen only slightly over the past decade in the United States, the increase has been larger in many other OECD countries. Moreover, socio-economic status, gender, and health and disability importantly determine employment rates and exit paths of older Americans out of the labour market (see Chapter 1).

Government policies play a role on several levels in influencing the employment policies of employers with respect to the hiring and retention of older workers. Some measures are specifically designed to promote more and better jobs for older workers (e.g. age discrimination legislation). More general labour market policies and institutions (e.g. labour taxes, Paid Time Off benefits, and health-insurance contributions) may nevertheless have an even bigger impact on the recruitment and retention of older workers. Most fundamentally, employment chances of older workers depend on how firms can better manage age diversity and ensure high levels of productivity in a diverse workforce, including older workers. Older workers' skills and how workers and firms adapt to changing abilities is therefore a particular focus of this chapter.

US labour market for older workers in an international perspective

Compared with other OECD countries, the US labour market is quite dynamic. While just over 60 million job separations took place in 2016 (equivalent to 42% of all non-farm jobs), close to 63 million new hires also occurred (OECD, 2016[1]). This dynamism is also reflected in higher job mobility by older workers in the United States than in other OECD countries, although lower than for younger workers. Only around 54% of older American men and 53% of older American women have 10 years or more of job tenure compared to 60% and 59% on average for the OECD. Over recent decades, however, mobility has declined for most workers – a trend not observed for older workers (Davis and Haltiwanger, 2014[2]).

Retention rates increasing slowly, hiring recovering from recession

The past decade was decisively influenced by the Great Recession that saw a decrease in job mobility. This has resulted in a shift in the US job tenure distribution toward longer-duration jobs since 2000 (Hyatt and Spletzer, 2016[3]). Figure 2.1 shows that changes in tenure were driven by declines in the hiring rate (Panel A), as well as by a rise in retention rates (Panel B).

In fact, initially after the global crisis hit the United States, hiring rates of older workers decreased more markedly than in other countries (Figure 2.1 Panel A) and the incidence of long-term unemployment among older workers rose notably during the Great Recession (Monge-Naranjo and Sohail, 2015[4]), although it has almost recovered its pre-crisis levels (see Annex Table 2.A.1). Thus, Hairault et al. (2014[5]) find that older workers' jobs are characterised by a higher responsiveness to business cycles than those of their younger counterparts. In particular, hiring of older workers is very sensitive to the cycle. The hiring rate of older workers in the United States has been picking up since

2010, but it was still below its pre-recession high in 2016s (Figure 2.1). The trend increase in the retention rates for older workers implies increased willingness to retain older workers. Burtless (2016[6]) finds a sizeable decline in exits to inactivity during the Great Recession for older workers in the United States. This tended to hold up their labour force participation rates and employment rates relative to younger people. Meanwhile, increases in retention rates have been greater in other countries.

Figure 2.1. The Great Recession coincided with large fall in hiring of older US workers

Hiring and retention rates of workers aged 55-64 over the past two decades, selected OECD countries

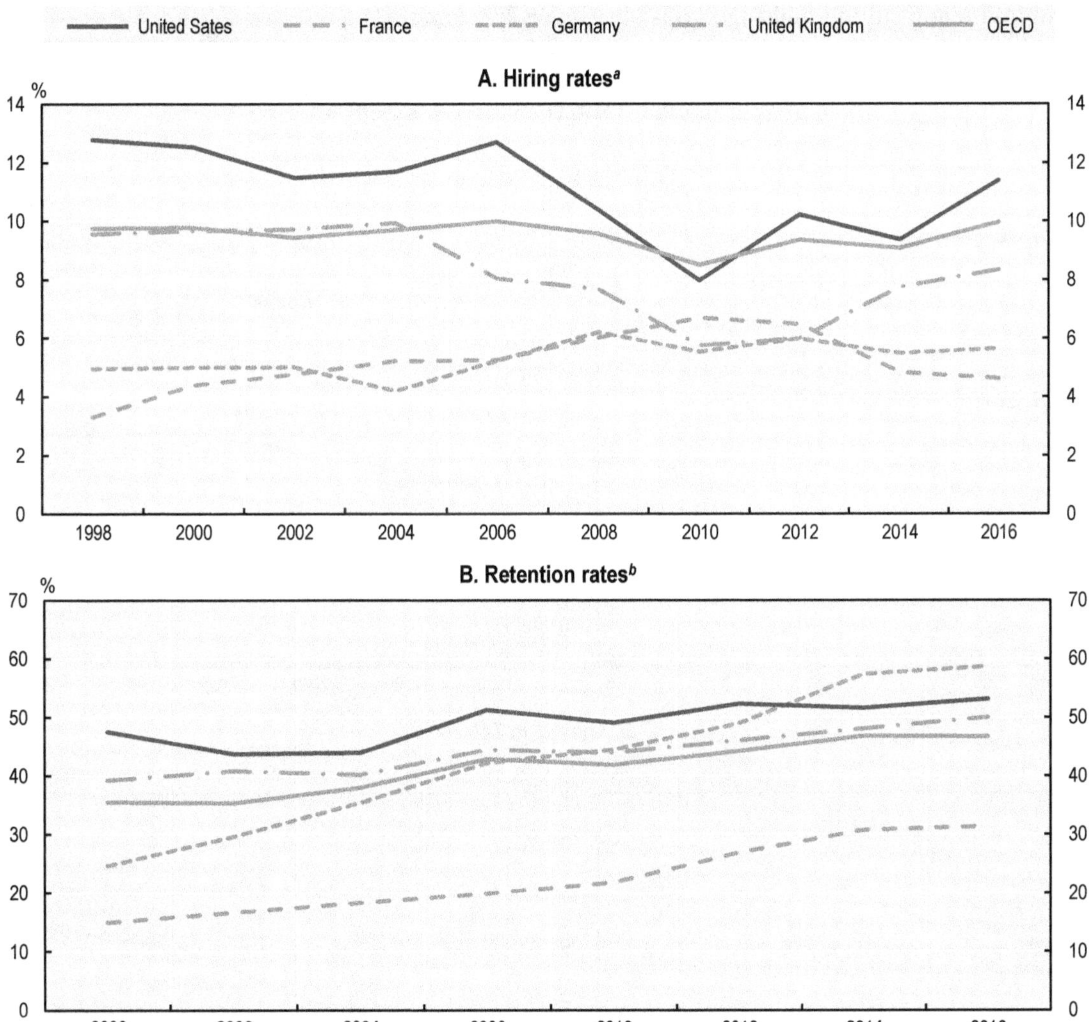

a) All employees aged 55-64 with tenure of less than one year as a percentage of the total number of employees two years before within the same age groups.

b) All employees currently aged 60-64 with job tenure of five years or more as a percentage of all employees aged 55-59 4-years previously. The accurate calculation should be 5-years previously but this has been modified for this figure in order to render the United States' biennial data comparable with the other countries.

Source: OECD calculations based on the *OECD Job Tenure Database*, http://stats.oecd.org//Index.aspx?QueryId=54562.

StatLink http://dx.doi.org/10.1787/888933643901

Older workers also face more difficulties finding a new job after displacement: once other characteristics are controlled for, workers aged 55-64 have a probability of re-employment that is some 19 percentage points lower than for people aged 25-34; with many displaced older workers retiring completely from the labour force (OECD, 2016[1]).

Trends in hiring and retention together determine employment. Figure 2.2 compares employment rates of older people in the United States to three other major OECD countries and the OECD average. Historically, employment of people aged 55-64 in the United States has been higher than in most other OECD countries, but whereas many OECD countries, especially Germany, have seen increases over the past decade, there has been little change in the United States for the group aged 55-64, with an increase of the employment of individuals aged 65-74 (Figure 2.2, Panel B) [1].

Figure 2.2. High employment rates of older US people but little change in recent years compared to other OECD countries, except after 65

As a percentage of each age group

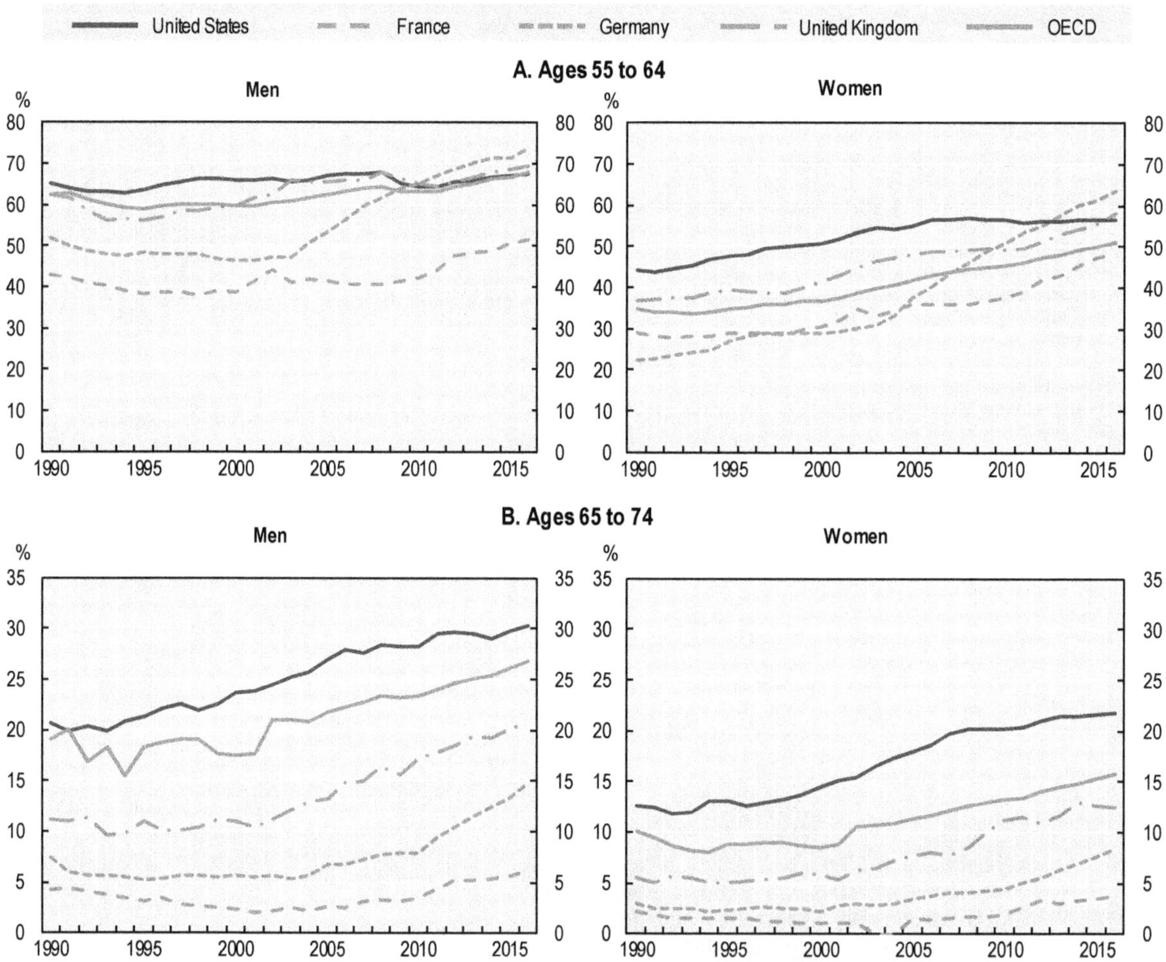

Source: *OECD Employment Database*, www.oecd.org/employment/database.

StatLink http://dx.doi.org/10.1787/888933643920

Figure 2.3. US workers retire across a wider age range than workers in other large OECD countries

Labour market status by age (50-69) and gender, selected OECD countries

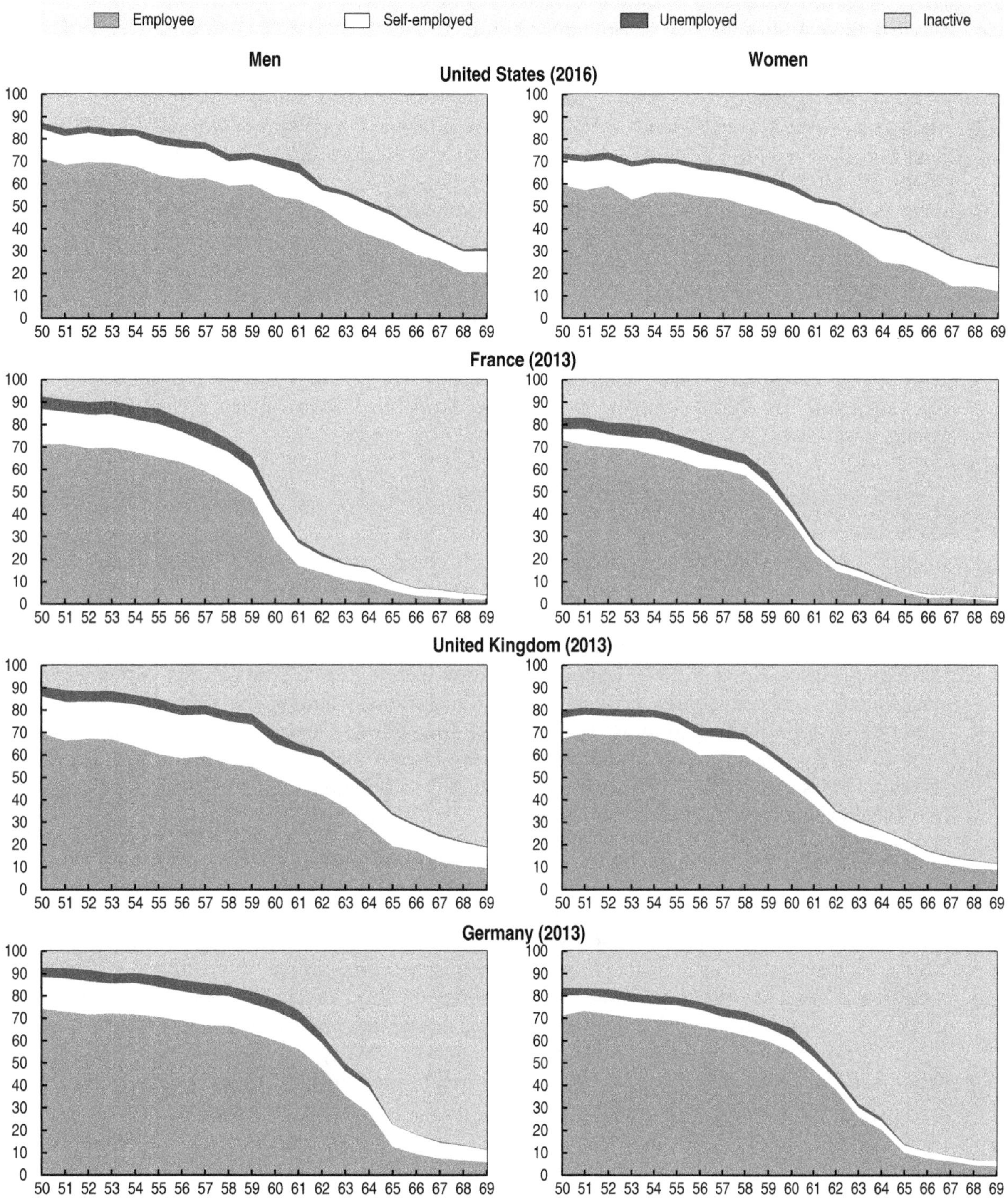

Source: OECD calculations based on the European Union Labour Force Survey for European countries and the Current Population Survey for the United States.

StatLink http://dx.doi.org/10.1787/888933643939

In absence of a mandatory retirement age in the United States, the pattern of changes in labour force status over the life cycle shows more variation in the effective age of retirement than in other major OECD countries (Figure 2.3). Moreover, the self-employed retire particularly late in the United States. Nevertheless, even in the United States, labour force participation rates fall considerably before the age at which workers receive full social security pensions (currently 66).

The increase in employment rates of older people across OECD countries partly reflects a number of measures that countries have taken to encourage and enable workers to retire later (see Chapter 1). But has this been at the expense of worsening job opportunities for young people? According to Gruber and Milligan (2010[7]) using US state-level data, there is little evidence of substitution between younger and older workers. Munnel and Yanyuan Wu (2012[8]) also show that there are no significant changes in the relationship between youth and older worker employment as a result of the Great Recession. Evidence for 25 OECD countries (including the United States) over the period 1997-2011 suggests that increases in the employment rate of older workers are either associated with increases in the youth employment rate or have no impact at all (OECD, 2013[9]).This suggests that with the right policies in place, employment prospects can be increased at the same time for all age groups and that more jobs for older workers does not mean fewer jobs for younger workers.

Unequal access to good jobs for older workers

Older workers are a very diverse group and average outcomes mask important divergences according to socio-economic and demographic characteristics such as gender, education, race and disability (Figure 2.4). Are these differences more marked in the United States than in other OECD countries? While the employment rate of women aged 60-64 is nearly 30% lower than for men across the OECD and the EU, the value in the United States is under 20%. For education, the differences in employment outcomes for older workers are slightly greater in the OECD area, including the United States – tertiary education leading to around 30% higher likelihood of employment for men and over 40% for women. For older individuals in the United States, the gap in employment rates by race is smaller than by education, albeit still substantial (with a 20% gap for men and 10% for women – data for other countries is not comparable).

A striking difference is the low level of employment of disabled individuals in the United States compared to other countries. Figure 2.4 shows that older disabled people in the United States are two thirds less likely to be employed than older able-bodied people – a much greater difference than that across the EU (44% – no OECD average is available). This gap may partly be explained by differences in employment protection, making retention of workers in the United States more sensitive to changes in individuals' productivity. Furthermore, other OECD countries have implemented measures seeking to better integrate disabled people into the labour market. Many EU countries as well as Japan and Korea operate quotas with penalties for firms who miss them (Lee and Lee, 2016[10]). Switzerland with an employment gap of only 20% has an insurance system to cover additional expenses employers may face when adapting workspaces for disabled individuals (for more examples on policies in this area, see below in the section on Public Policies).

Figure 2.4. Large disparities in employment rates by education and disability status in the United States

Employment gaps for adults aged 55-64 by selected socio-demographic characteristics, United States and OECD and EU averages, 2016

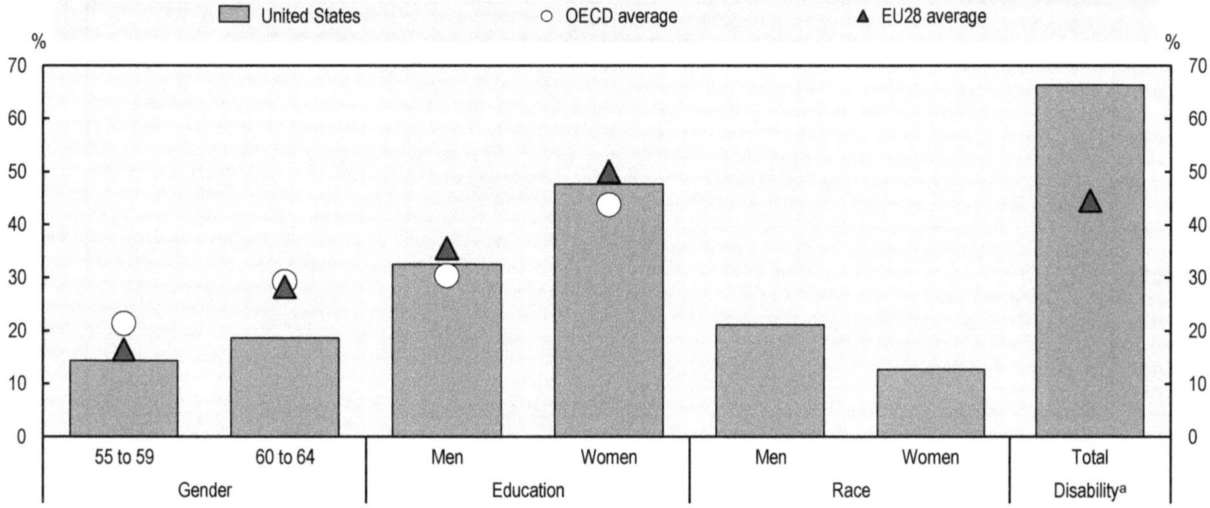

Note: *Employment gap by gender:* the difference between the employment rate (ER) of men and the ER of women, expressed as a percentage of the ER of men. *Employment gap by education:* the difference between the ER of men (women) with tertiary education and the ER of men (women) with less than upper secondary, expressed as a percentage of the ER of men (women) with tertiary education. *Employment gap by race:* the difference between the ER of white men (women) and the ER of black or African American men (women), expressed as a percentage of the ER of white men (women). *Employment gap by disability status:* the difference between the ER of people with no disabilities and the ER of people with disabilities, expressed as a percentage of the ER of people with no disabilities.

a) Data for the EU28 average refer to year 2011.

Source: *OECD Employment Database* (www.oecd.org/employment/database), *OECD Education at a Glance* (http://dx.doi.org/10.1787/eag-2017-en), Eurostat and the Current Population Survey (https://www.bls.gov/cps/).

StatLink http://dx.doi.org/10.1787/888933643958

Given the relative freedom with which firms in the United States determine wages, lack of demand for older workers may translate more immediately into lower wages than in other OECD countries with higher levels of minimum wages. Figure 2.5 shows that while mean hourly earnings of workers aged 55-65 in the United States are high, hourly earnings vary strongly. Inequality towards the extremes of the distribution is particularly marked – the 90-10 ratio comparing the top 10% (the 90th percentile) to the bottom 10% yields a multiple of 4.81 for the United States, but only 2.55 in France, 3.5 in the United Kingdom, 4.07 in Japan and 4.17 in Germany. Contrasting respectively the 90th percentile and 10th to the median reveals that the high US value is driven both by low earnings at the bottom of the distribution and by high earnings of the top 10%. Wage inequality of persons aged 55-65 generates considerable earnings inequality later in life via the pension system. Earnings inequality of over-65s is already amongst the highest in the OECD (OECD, 2017[11]). Measures increasing firms' demand for older workers could have long-lasting effects if this results in higher earnings especially for low-paid workers.

Figure 2.5. Germany and the United States have greater wage dispersion for older workers

Distribution of hourly wages in 2012 USD, workers aged 55-65

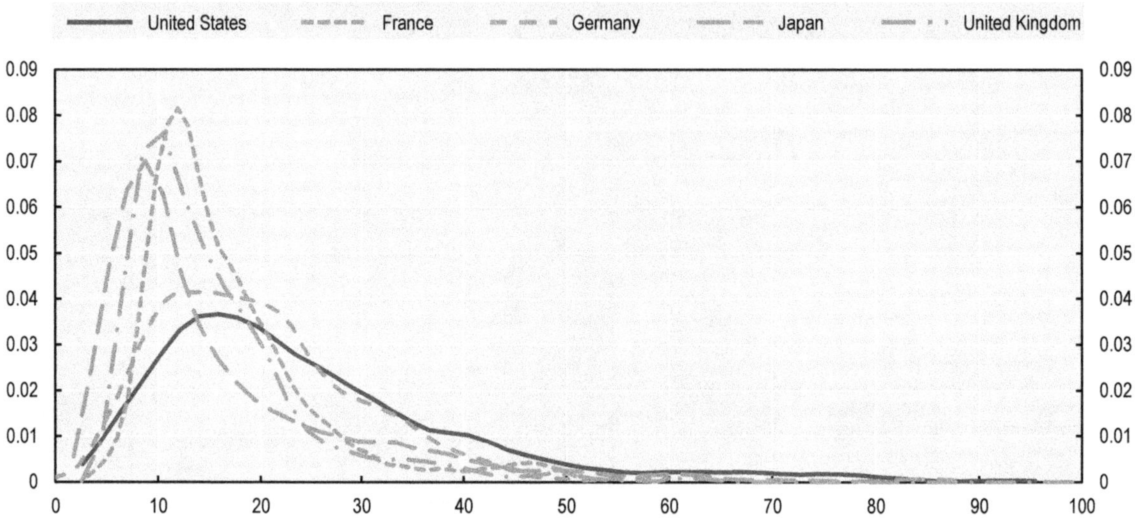

Note: Hourly wages are adjusted from national currency to 2012 US dollars, adjusted for purchasing power and trimmed of the top and bottom percentiles to control for extreme values.
Source: OECD calculations based on the Survey of Adult Skills (PIAAC) (2012, 2015), www.oecd.org/skills/piaac/.

StatLink http://dx.doi.org/10.1787/888933643977

Employment protection in the United States is relatively weak

In the United States, individual dismissals traditionally follow the doctrine of employment-at-will[2], although this principle has been softened in a number of US states. Furthermore, the threat of litigation by employees in combination with federal anti-discrimination law has generated a *de facto* need for firms to provide a legitimate reason for dismissal (Colvin, 2012[12]), – see below for more information on anti-age discrimination legislation). Rules governing dismissals are all the more relevant since there is no mandatory retirement age for most occupations in the United States[3], contrary to other OECD countries. Employers and workers could benefit from more support to cope with dismissals.

Employment Protection Legislation (EPL) in the United States is one of the least strict amongst OECD countries with respect to the ease and cost for employers of dismissing workers (Figure 2.6). Employers face no requirements to provide advance notice against individual dismissals; there is no requirement to consult with unions before dismissals take place; nor is there any provision to provide severance payments. Regulations in the case of mass dismissals are relatively stricter but remain rather lenient compared with other OECD countries. With less strict EPL, short-run reductions in a firm's production may result in lay-offs more readily than in other countries. Labour adjustment in the United States primarily takes place by reducing the number of people in work rather than adapting hours of work.

At the same time, strict EPL may reduce firms' willingness to hire workers in the first place. Uncertainty about older workers' capabilities may aggravate employers' caution in hiring older workers if there is a high level of EPL. Meanwhile, not all workers gain equally from the flexibility resulting from lower employment protection. Older workers experience particularly large income losses and suffer from lower re-employment rates after displacement. On balance, Autor et al. (2006[13]) find modest negative employment effects especially for older workers of the "implied contract doctrine (which limits employment at will by requiring good cause for dismissals), but no effects for two other restrictions on wrongful dismissal, the "good faith" and "public policy" exemptions.

In the absence of strong employment protection rules, schemes have been set up to prevent unnecessary job losses and connect laid-off workers to employment services immediately. These include rapid response services, layoff aversion schemes and recently also short-time work programmes. All of these schemes would benefit from wider coverage and greater effectiveness (OECD, 2016[1]).

Figure 2.6. Federal employment protection law is very limited in the United States

Protection of permanent workers against individual and collective dismissals, 2013

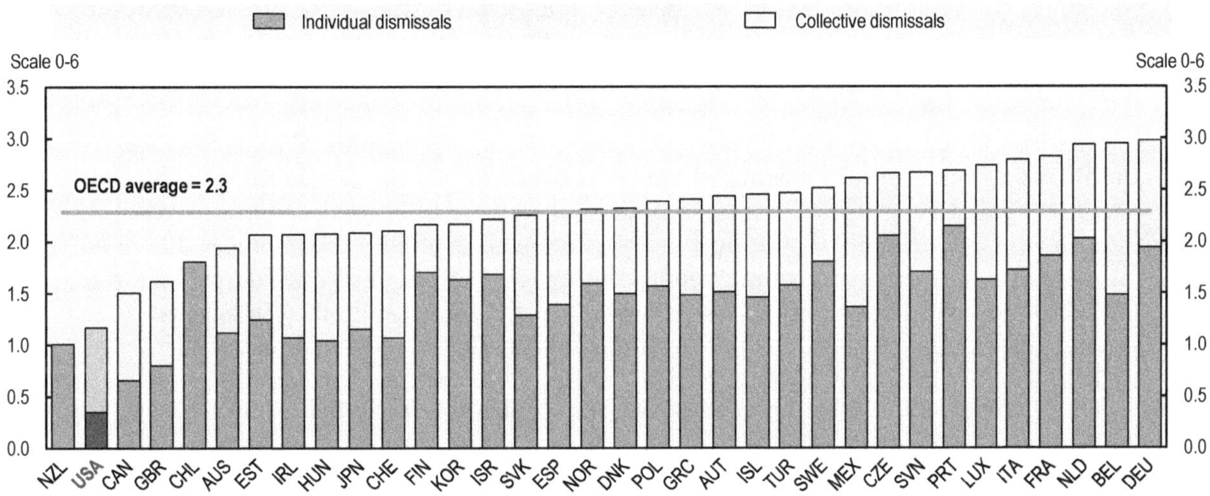

Note: The figure presents the contribution of employment protection for regular workers against individual dismissal and additional provisions for collective dismissal to the indicator of employment protection for regular workers against individual and collective dismissal. The height of the bar represents the value of the indicator.

Source: *OECD Employment Protection Database*, http://dx.doi.org/10.1787/lfs-epl-data-en.

StatLink http://dx.doi.org/10.1787/888933643996

Skills and productivity of older workers

Firms' willingness to retain and hire older workers depends importantly on the balance between older workers' labour costs and their productivity. There is a paucity of research in the United States that explains why employers hire and retain older workers (Agbayani et al., 2016[14]). One of the main constraints is the lack of linked employer-employee data. This section considers age differences in productivity and labour cost from an international perspective based on the OECD Survey on adult skills (Programme for the International Assessment of Adult Competencies, PIAAC). In comparison to other large OECD countries, older workers in the United States perform well in skill tests and use these skills as much as younger workers. This is related to better educational outcomes and more mobility across occupations and jobs. While job mobility remains high, special attention ought to be paid to the role of non-labour costs, in particular employer-provided health, in reducing job mobility.

The first part of this section presents age differences in workers' information processing skills, since data on individual productivity levels are not available for most jobs. However, older workers' individual skills do not directly translate to productivity. Rather, productivity depends also on technological and organisational choices. Changing tasks or responsibilities within a job or moving across occupations can preserve older workers' productivity. Therefore, the second part of this section considers workers' and firms' strategies in adapting to ageing.

Older workers' skills

There is consistent evidence of an age differentials in skills, with workers' skills peaking at ages 20-30 across different countries (for an overview, see Desjardins and Warnke (2012[15])). This chapter extensively uses PIAAC data on skill levels in 28 OECD countries. By administering tests to measure individuals' skills, PIAAC goes beyond subjective assessments and formal qualifications, increasing the reliability of cross-country comparisons. Individuals are required to perform information-processing tasks across different domains. Results from different tests have been usefully summarised in indicators for literacy and numeracy skills (Quintini, 2014[16]). Figure 2.7 and Figure 2.8 present respondents' average scores of these indices across different ages and countries. It is important to note that these data were only collected at one point in time, making it difficult to attribute age differences in skills to ageing, rather than differences across cohorts or time periods (Paccagnella, 2016[17]). While individuals over the age of 30 show lower skill levels on average, the differences in the United States are amongst the smallest across all countries studied, for both literacy and numeracy.

Figure 2.7. Age differences in literacy are small in the United States

Average literacy score by age

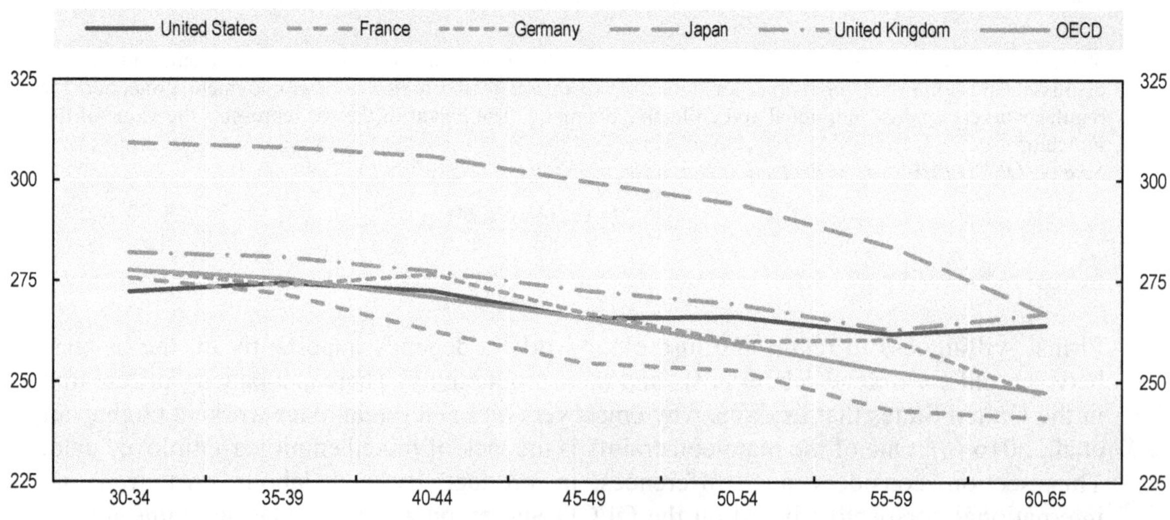

Note: The OECD is an unweighted average and excludes Hungary, Iceland, Latvia, Luxembourg, Mexico, Portugal and Switzerland. Data for the United Kingdom refer to England and Northern Ireland.
Source: OECD calculations based on the Survey of Adult Skills (PIAAC) (2012, 2015), www.oecd.org/skills/piaac/.

StatLink http://dx.doi.org/10.1787/888933644015

Figure 2.8. Age differences in numeracy are small in the United States

Average numeracy score by age

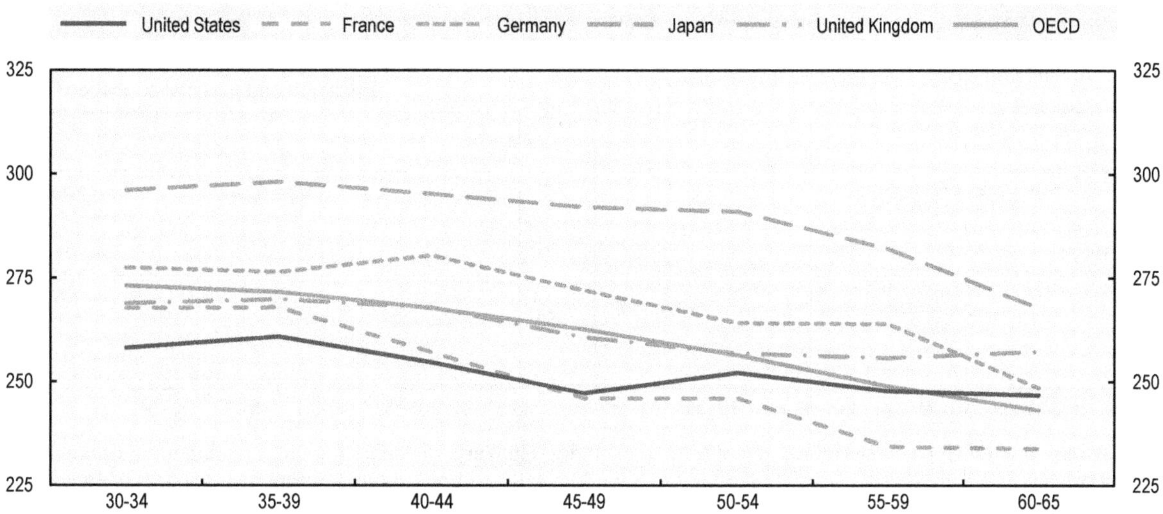

Note: The OECD is an unweighted average and excludes Hungary, Iceland, Latvia, Luxembourg, Mexico, Portugal and Switzerland. Data for the United Kingdom refer to England and Northern Ireland.
Source: OECD calculations based on the Survey of Adult Skills (PIAAC) (2012, 2015), www.oecd.org/skills/piaac/.

StatLink http://dx.doi.org/10.1787/888933644034

Older individuals' higher levels of education in the United States are partly responsible for the smaller age differential in skills compared to other countries. In other countries younger cohorts have much higher levels of educational outcomes than older cohorts (e.g. Japan), whereas educational outcomes across generations are more similar in the United States. In Figure 2.9 and Figure 2.10, Panel A shows the normalized age differential for literacy and numeracy, respectively, where in each case the skill level of the age bracket 30-34 is normalized to 100 but before adjusting for different levels of education.[4] For both literacy and numeracy, the skill level of the age group 60-65 is at least 10% below the level of 30-34 year olds in Germany, France and Japan, while the reduction in the United States is less than 5%. Controlling for educational differences across different age groups completely eliminates age differences in literacy and numeracy in the United States and the United Kingdom (Panel B of Figure 2.9 and Figure 2.10), while age differences are only attenuated in Germany, France and Japan.

Figure 2.9. Older US workers with same education are no less literate than young

Index of literacy skills, whole sample (aged 30-34=100)

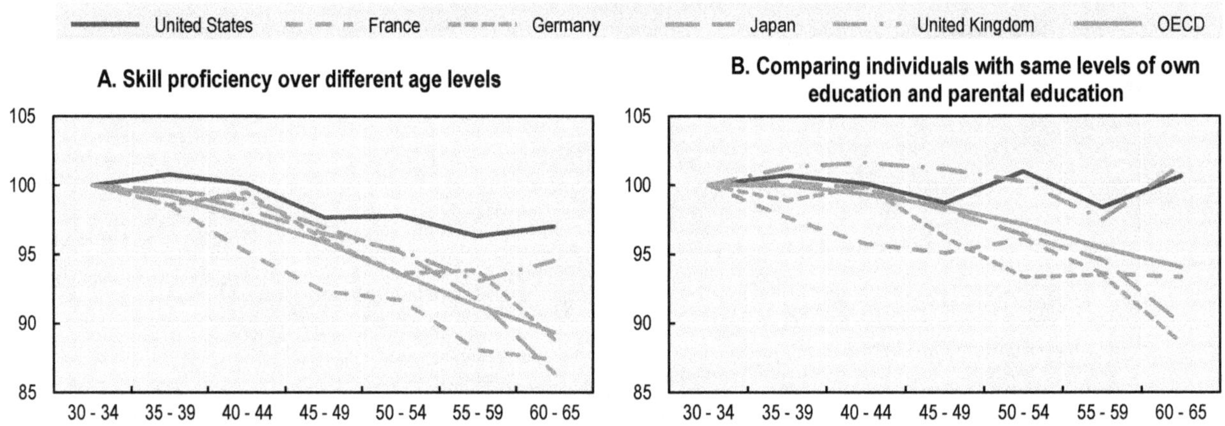

Note: The OECD is a weighted average and excludes Hungary, Iceland, Latvia, Luxembourg, Mexico, Portugal and Switzerland. Data for the United Kingdom refer to England and Northern Ireland. Results are presented as an index relative to the response of those respondents aged 30 to 34 years. **Panel A**: Estimates were obtained by regressing factor variables indicating age, gender, and country on literacy proficiency. **Panel B**: Estimates were obtained by regressing age, gender, and country dummies, as well as factor variables indicating the educational attainment of the respondent, their mother, and their father on literacy proficiency.
Source: OECD calculations based on the Survey of Adult Skills (PIAAC) (2012, 2015), www.oecd.org/skills/piaac/.

StatLink http://dx.doi.org/10.1787/888933644053

Figure 2.10. Older workers' lower numeracy skills also driven by lower educational outcomes

Index of literacy skills, whole sample (aged 30-34=100)

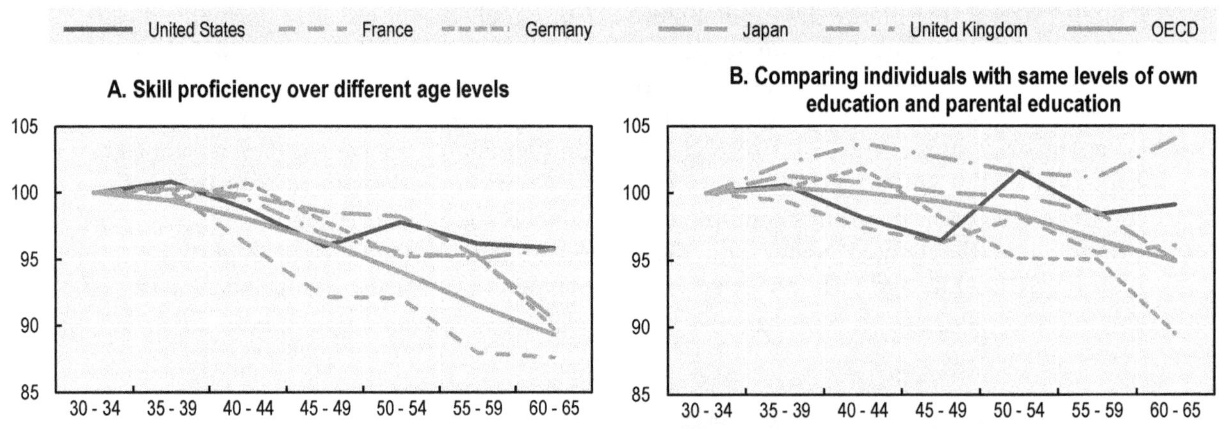

Note: The OECD is a weighted average and excludes Hungary, Iceland, Latvia, Luxembourg, Mexico, Portugal and Switzerland. Data for the United Kingdom refer to England and Northern Ireland. Results are presented as an index relative to the response of those respondents aged 30 to 34 years. **Panel A:** Estimates were obtained by regressing factor variables indicating age, gender, and country on numeracy proficiency. **Panel B**: Estimates were obtained by regressing age, gender, and country dummies, as well as factor variables indicating the educational attainment of the respondent, their mother, and their father on numeracy proficiency.
Source: OECD calculations based on the Survey of Adult Skills (PIAAC) (2012, 2015), www.oecd.org/skills/piaac/.

StatLink http://dx.doi.org/10.1787/888933644072

The small disadvantage of older US workers by international standards is remarkable but should be interpreted with caution. It is also consistent with lower levels of literacy of recent cohorts. The Society for Human Resource Management (SHRM) (2015[18]) presents a survey of a non-representative sample of US human resource managers who were asked to assess the strong points of employees over the age of 55. From a wide range of basic skills, the three most frequently cited skills relate to different dimensions of literacy. Older workers in the future may then have lower skill levels than current older workers. Furthermore, if there is a cohort effect in favour of current older generations, this implies that ageing has a more negative effect on skill levels than Figure 2.9 and Figure 2.10 suggest.

Age differences in skills among workforce and population

The analysis so far has considered age differences in skills across the whole population. However, for firms' retention decision, skills of the labour force are relevant. Older individuals' skills may be lower than those of younger workers as a result of specific workers retiring. This could mean that average skill levels in the workforce are constant across age groups despite differences in skill levels across age groups of the whole population. A great advantage of the PIAAC data is that it contains information from both individuals in and out of the labour force – thus including the retired population. Figure 2.11 contrasts age differences in skills in the workforce (Panels B) with age differences in skills across the whole population (Panels A). Both the pattern and the level of the left and right Panels are similar across all countries studied. Across the OECD, as well as in France, Germany and Japan, the employed population shows slightly larger differences in skill levels between the youngest (30-34) and oldest (60-65) age groups. This is in line with the idea that less skilled workers may be more likely to be non-employed. This pattern is not found for the United States and the United Kingdom, but in all countries the differences appear small. This suggests that different rates of labour force participation at different ages are not driving skill differences across ages. This also suggests that pre-retirement of workers in the age range 60-65 is not importantly driven by lower skill levels. Older unemployed individuals may nevertheless face particular challenges – an issue discussed in detail in Chapter 3.

Figure 2.11. Differences in participation are not driving age differences in literacy and numeracy proficiency

Literacy and numeracy proficiency, individuals aged 30-65

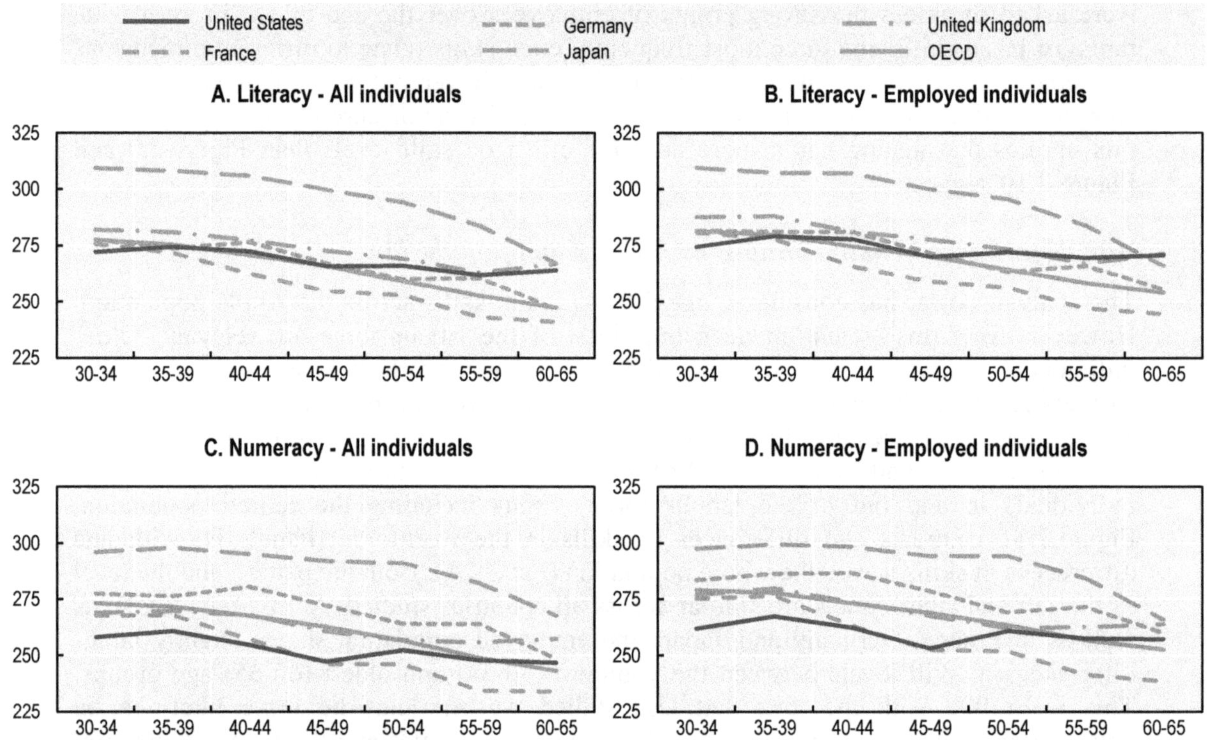

Note: The OECD is an unweighted average and excludes Hungary, Iceland, Latvia, Luxembourg, Mexico, Portugal and Switzerland. Data for the United Kingdom refer to England and Northern Ireland.
Source: OECD calculations based on the Survey of Adult Skills (PIAAC) (2012, 2015), www.oecd.org/skills/piaac/.

StatLink http://dx.doi.org/10.1787/888933644091

Adapting to ageing: Changing jobs, occupations and technologies

Despite the reduction in observable skills across several countries documented above, there is mixed evidence on the effect of the age composition of the workforce on firm-level productivity. Mahlberg et al. (2013[19]) find no evidence that a larger share of older Austrian workers is associated with lower productivity while Aubert and Crépon (2006[20]) find reductions in productivity occur after age 55 in France. Recorded skill declines concern information-processing skills such as literacy and numeracy. The difficulty of finding associated firm productivity differentials points to factors mitigating the effect of these skills on productivity – at least amongst firms that *do* employ older workers[5]. First, while proficiency in information-processing skills such as literacy and numeracy appears to decline somewhat with age, other skills used by firms do not. Second, workers may not only change the skills they use in their current job, but move to activities where these skills are more highly valued. Sanzenbacher et al. (2017[21]) argue that workers over 55 who change jobs retire later, suggesting that they benefit from finding a better match. Third, this may be actively encouraged by firms changing the tasks older workers perform to enable them to remain productive. Fourth, firms' technology choices will depend on the relative skills of the workforce. For example, technologies reducing the physical demands of work may be particularly suited to firms facing an ageing workforce. The following sections discuss these in turn.

Older workers use different skills

Older workers collect experience that can counterbalance the loss of skills. Thus speed in reading and writing may be compensated by skill in managing workers or taking decisions. Börsch-Supan and Weiss (2016[22]) test the productivity of workers of different ages in an assembly line setting and find that older workers made significantly fewer important errors, and that this was mainly a result of experience. AARP (2015[23]) presents US evidence that workers aged over 50 are more committed to their employers.

In response to lower levels of skill proficiency in certain areas, older workers may move to tasks which require less of these skills. Romeu Gordo and Skirbekk (2013[24]) find that older German workers are less likely to engage in physically demanding jobs and those requiring fluid forms of intelligence (the capacity to solve new problems) than crystallized intelligence (accumulated knowledge and skills). The differences across age groups were however overshadowed by large differences over time. The distribution of tasks across different age groups was found to be much more similar in 2006 than in 1986, suggesting that technological change may have allowed older workers to increasingly perform similar tasks to younger workers. A survey showed that the number one new skill identified by Human Resource professionals in the United States was soft skills (interpersonal skills, communication, teamwork and leadership), for which the PIAAC data allow studying skill use across workers of different ages. Respondents were not only tested on their capacity to perform certain tasks, but also asked how often they perform these kinds of tasks. Figure 2.12 presents US respondents' answers. While Panels E and F in Figure 2.12 indicate that younger workers (aged 30-34) use numeracy skills more often, Panels A and B indicate that older workers (aged 55-65) are more likely to frequently read mails, memos and manuals. Panels C and D indicate that young workers are both more likely to never write reports and fill in forms, but also more likely to do so every day. This may be explained by a combination of two factors: First, older workers may more often occupy positions with more responsibility which requires frequently executing administrative tasks. Second, more junior staff may be more likely to be either specialized office assistants (with associated administrative tasks) or work in more manual occupations with little exposure to administrative work. The pattern is consistent with workers specializing in tasks according to their relative skills. Interestingly, though, the nuanced pattern of skill use in the United States presented in Figure 2.12 is not found across all OECD countries: Across 20 EU countries in which PIAAC data was collected, skill use by younger workers was higher in *all* categories corresponding to Panels A-F in Figure 2.12 (although differences were small). This suggests that US labour markets are relatively efficient at making use of older workers' skills compared to other labour markets.

Figure 2.12. Differences in reading, writing and numeracy tasks performed at work

Distribution of responses, percent of total responses within the United States

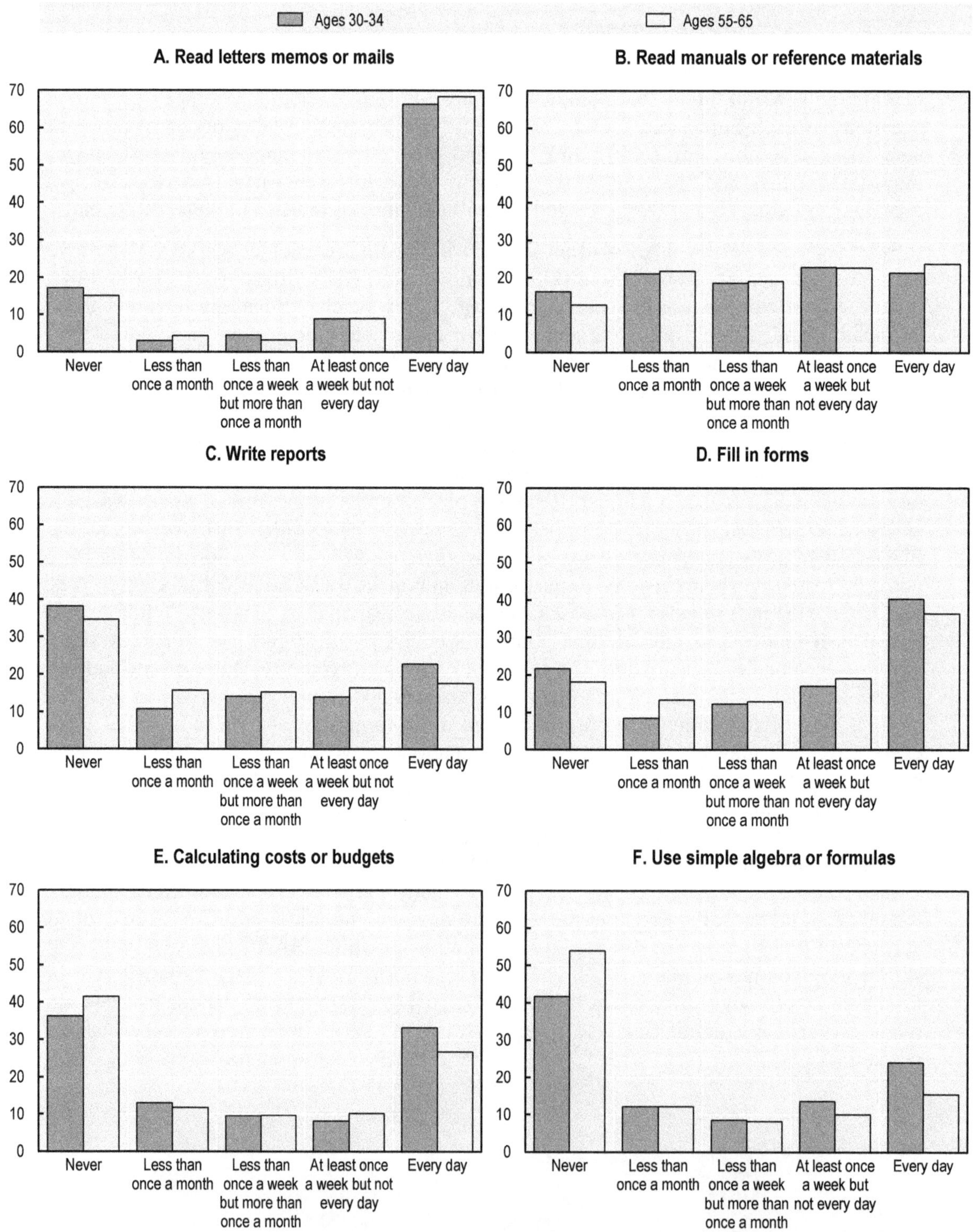

Source: OECD calculations based on the Survey of Adult Skills (PIAAC) (2012, 2015), www.oecd.org/skills/piaac/.

StatLink http://dx.doi.org/10.1787/888933644110

Figure 2.13 combines the use of literacy and numeracy skills into one indicator of basic skill use. Figure 2.13 compares age differences across countries, with the value of young respondents' skill use set to 100. (Given that the index is based on country-level normalization, comparisons of levels of skill use across countries should not be made, see Quintini (2014[16])). Panel A of Figure 2.13 shows that skill use is lower for successively older workers in nearly each age group and across all countries presented here. The reduction in skill use of older workers is much lower in the United States than in the other countries presented here. For individuals with the same levels of educational attainment (Panel B), we only see a skill reduction for workers over the age of 60. Older workers in the United States are more likely to use their basic skills because they have higher educational levels than in other countries. Note that the encouraging performance of older US workers vis-à-vis younger workers may partly be a result of low levels of skills of younger workers. This raises questions about older workers' employability in the future – Chapter 3 looks into this aspect in more detail. How do US workers achieve a high level of skill use?

Figure 2.13. In the United States, skill use of older workers declines less than in other countries, due to smaller educational differences across generations

Index of basic skill use at work, employed individuals (age group 30-34 = 100)

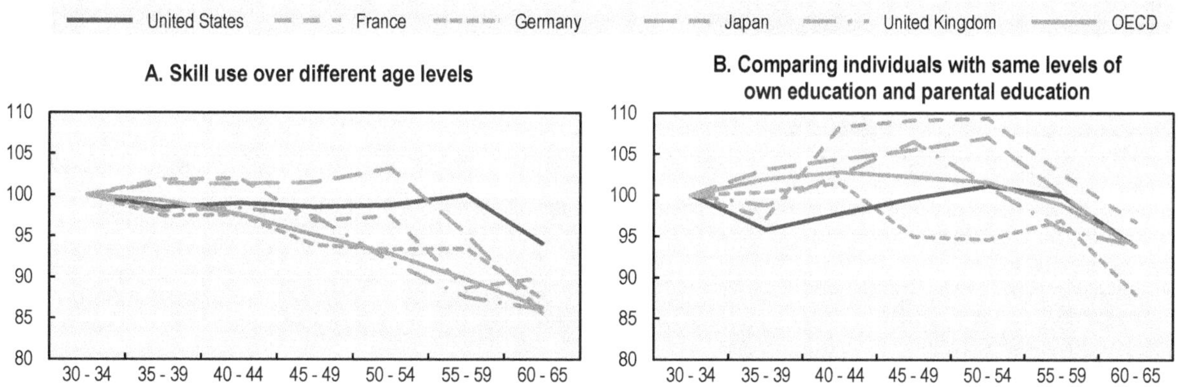

Note: The OECD is a weighted average and excludes Hungary, Iceland, Latvia, Luxembourg, Mexico, Portugal and Switzerland. Data for the United Kingdom refer to England and Northern Ireland. Results are presented as an index relative to the response of those respondents aged 30 to 34 years. **Panel A**: Estimates were obtained by regressing factor variables indicating age, gender, and country on basic skill use at work. **Panel B**: Estimates were obtained by regressing age, gender, and country dummies, as well as factor variables indicating the educational attainment of the respondent, their mother, and their father on basic skill use at work.

Source: OECD calculations based on the Survey of Adult Skills (PIAAC) (2012, 2015), www.oecd.org/skills/piaac/.

StatLink http://dx.doi.org/10.1787/888933644129

Older workers' occupations ensure high skill use

Investigating the determinants of differences in skill use may provide indications about how different labour markets ensure high levels of skill use among older workers. One reason for the high levels of skill use of older workers in the United States is simply that workers have better available skills. Furthermore, occupations seem to play an important role.

Figure 2.14 contrasts three sets of age differences in skill use: First, the bars represent the standardized difference in skill use comparing workers aged 55-65 to those aged 30-34, corresponding to the slope of skill use in Figure 2.13. As already noted, the United States is characterised by particularly small age differences in skill use. For numerical skills only Denmark, Sweden, Norway and Canada show smaller mean age differences. With respect to literary skills, older US workers are in fact more likely to use them at work than younger workers – a pattern not found for any other country.

Figure 2.14. Older workers use skills less because they have lower skill levels, but are over-proportionally found in occupations that use their skills efficiently

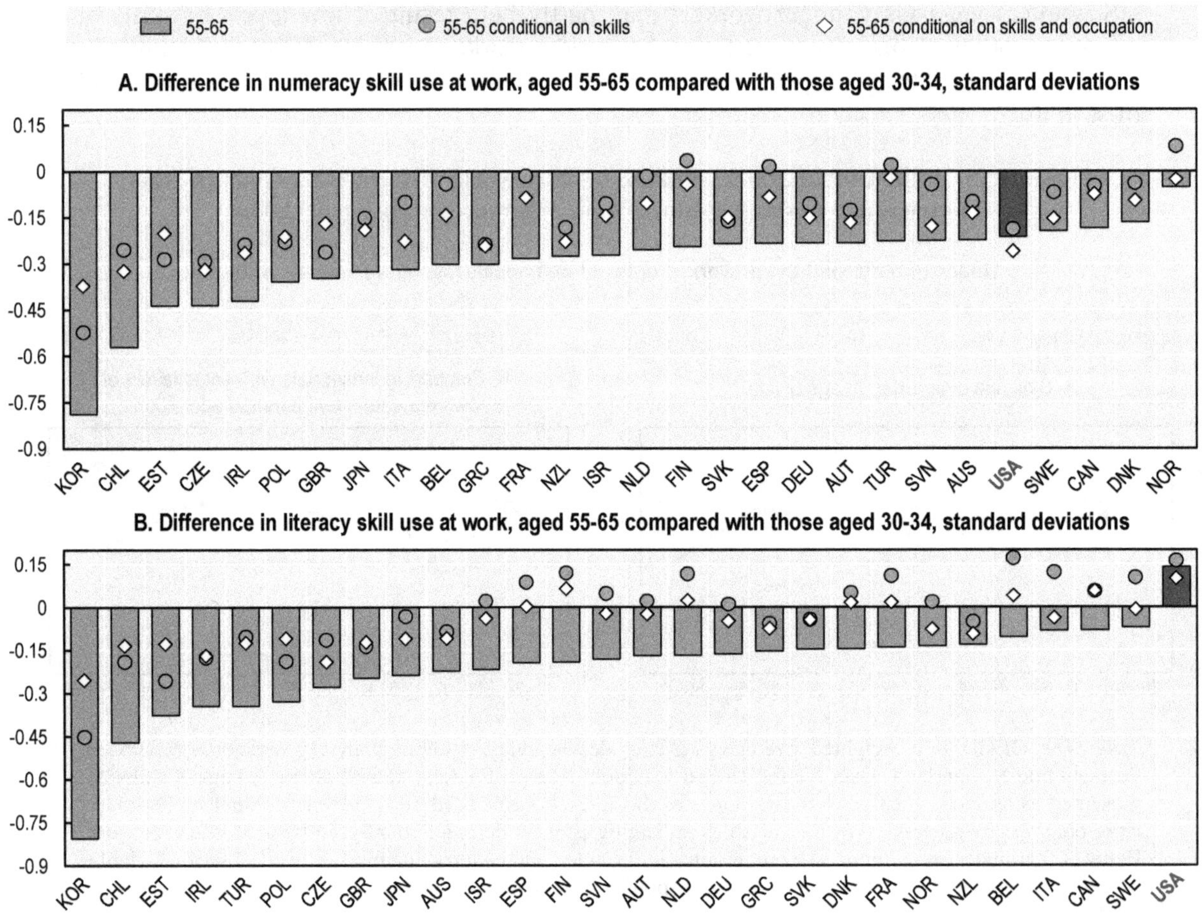

Note: The figure depicts the estimated coefficient of an indicator for those aged 55 to 65 within a regression including various other variables. For each model the dependent variable is a constructed index of the use of numeracy/reading skills at work, normalized by country. The model "55-65 conditional on skills" controls for numeracy/literacy proficiency as well as the age dummies in a regression framework. The model "55-65 conditional on skills and occupation" additionally contains controls for 1 digit ISCO-08 occupational groupings. Belgium refers to Flanders and the United Kingdom to England and Northern Ireland. Values on the vertical axis can be interpreted as the difference in literacy use of those workers aged 55 to 65 as compared with their peers aged 30 to 34, measured in standard deviations.

Source: OECD calculations based on the Survey of Adult Skills (PIAAC) (2012, 2015), www.oecd.org/skills/piaac/.

StatLink http://dx.doi.org/10.1787/888933644148

Second, the white squares in Figure 2.14 indicate age differences in skill use for individuals with the same level of skill. Do older workers who have the same level of skills use these less? Mean age differences in skill use become more favourable for older workers in all countries, suggesting that an important part of age differences in skill use is associated with differences in available skills. In fact, in four countries (Finland, Spain, Turkey and Norway), older workers are more likely to use numeracy skills than younger workers if they have the same level of skills. For literary skills, this is true for nearly half of countries in Figure 2.14. Since age differences in skills are relatively small in the United States, results for the conditional age differences in skill use are fairly similar to the unconditional ones.

Third, the black squares show age differences in skill use for individuals with the same skill levels and who share the same occupation. Interestingly, in most OECD countries (including the United States), age differences in skill use within a given occupation are larger than age differences overall. The fact that younger and older workers are found in different occupations diminishes age differences in skill usage. In fact, Panel B of Figure 2.14 shows that in a given occupation, older workers in the United States, Spain, Finland, the Netherlands, Denmark, France, Belgium, Italy, Sweden, Norway and Israel use literary skills more often.

The role of occupations in mediating skill use suggests international differences in patterns of occupational sorting with age. Figure 2.15 presents age distributions across specific occupations across five large OECD countries. The United States stands out as a country where young people under the age of 30 are over-proportionally employed in service and sales jobs (Figure 2.15, Panel A) as well as elementary occupations such as basic labourer (Panel B). At the same time, presumably in relation to the high rates of non-regular work among older workers, a large proportion of elementary occupations in Japan are carried out by workers over the age of 60. By contrast, management tasks are more strongly reserved to older workers in the United States than in Germany or the United Kingdom - an even stronger association between management and seniority is only found in Japan (Panel D). Professionals such as doctors or lawyers are far less likely to change their career. Consistent with this, differences across countries are particularly small for this group (Panel C).

Note that this pattern of occupational sorting by age is not *necessarily* a result of occupational mobility, with older workers moving to occupations that fit their relative skills. Given the cross-sectional nature of the data, it is not possible to identify potential generational (or cohort) effects which could produce the same pattern of age differences across occupations. For example, young workers may prefer different occupations today than previous generations. However, evidence from panel data also points to the importance of occupational mobility in explaining the types of jobs older workers hold. In line with the evidence discussed here, Sonnega et al. (2016[25]) and Johnson and Kawachi (2007[26]) show that workers' changing skills and preferences determine movements across occupations, and that this does not necessarily imply moving to higher-status or higher-income jobs.

Figure 2.15. Worker age profiles differ across countries and occupations

Age distribution by country and occupation, density

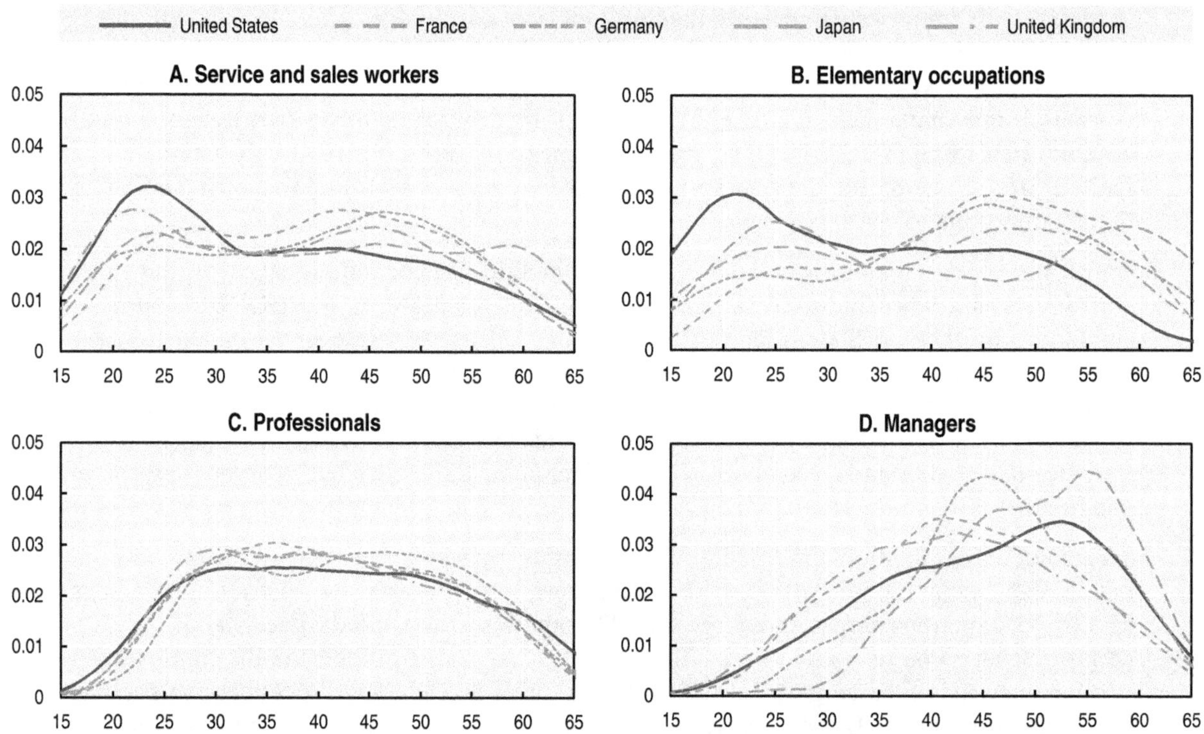

Note: Figures depict the smoothed age distribution of workers within a specified 1 digit ISCO 08 occupation group. Data for the United Kingdom refer to England and Northern Ireland.
Source: OECD calculations based on the Survey of Adult Skills (PIAAC) (2012, 2015), www.oecd.org/skills/piaac/.

StatLink http://dx.doi.org/10.1787/888933644167

Older workers' jobs involve more complex tasks

The previous section has shown that occupational mobility may play a role in ensuring good labour market outcomes for older workers. Whilst occupational classifications are rather broad, the PIAAC questionnaire additionally asks questions about individuals' specific tasks. Based on answers to these questions, four dimensions of job complexity have been constructed: i) how often workers *supervise* colleagues; ii) the extent to which individuals engage in *planning*; iii) the degree of *task discretion* workers have in their work; and iv) whether a job requires workers to *influence* others. Greater job complexity implies more abstract and less routine tasks in the semantics of the recent "task-based" literature (for an overview, see Autor and Handel (2013[27])). These tasks also require more so-called soft skills (interpersonal skills, communication, teamwork and leadership). According to a non-representative sample of US Human Resources professionals, these types of skill have been found to be particularly important for firms' hiring in response to skills shortages (SHRM, 2016[28]).

Figure 2.16. Older workers more likely to supervise colleagues, have higher task discretion, use planning skills and influencing others more often

Skill use at work, employed individuals (age group 30-34 = 100)

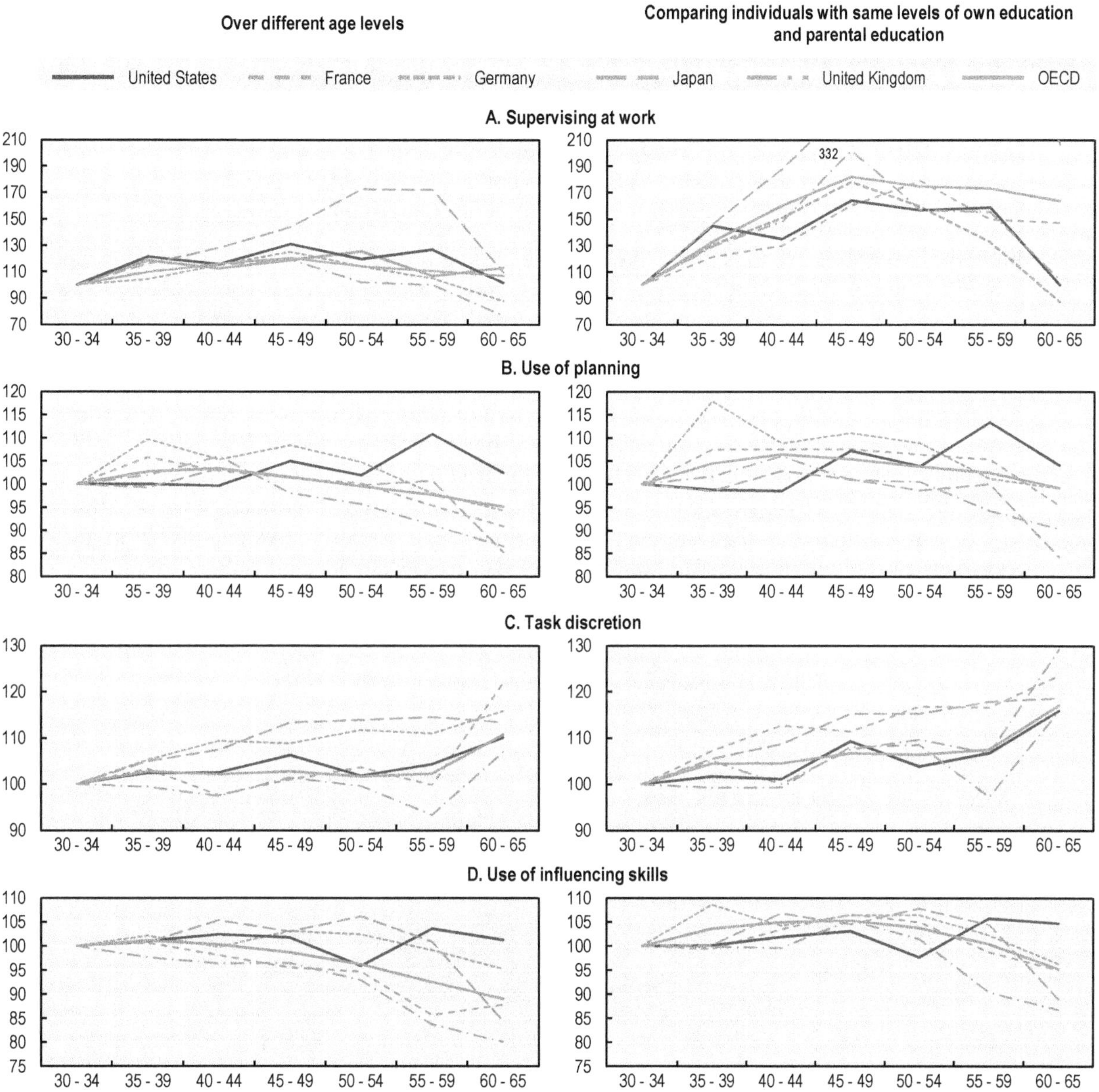

Note: The OECD is an unweighted average and excludes Hungary, Iceland, Latvia, Luxembourg, Mexico, Portugal and Switzerland. Data for the United Kingdom refer to England and Northern Ireland. Results are presented as an index relative to the response of those respondents aged 30 to 34 years. **Left-hand panels:** Estimates were obtained by regressing factor variables indicating age, gender, country and skill index. **Right-hand panels:** Estimates were obtained by regressing age, gender, country dummies, as well as factor variables indicating the educational attainment of the respondent, their mother, and their father on the skill index.

Source: OECD calculations based on the Survey of Adult Skills (PIAAC) (2012, 2015), www.oecd.org/skills/piaac/.

StatLink http://dx.doi.org/10.1787/888933644186

Figure 2.16 shows that older workers up to the age of 60 are more likely to be engaged in supervision (Panel A) and planning (Panel B) and are more likely to have jobs that that benefit from high levels of task discretion (Panel C) and that involve influencing others (Panel D). Compared to other large OECD countries, the age differential in these abstract tasks appears to be greater (in favour of older workers) in the United States with respect to planning and influencing, whilst the age differential in supervisory tasks appears relatively modest in the United States. Comparing only individuals with the same level of education (Figure 2.16, right-hand panels) reveals limited mean age differences in the United States except for supervision, where controlling for education increases the advantage of workers aged 45-55. This suggests that these workers perform supervisory duties mainly if they have better educational outcomes than older workers.

While older workers are thus more likely to use certain abstract tasks, their physical effort at work declines slightly on average for US workers, as Figure 2.17 shows. While the patterns appear to be rather different in the other OECD countries presented here, Panel B of Figure 2.17 shows that the age differences across different countries are more similar when young and older workers with the same educational levels are compared. US survey data from the Health and Retirement survey show large differences across different demographic characteristics, with half of older black workers describing their work as including "lots of physical effort" in 2014, compared to only one third of white workers (Ghilarducci et al., 2016[29]). The relationship between ageing and reduced physical effort may be larger than the data suggest if the time trend to less physical effort in the workplace affects younger workers before older workers (Bucknor and Baker, 2016[30]).

Figure 2.17. Older workers only see a small reduction in physical effort

Skill use at work, employed individuals (age group 30-34 = 100)

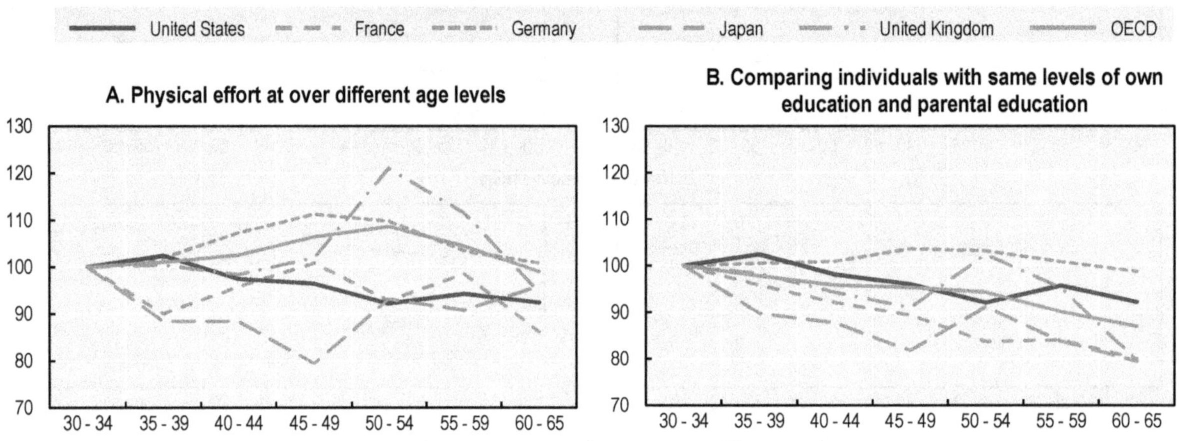

Note: The OECD is a weighted average and excludes Hungary, Iceland, Latvia, Luxembourg, Mexico, Portugal and Switzerland. Data for the United Kingdom refer to England and Northern Ireland. The data depicts survey takers response to the following question: "How often at work do you work physically for long periods of time?" Results are presented as an index relative to the response of those respondents aged 30 to 34 years. **Panel A**: Estimates were obtained by regressing factor variables indicating age, gender, and country on physical effort at work. **Panel B**: Estimates were obtained by regressing age, gender, and country dummies, as well as factor variables indicating the educational attainment of the respondent, their mother, and their father on physical effort at work.

Source: OECD calculations based on the Survey of Adult Skills (2012, 2015), www.oecd.org/skills/piaac/.

StatLink http://dx.doi.org/10.1787/888933644205

Policy makers have been concerned about older workers being side-lined due to lacking computing skills (or, more generally, skills relating to information and communications technologies (ICT)). Young people have been exposed to mobile phones, computer and social media early in life. This could put older workers at a disadvantage when these technologies are used in the workspace, opening a "digital divide" (Olphert and Damodaran, 2013[31]). Figure 2.18 reveals a clear pattern across five OECD countries: Older workers less often use information and communications tools (ICT) at work. However, the United States has the lowest differential, very close to zero. There is thus a remarkable equality in terms of ICT use across age groups in the United States, with only for the oldest age group in the sample displaying particularly low ICT usage. However, note that the measure of ICT use here does not differentiate between simple tasks such using emails and more advanced computing skills (e.g. programming).

Figure 2.18. Use of ICT at work

ICT skill use at work, employed individuals aged 55-65 compared with peers aged 30-34, standard deviations

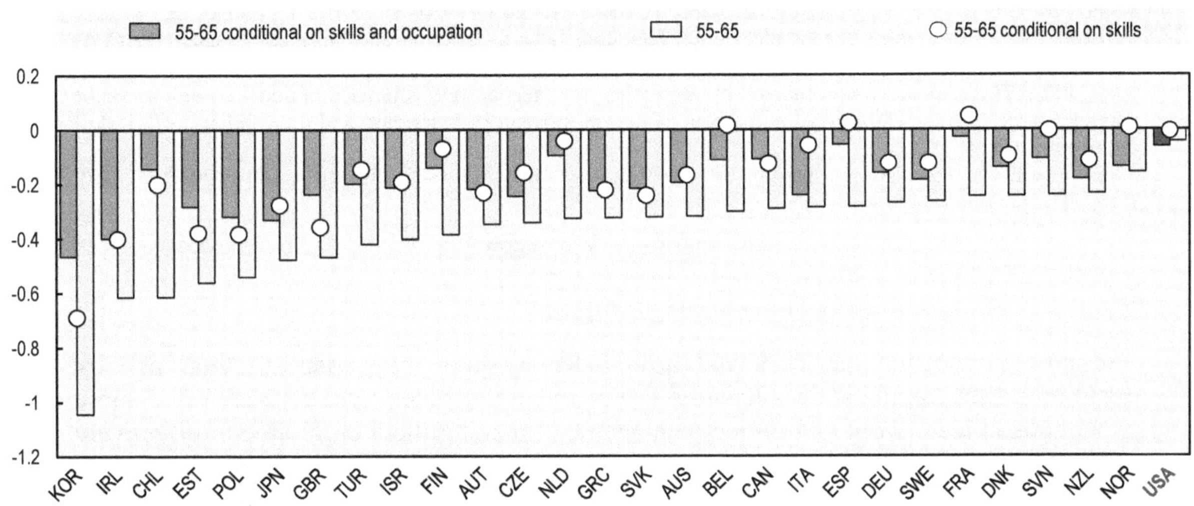

Note: The figure depicts the estimated coefficient of an indicator for those aged 55 to 65 within a regression including various other variables. For each model the dependent variable is an index of the use of ICT skill use at work, normalized by country. The model "55-65 conditional on skills" controls for numeracy/literacy proficiency as well as the age dummies in a regression framework. The model "55-65 conditional on skills and occupation" additionally contains controls for 1-digit ISCO-08 occupational groupings. Belgium refers to Flanders and the United Kingdom to England and Northern Ireland. Values on the vertical axis can be interpreted as the difference in literacy use of those workers aged 55 to 65 as compared with their peers aged 30 to 34, measured in standard deviations.
Source: OECD calculations based on the Survey of Adult Skills (PIAAC) (2012, 2015), www.oecd.org/skills/piaac/.

StatLink http://dx.doi.org/10.1787/888933644224

Figure 2.19 compares the pattern of ICT usage across different age groups in more detail in five large OECD countries. Lower levels of ICT use are found mainly for individuals in the 60-65 year bracket. Consistent with Figure 2.18, Figure 2.19 also shows that the United States alongside France and Germany has a very small age differential in ICT usage at work. Given that ICT skills are not an integral part of curricula in most OECD countries, it is maybe not surprising that, contrary to other types of skill, comparing individuals with the same level of educational attainment does not change the picture much (Figure 2.19, Panel B).

Figure 2.19. Modest age differences in ICT use except for 60-65 year olds

Index of ICT skill use at work, employed individuals (age group 30-34 = 100)

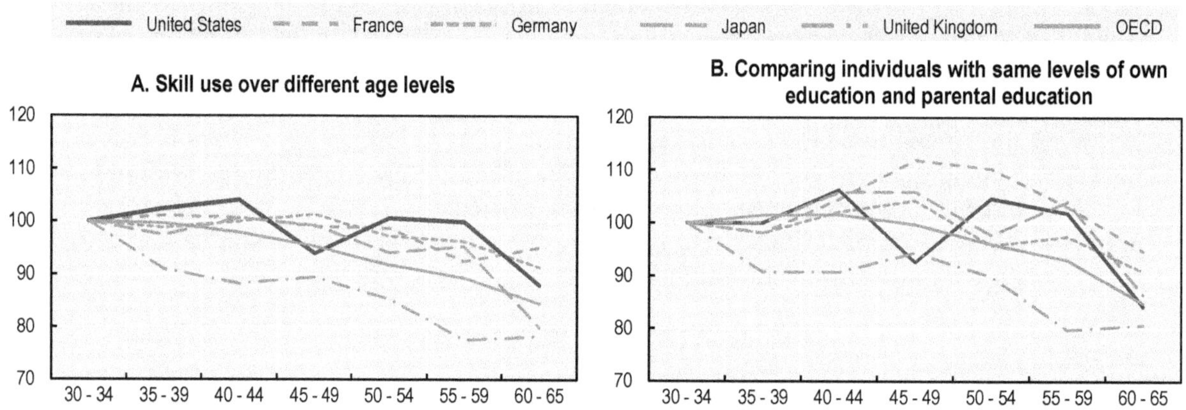

Note: The OECD is a weighted average and excludes Hungary, Iceland, Latvia, Luxembourg, Mexico, Portugal and Switzerland. Data for the United Kingdom refer to England and Northern Ireland. **Panel A**: Estimates were obtained by regressing factor variables indicating age, gender, and country on ICT skill use at work. **Panel B**: Estimates were obtained by regressing age, gender, and country dummies, as well as factor variables indicating the educational attainment of the respondent, their mother, and their father on ICT skill use at work.

Source: OECD calculations based on the Survey of Adult Skills (PIAAC) (2012, 2015), www.oecd.org/skills/piaac/.

StatLink http://dx.doi.org/10.1787/888933644243

Adapting to ageing by changing technologies

The previous section has reviewed how older workers may adapt to their age by exploiting their comparative advantages: For example, older workers may have more experience in team work and project management, making them more able to effectively supervise colleagues, while younger workers' physical strength may be greater. While part of adapting to ageing may thus consist in changing occupation or job tasks, firms employing older workers can also change working conditions to accommodate older workers' needs. The number one successful strategy concerns workplace flexibility (Whitman, 2014[32])

Telework

Telework can enable workers to have a better work-life balance (with some important caveats, see the literature review by Tavares (2017[33])) and may be particularly valuable for accommodating older workers' needs (AARP, 2015[23]). There is a trend to increased telework throughout OECD countries, including the United States (Eurofound and ILO, 2017[34]). With around 20% of US workers regularly working from home, the United States characterised by wide-spread use telework, though less than in Sweden and Finland. While few countries have specific telework legislation (for example Hungary, Italy and Spain), EU countries agreed a Framework Agreement on Telework in 2002. In many countries, telework is part of sectoral agreements between trade unions and employers (e.g. in Belgium, Italy, the Netherlands and Spain). Finland and Sweden organised a tripartite agreement with the national government and the social partners. Where private-sector agreements regarding telework are more difficult, the public sector can take a lead in creating social norms and establishing standards. In the United States, the Telework Enhancement Act of 2010 requires that all federal executive agencies create official teleworking policies, specify telework eligibility requirements, and disseminate information about telework opportunities to all employees. A report to the US Congress showed that 25% of federal workers age 60 and over teleworked in 2013, increasing from 21% in 2011 and similar to other age groups.[6]

Use of robots

Firms may respond to the long-term trend of an ageing workforce by more substantive changes in production technologies to ensure a high level of productivity. Bucknor and Baker (2016[30]) show a significant reduction between 2009 and 2014 in the share of older workers in physically demanding jobs. This development may be a result of technological progress favouring less physical work. However, it may also be a sign of firms' adapting to workforce ageing. Acemoglu and Restreppo (2017[35]) argue that the rate of technological adoption is a function of countries' demographic composition and relate this to the use of robots. Countries with higher levels of population ageing are thus more likely to show a large number of robots (Figure 2.20). They find this correlation across different OECD countries, even when they exclude Japan, the most emblematic case given rapid ageing and extensive use of robots. Drawing on related theoretical work, Acemoglu and Restreppo (2017[35]) also argue that the adoption of modern technology more than compensates for the reductions in per-capita labour supply, such that labour productivity actually increases with population ageing. They present suggestive cross-country evidence for the hypothesis that robots more than offset the effect of a smaller workforce on GDP levels (Figure 2.21). Not all researchers are as optimistic, however. Based on macroeconomic time-series data, Aiyar et al. (2016[36]) argue that population ageing causes lower total factor productivity.

Figure 2.20. Population ageing is associated with the introduction of robots

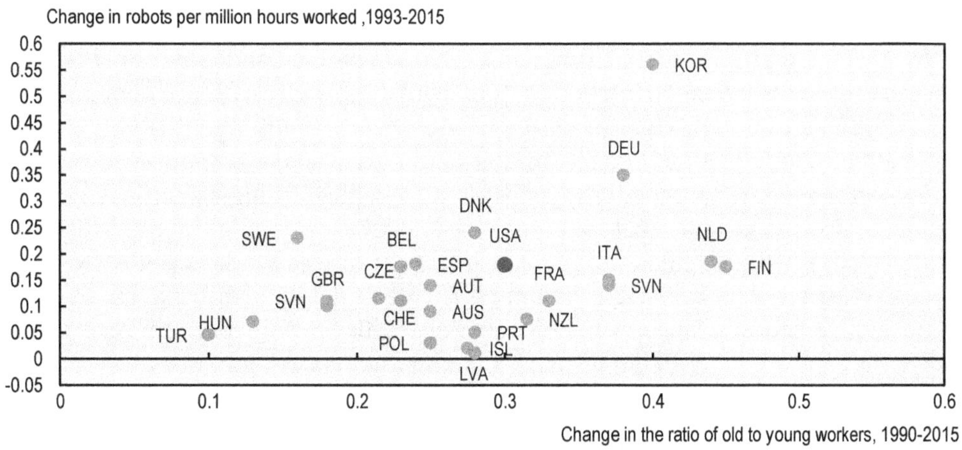

Note: Correlation between change in the ratio of old to young workers between 1990 and 2015 and change in the number of robots per million hours worked between 1993 and 2015.

Source: Acemoglu, D. and P. Restrepo (2017), "Secular Stagnation? The Effect of Aging on Economic Growth in the Age of Automation", *NBER Working Paper*, No. 23077, https://economics.mit.edu/files/12536.

StatLink http://dx.doi.org/10.1787/888933644262

Figure 2.21. Population ageing is not associated with lower growth rates

Correlation between ageing and growth in GDP per capita (in constant dollars)

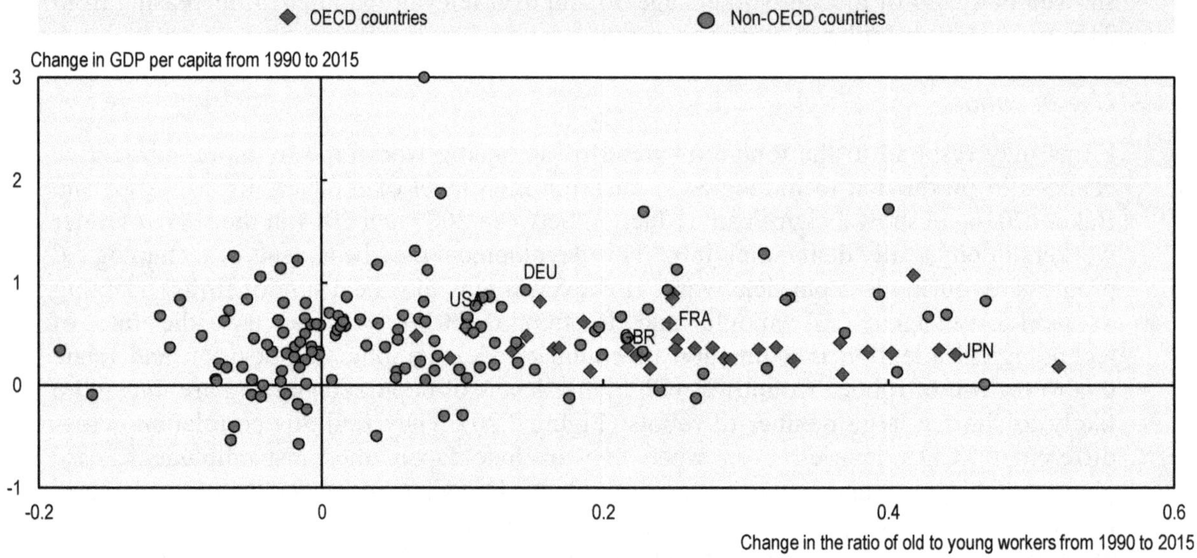

Note: Ageing is defined as the change in the ratio of the population above 50 years old to the population between aged 20 and 49.

Source: Acemoglu, D. and P. Restrepo (2017), "Secular Stagnation? The Effect of Aging on Economic Growth in the Age of Automation", *NBER Working Paper*, No. 23077, https://economics.mit.edu/files/12536.

StatLink http://dx.doi.org/10.1787/888933644281

Key stylised facts

Older workers in the United States have relatively higher skill levels compared with their younger counterparts than in other OECD countries. This small age differential is largely driven by more equal educational outcomes across younger and older workers in the United States than in other countries. In line with this, older US workers report high levels of skill use. The high level of skill use is associated with age differences in tasks and occupational composition. Older workers may partly adapt to their specific skill set by sorting into specific occupations, as well as by performing specific tasks within occupations. However, note that data on basic skills is available for workers and non-workers alike (in particular, retirees), while skill use at work is collected only for employees. With the data in hand, it is thus difficult to distinguish between adjustments over time and selection effects, whereby workers with specific occupations, tasks and skill usage patterns are more likely to remain in employment at older ages.

Within occupations, older workers are more likely to be found in jobs with higher job complexity. The data show that use of planning skills remains high for older workers, while their task discretion is higher and they are more likely to be supervising other workers than younger employees. These increases in job complexity may serve to raise older workers' productivity relative to younger colleagues. Patterns of ICT usage across ages suggest that concerns about ICT skills of older workers may be less a problem in the United States than in other major OECD countries – again related to the smaller generational gap in education in the United States.

Labour costs of older workers

Firms' willingness to retain and hire older workers depends on the relationship between their productivity and labour costs. While US employers have a high degree of flexibility in setting wages compared to other countries, other dimensions of labour cost may deter employment of older workers, especially health costs. The final part of the section thus considers paid leave, sick leave and employer healthcare benefits. Removing the Secondary Payer rule for Medicare would decrease labour costs for older workers. Special attention needs to be paid to any changes in the rules governing employer-provided health insurance. Relaxing the rules on coverage of workers with pre-existing health conditions, for example, may lead to "job lock" of older workers in their current jobs.

Seniority wages

In many OECD countries, concerns have been raised that seniority-based pay schemes may create a barrier to employment of older workers (Frimmel et al., 2015[37]). In the United States, fewer employment contracts are subject to seniority pay schemes than in other countries, mainly for unionised jobs and in the public sector. Seniority-based pay schemes thus exist for US teachers in most states and in the military. Federal employees are subject to the so-called General Schedule where wages increase regularly according to steps, unless workers' performance is unsatisfactory, which happens very rarely in practice. Paying more senior workers higher wages may provide incentives for workers to exert effort to stay in an organization and can thus encourage worker tenure – making it an interesting proposition for employers in jobs in which experience is valuable and monitoring performance is difficult. Analysis of earnings data from several large US employers reveals that, on average, earnings increase until around 30 years of tenure, but with considerable variation across industries (AARP, 2015[23]). While on average earnings increase to twice their initial level over the first 30 years of tenure, pay levels in some industries peak at 15 years of service and decrease after that. Tenure and experience effects importantly contribute to earnings differential by age, which using PIAAC-data appear to be small relative to the situation in other major OECD countries (Figure 2.22).[7]

Paid time off is a significant component of wage costs. Average levels of paid vacation are lower in the United States than in other OECD countries. Uniquely among OECD countries, there is no minimum number of paid vacations. Nevertheless, paid holidays and sick leave are provided to over 80% of private industry workers, with benefits estimated to make up 6.9% of total compensation (Van Giezen, 2013[38]). Many companies increase vacation allowances according to firm tenure. Based on the National Compensation Survey, Van Giezen (2013[38]) reports increases in the average number of vacation days from 10 to 20 days after 20 years of tenure. Using a regression framework taking into account selection effects of workers, Altonji and Usui (2007[39]) find similar increases in the amount of vacation taken – by 0.6, 1.1 and 1.6 weeks after 5, 10 and 20 years of tenure. Although limited in scope, the increase in paid time off for older workers may affect retention of older workers, akin to seniority pay scales. While these practices create a differential in labour costs, these rules may also constitute firms' best response to changing worker demands for days off.

Figure 2.22. Moderate variation in average earnings over the life cycle

Employed persons, hourly and monthly wages in 2012 USD

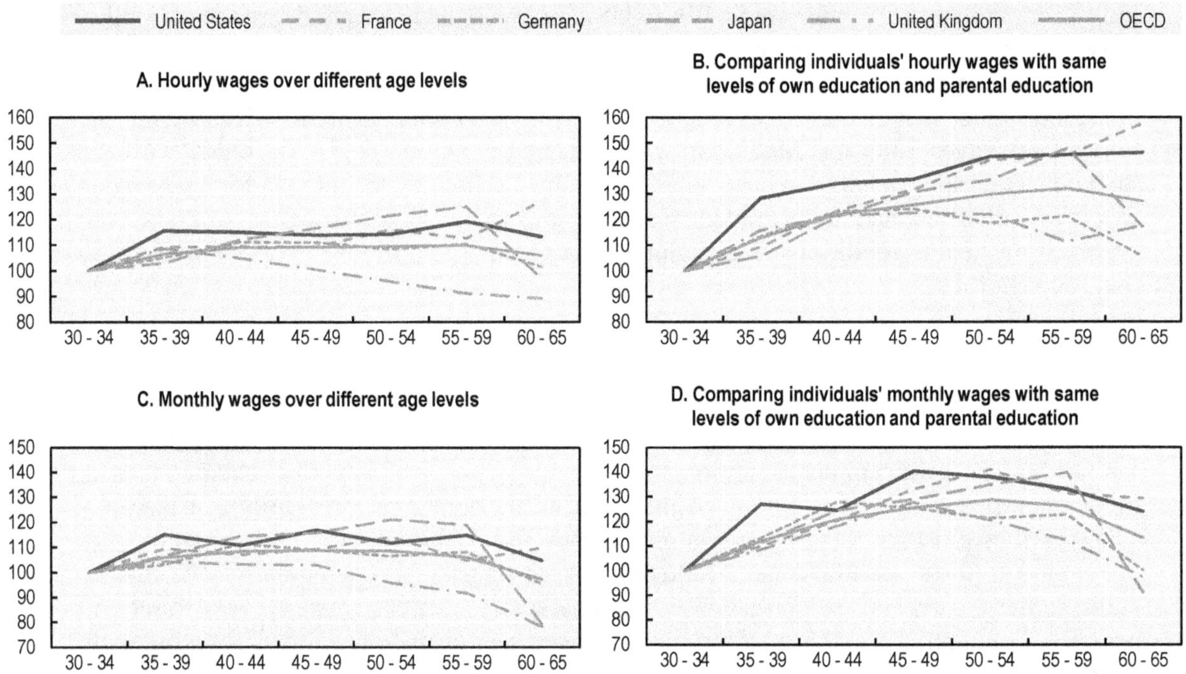

Note: The OECD is a weighted average and excludes Hungary, Iceland, Latvia, Luxembourg, Mexico, Portugal and Switzerland. Data for the United Kingdom refer to England and Northern Ireland. Hourly and monthly earnings are adjusted from national currency to 2012 US dollars, adjusted for purchasing power and trimmed of the top and bottom percentiles to control for extreme values. **Panel A**: Estimates were obtained by regressing factor variables indicating age, gender, and country on log hourly wages. **Panel B**: Estimates were obtained by regressing age, gender, and country dummies, as well as factor variables indicating the educational attainment of the respondent, their mother, and their father on log hourly wages. **Panel C**: Estimates were obtained by regressing factor variables indicating age, gender, and country on log monthly wages. **Panel D**: Estimates were obtained by regressing age, gender, and country dummies, as well as factor variables indicating the educational attainment of the respondent, their mother, and their father on log monthly wages.

Source: OECD calculations based on the Survey of Adult Skills (PIAAC) (2012, 2015), www.oecd.org/skills/piaac/.

StatLink http://dx.doi.org/10.1787/888933644300

The importance especially for older workers of paid time off is partly a result of the long working hours in the United States. Average annual working hours per US worker have remained constant over the past decades, contrary to reductions seen in the United Kingdom and France (Blundell, Bozio and Laroque, 2013[40]). Note that demographic composition and educational levels may contribute to these cross-country differences (Bick, Brüggemann and Fuchs-Schündeln, 2017[41]). The decreasing value (in real terms) of the threshold above which salaried US workers' overtime hours go unpaid (under the white-collar exception) makes it easier for employers to increase workers' weekly hours. While older workers may find the relatively long hours in the United States strenuous, thus affecting job quality and labour supply, there is no evidence that increased paid time off for older workers constitutes an important disincentive for firms to hire and retain older workers.

Health care, pension contributions and labour taxes

Non-wage costs are an important part of labour costs in all OECD countries, especially unemployment and health insurance as well as pension contributions. In the United States the so-called "tax wedge" that firms pay on top of workers' net wages consisting in income tax and social security contributions is low by international comparisons, at under 32% for an average worker, compared to an OECD average of 36% (OECD, 2017[42]). However, this does not include non-statutory health care costs that employers pay for workers. Contrary to other OECD countries, these account for a significant fraction of labour costs.

Figure 2.23. The United States has low levels of non-wage labour costs when employer health care is not included

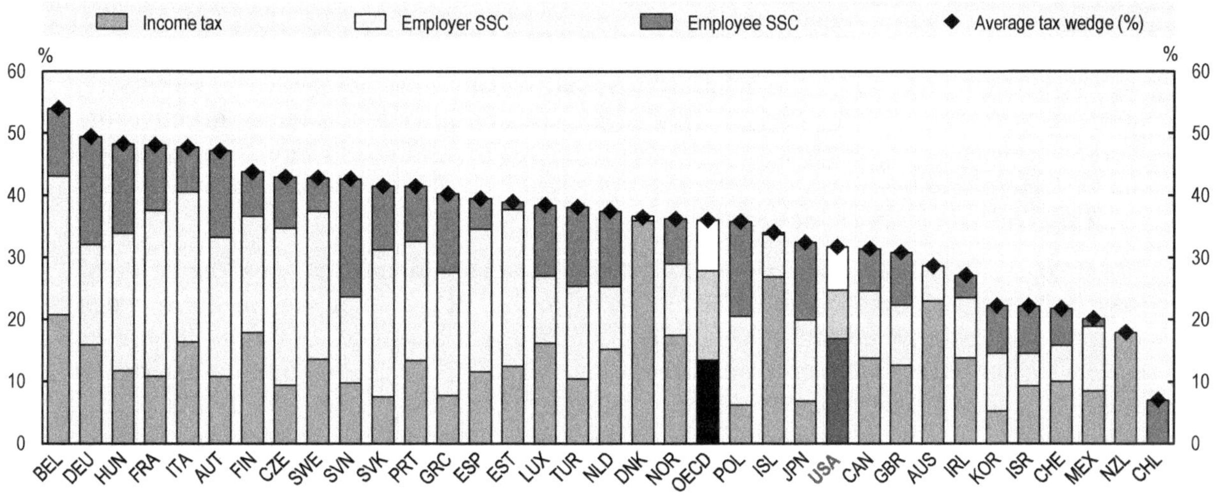

SSC: Social Security Contributions.

Note: Tax wedge for an average single worker, no children. The tax wedge gives the fraction of total labour costs (gross wages and employer social security contributions) that consist of personal income tax and employee and employer social security contributions. The three categories shown in the chart do not total the average tax wedge in Denmark due to the incidence of cash transfers, which are not shown.

Source: OECD Taxing Wages, www.oecd.org/tax/tax-policy/taxing-wages-united-states.pdf.

StatLink http://dx.doi.org/10.1787/888933644319

Both firms and workers may benefit from employers contributing to employees' health care expenditure, since this part of compensation is subject neither to social security contributions nor to income tax (at the expense of lower tax revenues for the government). While few firms directly pay for workers' health care expenditure, many firms cover some of employees' insurance premiums. The Affordable Care Act of 2010 limits which factors may determine insurance premiums - importantly, health rating based on pre-existing health conditions is not allowed, but age is a permitted factor. Thus there remains a link between firms' age composition and the payments made to insurance companies. Firms with an older workforce pay more for healthcare. This contrasts to the universal health insurance in all other OECD countries. While many systems include multiple payers (e.g. public and private health insurance systems), insurance payments typically depend only on workers' earnings, and not, for example, their health status or age. Older workers thus cause employers an additional cost in the US-American system. As a result, health care costs for older workers remain considerably higher than for younger workers. For instance, the average cost of health care claims paid by large employers was USD 10 497 for workers in the age group 60-64, compared with USD 3 781 for workers in the age group 25-29 and USD 7 600 for workers in the age group 40-44.[8]

Between 2003 and 2011, growth in health care costs has been lower for older workers than for other age groups – although in absolute terms the increase in health costs is hump-shaped in age, peaking at around 55 years (around 50% higher than for workers aged over 60 or under 30 years of age (AARP, 2015[23])[9]). Meanwhile, employers have reduced the percentage of health care costs they pay to workers' health care, with only 9% of firms reimbursing their workers completely (Kaiser Family Foundation and Health Research & Educational Trust, 2016[43]). This limits the age differential in labour costs between younger and older employees. This differentiation of health care costs by workers' health status should reduce the risk of health care costs lowering firms' willingness to employ older workers. This differentiation, however, also reduces the insurance value for workers. Furthermore, labour supply may decrease as a result of higher insurance premiums for older workers as workers now pay for more expensive health care costs out of their wages. For older workers this may decrease incentives to work. This contrasts to fixed insurance rates in most universal health care systems across the OECD. In these systems, older workers pay relatively less and have relatively higher net wages than their US counterparts.

Negative labour supply incentives due to higher insurance premiums for older workers may be moderated by the limited coverage when they leave employment. Some older workers may be covered under Medicaid. Medicaid is a means-tested health insurance system mainly for the poor administered by individual states who also determine eligibility rules. Workers over the age of 65 are covered by the federal Medicare system independent of their resources. However, employer health care is considered more desirable than Medicare, as indicated by the extensive use of "Medigap" insurance schemes that supplement Medicare. In fact, one of the much-discussed welfare costs of employer-provided health care is its potential to give rise to "job lock", whereby workers prefer to remain in their current job for fear of losing their health care benefits. This may result in inefficiently low levels of job mobility, reducing productivity by preventing optimal matches between firms and workers. While several studies find this effect, the magnitude is somewhat uncertain (for a thorough review of the issues, see Gruber and Madrian (2004[44]), for recent evidence, see Garthwaite et al. (2014[45]) and Baker (2015[46])). Nevertheless, the conditions under which Medicare provides individuals with healthcare have been viewed as an "implicit tax" on older workers.[10] Healthcare costs are covered by the Medicare system for individuals over the age of 65 only if they are not covered by an employer healthcare scheme, the primary payer. Removing this "Secondary Payer" rule would imply also providing Medicare benefits to employees aged over 65. Shah Goda et al. (2011[47]) estimate that Medicare expenses would increase by 4.4% in this case, but that additional revenues from higher income taxes may be generated at a similar magnitude as a result of increased work incentives for older workers. Since workers would have benefitted from free healthcare anyway, the value of health insurance no longer provides an incentive to work for individuals above the age of 65. The rules also depend on the size of employees on the payroll and whether the firm has a health plan for other workers or not.

The reduction of the value of employer health insurance above 65 years of age is compounded by the reduced value employer pension contributions. Since only the highest-paying 35 years of work are considered in calculating retirees' pensions, the marginal benefit of paying pension contributions decreases discontinuously once workers reach the 35-year threshold.

The United States has also seen a shift in recent years away from defined benefit (DB) pension plans and towards defined contribution (DC) retirement schemes, which generally have less relation to age and tenure (see Chapter 1). Some DC plans have "vesting" requirements based on tenure. The worker does not fully "own" the employer-contributed funds in their DC plan until they've worked at the company for a certain number of years. This could constitute a further barrier to retention of older workers.

Public policies and practices in firms towards older workers

In the United States, federal and state governments intervene in ways that change the regulatory environment confronting employers in some measures focusing on older worker employment such as age and disability discrimination. However according to Rix (2016[48]), public policy initiatives do not appear to be major contributors to rising labour force participation rates at older ages and an aspect that has received insufficient attention in policy discussions about longer working lives is the role of the employer. It is therefore important to better promote business case for employing older workers. The United States could learn from good practices implemented in other OECD countries to better manage age diversity in firms.

Discrimination and negative employer attitudes

Many firms' decisions may be subject to discrimination arising from stereotypical views of older workers on hiring, firing, compensation, training or promotion of older workers (OECD, 2006[49]). Besides, perceived age discrimination in the workplace may influence employment outcomes not only as a result of firms' decisions, but also by influencing workers' labour supply decisions (Angrisani et al., 2013[50]). For instance, barriers to hiring may induce older workers to accept poor quality jobs or stop searching for a new job altogether. Two broad approaches can be identified in tackling these issues: public policies, including anti-discrimination legislation; and initiatives to influence public opinion and to change employer attitude. To offer the same level of protection against discrimination requires broadening the scope of anti-age discrimination to all firms and ages as well as ensuring efficient access to legal expertise and counsel.

Age discrimination legislation in the United States

The United States was the pioneer among OECD countries in terms of specific legislation banning age discrimination with the Age Discrimination in Employment Act (ADEA) of 1967. The ADEA forbids discrimination against employees or job applicants who are 40 or older and who work for employers with 20 or more employees. Under the law, discrimination in the workplace may pertain to hiring, firing, promotions, training, wages, and benefits. Following contradicting jurisprudence by lower courts, the Supreme Court in 2005 clarified that firms may legitimately implement policies which affect older workers differentially, as long as they are motivated by "Reasonable Factors Other than Age" (RFOA). The Equal Employment Opportunity Commission (EEOC) is responsible for enforcing federal anti-discrimination laws, in particular the ADEA. In addition, the EEOC promotes awareness, understanding and compliance with the legislation by publishing guides and offering training programmes for employers. Finally, the EEOC offers Technical Assistance Programs (TAPS) to employers in cities across the country.

TAPS are designed to help human resource staff, business owners, managers, union officials, and government officials gain an understanding of their legal obligations in preventing all forms of employment discrimination, including age discrimination. Age discrimination has also been a topic for "customer-specific trainings", which are programmes customised to fit stakeholders' specific needs. In addition, EEOC field offices throughout the US conduct outreach in their local communities.

Despite the length of time since ADEA has been in operation, there is evidence that age discrimination on the part of employers persists in the United States. The results of a 2013 survey from AARP indicate that 64% of workers have either experienced or observed age discrimination. This is a slight increase from 2007 (60%). Age discrimination is not equally distributed. On the contrary, there is an intersection of different factors in discrimination, women and African Americans being more likely to report age discrimination in the workplace alongside workers over 50 (AARP, 2014[51]). The OECD recommended already in 2005 an expansion of federal age-based anti-discrimination law to cover all workers (OECD, 2005[52]). Many US states already go beyond the Age Discrimination in Employment Act. For instance, some state laws bar age discrimination in employment irrespective of the worker's or applicant's age and also cover business employers with fewer than 20 employees. Interestingly, Neumark and Song (2013[53]) show that the increase of the federal retirement age was most effective in raising actual retirement ages in States that provided anti-discrimination legislation beyond the ADEA. However, during the Great Recession stronger age discrimination laws may have been associated with worse employment outcomes for some older workers (Neumark and Button, 2014[54]).

Age discrimination, still a challenge in OECD countries

Age discrimination is banned by law in all OECD countries, but not in Switzerland where a proposal of anti-discrimination law was rejected by the Federal Council in 2009. Unlike most age discrimination legislation in the United States, the EU Directive issued in 2000 on equal treatment in employment and occupations does not target discrimination against older workers alone and in firms with 20 or more employees. Even though the EU Directive required all EU Member States to have anti age-discrimination legislation in place by 2006, a perception that age discrimination occurs, particularly in hiring, remains very common in Europe. According to a Eurobarometer Survey in 2015, 60% of all respondents and managers on average in Europe report that being older is a factor that puts job applicants at a disadvantage (Eurobarometer, 2015[55]).

In addition, laws against age discrimination in the workplace appear to have only limited impact. For example, Davey (2014[56]) argues that legislation against age discrimination in the workplace in New Zealand is hampered by difficulties in proving discrimination. Anti-discrimination laws will have more impact if the enforcement is not exclusively dependent on the initiative of individuals deprived of their rights. Indeed, individual victims of discrimination often face strong barriers to bring a case before the courts, as legal action remains a costly, complex, time-consuming and adversarial process. In particular, age discrimination in hiring should be subject to greater control and penalty by public authorities and unions, although it is inherently harder to prove discrimination in hiring than in dismissals.

This is confirmed by researchers. The field experiment of (Drydakis et al., 2017[57]) for the period 2013-2015 in the United Kingdom suggests that age discrimination persists at alarming levels. It shows that when two applicants engage in an identical job search, the older applicant would gain fewer invitations for interviews regardless of her/his experience or superiority for the appointment. Carlsson and Eriksson (2017[58]) conducted also a field experiment in Sweden, where over 6 000 fictitious resumes with randomly assigned information about age (in the interval 35-70) and gender were sent to employers with a vacancy and the employers' responses (callbacks) were recorded. They find that the callback rate starts to fall substantially early in the age interval considered. This decline is steeper for women than for men. These results indicate that age discrimination is a widespread phenomenon affecting workers already in their early 40s in many occupations. Ageism and occupational skill loss due to ageing are unlikely explanations of these effects. Instead, their employer survey suggests that employer stereotypes about three worker characteristics – ability to learn new tasks, flexibility/adaptability, and ambition – are important.

Disability-based discrimination in the United States

As disability becomes more frequent with age, older workers are also likely to be disproportionately affected by disability-based discrimination. The Americans with Disabilities Act (ADA) and the federal Rehabilitation Act thus have special significance for older workers.

The ADA of 1990, as amended by the Americans with Disabilities Amendments Act of 2008, protects people of all ages who have physical or mental disabilities or a record of such disability, or who are perceived as having such disability. The ADA prohibits discrimination in employment, public services, public accommodations, transportation, and telecommunications. It affords protections equivalent to those granted under prior civil rights laws to people facing bias on the grounds of race, colour, gender, religion, or national origin and seeks to end a legacy of segregation and degradation. However, since the requirements to be considered disabled remain demanding despite the expanded protection offered by the 2008 amendment, significant portion of individuals with less severe disabilities are not covered by disability discrimination laws.

In the United States, all workforce programmes are available to individuals with disabilities, including the Vocational Rehabilitation programme operated by the Department of Education that is specifically designed to provide services for persons with physical or mental impairment. However, despite the efforts made at the federal and state levels, a striking employment gap persists between Americans with and without disabilities. It is thus welcome that the Employment and Training Administration (ETA) and the Office of Disability Employment Policy (ODEP) at the Department of Labor (DOL) have been jointly funding since 2010 the Disability Employment Initiative (DEI).[11] DEI is a demonstration project that improves existing programmes for increasing employability for people with disabilities. Since its launch, DOL has awarded over USD 139 million to 55 projects in 30 states to improve the programmes that lead to training and employment outcomes for individuals with disabilities. DEI funded projects support several of the Workforce Innovation and Opportunity Act (WIOA) disability-related requirements, including strengthening the capacity of American Job Centres to serve individuals with disabilities through increased physical and programmatic access. For some of the grantees, DOL is currently conducting a random-assignment evaluation of DEI. The interim reports issued to date indicate that DEI pilot sites enrol more participants with disabilities in services.[12]

Recent research has explored the effects of disability discrimination laws which may do more to protect older workers than age discrimination laws on hiring of older workers.

Using state variation in disability discrimination protections, Neumark et al. (2015[59]) find little or no evidence that stronger disability discrimination laws lower the hiring of nondisabled older workers. Similarly, they find no evidence of adverse effects of disability anti-discrimination laws on hiring of disabled older workers.

Focus on back to work of those with remaining working capacities in OECD countries

As it has been pointed out in Chapter 1, many other OECD countries, particularly several EU countries, have shifted their policy objectives from merely paying benefits to people with disability towards helping them stay in or return to the labour market. For example, in Germany equally qualified individuals are treated preferentially when applying for a job. In France, employers that do not employ a certain number of disabled workers pay a fine. In Sweden, a clear, well-defined framework for the sick-listing process was established between 2008 and 2010, improving the possibilities for people on disability benefits to return to work. Besides, access to disability pensions has been restricted through recent reforms in several countries and combining work and the receipt of (partial) disability pensions promoted. An interesting example is Denmark, where a recent reform of the disability pension restricted its access to individuals over 40, and introduced a rehabilitation programme stipulation prior to being able to receive a disability benefit. The flexjob scheme introduced at the same time allows a reduction in working time or an adaptation of working conditions depending on the needs of individuals. The flexjob scheme is not targeted at older people in particular, although more than half of all people in flexjobs in 2013 were over 50. However, a feature of the scheme is the very low share of participants who return to regular jobs. The scheme was modified in 2013 to curb the risk of flexjobs replacing regular jobs. Regular assessments and not allowing flexjobs to become permanent positions for over 40s are essential to prevent misuse of flexjobs (OECD, 2015[60]). DOL has also funded research into different policy measures that could increase return-to-work after phases of disability in the United States, for example promoting US States to take action (Ben-Shalom, 2016[61]).

Initiatives to promote an age-diverse business culture

In the United States, successful strategies for integrating older workers in the workforce have taken various forms. AARP recently conducted a series of case studies of leading employers to examine promising practices for addressing the intergenerational workforce (Box 2.1). Many employers recognise the need to have a diversity and inclusion strategy. Age diversity focuses on the array of people of different ages while inclusion goes beyond the identification of differences by encouraging a work environment that allows people to be who they are and feel safe to do so. Companies have long recognised that there is a business case for building a diverse and inclusive workforce because it can lead to greater engagement, teamwork, performance, and innovation. The Sloane Center for Aging & Work (2013[62]) recommends the development of comprehensive age-management policies and provides practical guidance to implementing these. DOL and many of its grantees participate in an annual "National Employ Older Workers Week" to highlight innovative strategies for supporting and utilising older workers.

Box 2.1. Promising practices for Disrupting Ageing in the Workplace in the United States

AARP conducted interviews in February and March 2016 with human resources staff, diversity officers, and programme managers of five companies from a variety of industries and of different sizes. These companies were selected because they believe that promoting age diversity and addressing the intergenerational workforce are important and worthwhile for their business success. Several promising practices in diversity and inclusion strategies emerge as a result of this inquiry:

- Talent recruitment across all ages helps build a diverse and experienced workforce.
- Apprentice programmes open to people of all ages help recruit and retain talent.
- Special programmes designed to help older workers re-enter the workforce following an extended absence can provide an opportunity for permanent employment.
- Raising awareness of intergenerational differences (e.g. using videos, training programmes, events) enhances understanding and leads to better-functioning teams.
- Employee resource groups increase employee engagement and often house mentoring programs. Some have evolved into employee business resource groups that help further business goals. Some companies also use employee groups as a path for leadership development.
- Cross-generational mentoring programmes help facilitate knowledge transfer – a critical need for many companies.

Source: Trawinski, L. (2016), *Disrupting Aging in the Workplace: Profiles in Intergenerational Diversity Leadership*, AARP, Washington DC. and OECD (2016), *Recommendation of the OECD Council on Ageing and Employment Policies*, OECD Publishing, Paris.

Across OECD countries, results from surveys show that negative stereotypes about older workers persist.[13] It is thus important to raise awareness among employers, employees and society in general to address problems relating to the "image" of seniors, who are sometimes regarded, wrongly, as less likely to adapt to a job. In general in the OECD area, initiatives to change employer attitude include awareness campaigns, development of "tool kits", promotion of best-practices and co-operation with the social partners (Sonnet, Olsen and Manfredi, 2014[63]). However, despite these initiatives and awareness among stakeholders of the key elements of an inclusive age-diverse culture (Box 2.2), employers face a significant challenge implementing it (Box 2.3).

Box 2.2. Key elements of an age-diverse inclusive business culture

The aim is to create a workplace where people of all generations feel comfortable and appreciated by management and their peers, regardless of age. Key elements are the following:

- Policies cannot be implemented in isolation and it is not about targeting one age group at the perceived expense of another. Particularly promising are initiatives that start early in the career and persist throughout the working life. For instance, firms need to invest more in training their least-qualified workers, of whatever age.
- Older and younger workers have relative strengths and needs, which can give rise to positive externalities in the workforce between generations.
- The most obvious strengths of older workers are those that derive from maturity and experience whereas younger workers may have more up to-date skills and may be more able to carry out more physically and mentally demanding work, even if it is crucial to reduce early exposure to strenuous work.
- It is not just older workers who may have special needs in terms of how they work and at what rhythm but younger workers as well who may have their own specific needs in terms of balancing work and family commitments (e.g. when it comes to the distribution of night shifts across different groups of workers).

Source: OECD (2006), *Live Longer, Work Longer, Ageing and Employment Policies,* OECD Publishing, Paris http://dx.doi.org/10.1787/9789264035881-en; Sonnet, A., H. Olsen and T. Manfredi (2014), "Towards More Inclusive Ageing and Employment Policies: The Lessons from France, The Netherlands, Norway and Switzerland", *De Economist*, Vol. 162 http://dx.doi.org/10.1007/s10645-014-9240-x; OECD (2016), *Recommendation of the OECD Council on Ageing and Employment Policies* Paris; and OECD (2017), *Preventing Ageing Unequally,* OECD Publishing, Paris, http://dx.doi.org/10.1787/9789264279087-4-en.

Box 2.3. Challenges for implementing an age-diverse workforce: Evidence from OECD countries

In an overview of age-management practices among OECD countries, Duell (2015[64]) finds that in general, their implementation remains poor, particularly in small and medium-sized enterprises (SMEs). Only large companies have human resource management departments that can develop and implement age-management strategies. Guidance for age management in SMEs should be provided on a wider scale. Nevertheless, the "knowing-doing gap" is still wide. In particular, there is still room for improvement in sharing information on good practices and tools on this issue. However, too general guidelines for age management have their limitations and they should therefore take into account the different management styles and conditions of enterprises of different sizes.

In the United Kingdom, the Fuller Working Lives Business Strategy Group was set up by the Department of Work and Pensions (DWP) to drive change among employers and make recommendations to business on how to harness the benefits of a multi-generational workforce (DWP, 2017[65]). The Business Strategy Group attracted more than 50 members from some of the UK's most influential companies and organisations; all of whom committed to review their own policies and practices in relation to people aged 50 and over; and to talk to other employers about the benefits and challenges of employing older workers. The Business Strategy Group identified three areas to focus on: i) developing the business case for older workers; ii) improving manager education and iii) providing support for older workers with caring responsibilities.

The Chartered Institute of Personnel and Development (CIPD) also underlines that one important way of countering potential bias against older workers and fostering an age diverse workforce is to provide training for line managers. CIPD (2016[66]) has investigated how employers can best manage an increasingly older workforce in the context of their health and well-being and care responsibilities in five European countries (the Czech Republic, Denmark, France, Germany and the United Kingdom). Line managers are typically those who implement policies on a day to day basis and regulate access to support and adjustment mechanisms for older workers to enable them to extend their working lives. Line managers may not always have the skills required to ensure older workers feel comfortable discussing issues with them relating to ageing. It is important to improve their awareness of issues affecting older workers' employment, so that they can provide effective support.

Finally, also promoting intergenerational partnerships at work, in particular between young and older workers, is considered important in OECD countries. More specifically, public representatives in Europe recommend that businesses actively transfer knowledge between generations and encourage mentoring (reverse mentoring) (European Parliament, 2013[67]). Yet, few governments have taken formalised steps in this direction and the initiatives undertaken to date do not seem to have had a decisive and important impact. For example, the "generation contract" created by law in France in 2013, following the national multi-sector agreement signed by all the social partners in 2012, has gained strength much more slowly than the government expected (OECD, 2014[68]). Its purpose is to institute specific, negotiated measures to promote the employment of young people, older workers, and the transmission of knowledge and skills between generations within the firm.

Box 2.3. Challenges for implementing an age-diverse workforce: Evidence from OECD countries *(Cont.)*

Source: Duell, N. (2015), "Local economic strategies for ageing labour markets: Management practices for productivity gains of older workers", *OECD Employment Policy Papers*, No. 11, OECD Publishing, Paris, http://dx.doi.org/10.1787/5jrnwqkwpxjj-en; DWP (2017), Fuller Working Lives A Partnership Approach, Department for Work and Pensions, London, https://www.gov.uk/government/publications/fuller-working-lives-a-partnership-approach; CIPD (2016), *Creating longer, more fulfilling working lives: Employer practice in five European countries*, Chartered Institute of Personnel and Development, London, https://www.cipd.co.uk/Images/creating-longer-more-fulfilling-working-lives_2016-employer-practice-in-five-european-countries_tcm18-14265.pdf; European Parliament (2013), *Combining the Entry of Young People in the Labour Market with the Retention of Older Workers*, IP/A/EMPL/ST/2012-04, April; and OECD (2014), *Ageing and Employment Policies: France 2014: Working Better with Age*, Ageing and Employment Policies, OECD Publishing, Paris, http://dx.doi.org/10.1787/9789264207523-en.

Directions for policy

With respect to the previous OECD assessment of demand-side constraints on older workers' employment in 2005, few fundamental policy changes have been made. Nine federal agencies convened a taskforce on the challenges of workforce ageing in 2007 which proposed several approaches, many of which still appear relevant (U.S. Department of Labor, 2008[69]). A striking employment gap persists for disadvantaged older workers, in particular between those with and without disabilities.

There is a paucity of research in the United States that explains why employers and firms hire and retain older workers. This research gap is of particular concern to promote better and longer working lives. When employers need workers in case of labour shortages, they will do what is required to hire and retain them.

The appropriate balance needs to be found between protecting jobs of older workers and avoiding barriers to hiring older workers. While employment protection is very weak in the United States, older workers are protected against discriminatory dismissals by the ADEA. However, unequal access to justice and difficulties in establishing discrimination reduce the effectiveness of this protection.

Older workers' patterns of skill utilisation suggest a role for occupational mobility in ensuring that older workers efficiently use their skills. By moving across occupations and jobs, older workers may benefit from the large degree of flexibility on the labour market, allowing them to find jobs that better match their specific skills. Barriers to worker mobility may arise as a result of employer-provided health care in particular.

Adapting to ageing is a challenge both for individuals, firms and industrial structure more broadly. Contrary to often-voiced concerns, and contrary to other OECD countries, there is little evidence of a digital divide between younger and older workers in the United States. Certain opportunities provided by digitalisation of the workplace, for example the expanded possibilities to use telework, may in fact favour older workers. Policymakers should not only consider policies for specific age-based policies, but accommodate the role of changing forms of industrial production on older workers' chances of finding a productive and rewarding job.

The following actions could support firms in hiring and retaining older workers:

- *Expand the federal age-based anti-discrimination law to cover all workers in all firms*. Protection under ADEA should be extended to people of any age rather than to just those aged 40 and over. This could help remove artificial distinctions between younger and older people and reduce the risk that all people aged 40 and over viewed as being old and disadvantaged and therefore in need of protection. The exemption of smaller companies should also be reconsidered. The 2000 EU directive concerning age discrimination extends protection to people of all ages and in all firms. Options ought to be considered to extend the coverage of the ADEA to apply also to cases where discrimination is based on more than one characteristic (e.g. both age and gender).
- *Make anti-discrimination legislation more easily enforceable for workers.* Compared to countries with greater employment protection legislation, the role of anti-discrimination legislation is greater in the United States. Removing barriers to legal expertise and counsel are thus important for all workers to benefit from the same protection.
- *Continue and expand the Disability Employment Initiative*. DEI is a pilot programme that numerous states use to promote employability for people with disabilities. Older disabled workers are particularly vulnerable – policy should aim at increasing the full or partial return to work for those with remaining working capacities. Conditional on a positive evaluation of the DEI, this programme should be rolled out also in currently non-participating US states. Future activities under the DEI ought to focus on the particular needs of older disabled workers.
- *Eliminate the Medicare as a second-payer rule*. For workers over the age of 65 this will lower the effective cost of employing older workers. While Medicare expenses would increase, additional revenues from higher income taxes may be generated at a similar magnitude as a result of increased work incentives for older workers.
- *Avoid job lock for workers with pre-existing health conditions.* Avoid changes to rules governing health insurance that may discourage workers with pre-existing health conditions from changing jobs.
- *Support the business case for promoting longer and better working lives*. The business world has an important role to play to implement successful strategies for integrating older workers in the workforce and for adapting to ageing. The outreach and educational activities of the EEOC should continue to be expanded. Key stakeholders in the United States, including NGOs, should identify firms' best policies to retain, retrain, and recruit older workers and learn from good practices implemented in other OECD countries. AARP experience in this area is very helpful.
- *Encourage research on firms' decisions of employing older workers.* There is a paucity of research into why employers hire and retain older workers. One of the main constraints is the lack of available linked employer–employee data. Collaborative efforts among different governmental agencies and other external institutions would be crucial to tackle this issue.

Notes

1. On the other hand, these rising trends are not being driven by composition effects of the large cohort of baby boomers moving into the age groups 65, 66, 67, etc. where labour force participation and employment rates are still significantly higher than for people at an older age.

2. Employment-at-will is a common law doctrine which holds that "an employer may hire or discharge an individual for 'a good reason, a bad reason, or no reason at all' emphasizing employers' unilateral power to decide whether to initially employ or continue to employ an individual. In other words, the employer has no obligation to make rational hiring decisions or to discharge employees only for "just cause" (Lieberwitz, 2008[74]).

3. The 1986 prohibition on mandatory retirement contained exemptions for certain types of employment, including for firefighters, police officers, top executives and policy making officials who receive substantial retirement benefits, and tenured faculty members. Mandatory retirement for tenured faculty was permissible at the age of 70 until the exemption was repealed at the end of 1993. For more information, see: http://www.eeoc.gov/eeoc/history/35th/thelaw/adea_amendments_1986.html. Mandatory retirement also may exist where age is a "bona fide occupational qualification" for the position, which generally has been found in public safety positions such as pilots. Other federal laws also have imposed mandatory retirement ages for certain federal government employment, including for air traffic controllers, federal law enforcement positions, most foreign service officers, and military personnel.

4. Results are based on predicted values of skills from an OLS regression of skill levels on factor variables indicating 5-year age groups, gender. Adjusting for education here means adding controls in the regression for the highest educational attainment of the respondent, their mother, and their father. Educational attainment is separated into three groups: less than high school, high school but less than tertiary, and tertiary.

5. The lack of clear empirical evidence is certainly partly a result of the challenge of establishing a causal link between firm demography and productivity. Studies require differences in age composition across firms that are otherwise very similar. A lack of productivity differences could otherwise be caused by differences in other inputs such as work intensity or the use of different technologies.

6. See: https://www.telework.gov/reports-studies/reports-to-congress/2014-report-to-congress.pdf

7. The quality of teaching used to be hard to evaluate, but centralised testing of students has removed some of these constraints. Biasi (2017[72]) shows the result of one region moving from a seniority-based pay scheme to a performance-based pay system can increase teacher quality, an effect due mainly to lower-performance teachers moving to other areas. The effects on older teachers were not specifically studied.

8. The analysis is based on health claims of 14.6 million medical plan participants (employees and dependents) in 2011 (AARP, 2015[23]).

9. This is easily confirmed using back-of-the-envelope calculations based on Figures III-8 and III-9 in (AARP, 2015[23]). Health costs for individuals aged 60 are shown to be around USD 10 000. For individuals aged 30 they are around USD 5 000. Given growth rates are around 4% and 8% for these two groups, absolute increases in health care costs are USD 400 for both of these groups. From the limited number of categories presented, increases in absolute terms actually peak at around USD 560 for workers aged 55 (since spending levels in 2011 were USD 9 800 and the growth rate was 6%).

10. The rules about eligibility for Medicare are intricate. Employees in small firms, in firms without an employer health plan or working part time may also be eligible for Medicare coverage despite being employed.

11. http://www.ncsl.org/research/labor-and-employment/employing-people-with-disabilities.aspx.

12. https://www.dol.gov/odep/topics/Stay-at-Work-Return-to-Work.htm.

13, For example, see for European countries (2012[73]), for Australia (2015[70]) and for Canada (2012[71]).

References

AARP (2014), *Staying Ahead of the Curve 2013: The AARP work and career study: Older workers in an uneasy job market*, http://www.aarp.org/content/dam/aarp/research/surveys_statistics/general/2014/Staying-Ahead-of-the-Curve-2013-The-Work-and-Career-Study-AARP-res-gen.pdf. [51]

AARP (2015), *A Business Case for Workers Age 50+: A Look at the Value of Experience*, http://states.aarp.org/wp-content/uploads/2015/08/A-Business-Case-for-Older-Workers-Age-50-A-Look-at-the-Value-of-Experience.pdf. [23]

Acemoglu, D. and P. Restrepo (2017), "Secular Stagnation? The effect of aging on economic growth in the age of automation", *NBER working paper*, No. 23077, https://economics.mit.edu/files/12536. [35]

Agbayani, C. et al. (2016), *Labor Market and DOL-Funded Employment Assistance for Older Workers Literature Review Report*, IMPAQ International, Columbia, https://www.impaq.cg-dev2.com/sites/default/files/project-reports/Lit_Review_Older_Workers_Labor_force.pdf. [14]

Aiyar, S., C. Ebeke and X. Shao (2016), "The Impact of Workforce Aging on European Productivity The Impact of Workforce Aging on European Productivity 1 Prepared by", *IMF Working Papers*, No. WP/16/238, International Monetary Fund, https://www.imf.org/external/pubs/ft/wp/2016/wp16238.pdf. [36]

Altonji, J. and E. Usui (2007), "Work Hours, Wages, and Vacation Leave", *ILR Review*, Vol. 60/3, pp. 408-428, http://dx.doi.org/10.1177/001979390706000306. [39]

Angrisani, M. et al. (2013), "Labor Force Transitions at Older Ages: The Roles of Work Environment and Personality", No. 295, University of Michigan: Michigan Retirement Research Center , Ann Arbor, http://www.mrrc.isr.umich.edu/publications/papers/pdf/wp295.pdf. [50]

Aubert, P. and B. Crépon (2006), "Age, Wage and Productivity: Firm-Level Evidence", *Crest working paper*, http://citeseerx.ist.psu.edu/viewdoc/download?doi=10.1.1.461.4177&rep=rep1&type=pdf. [20]

Australian Human Rights Commission (2015), *National prevalence survey of age discrimination in the workplace*, https://www.humanrights.gov.au/sites/default/files/document/publication/AgePrevalenceReport2015.pdf. [70]

Autor, D., J. Donohue III and S. Schwab (2006), "The costs of wrongful-discharge laws", *The Review of Economics and Statistics* 88(2), https://economics.mit.edu/files/11580. [13]

Autor, D. and M. Handel (2013), "Putting Tasks to the Test: Human Capital, Job Tasks, and Wages", *Journal of Labor Economics*, Vol. 31/S1, pp. S59-S96, http://dx.doi.org/10.1086/669332. [27]

Baker, D. (2015), *Job Lock and Employer-Provided Health Insurance*, AARP, Washington DC, http://www.aarp.org/ppi/info-2015/job-lock-and-employer-provided-healthcare.html. [46]

Ben-Shalom, Y. (2016), "Steps States Can Take to Help Workers Keep Their Jobs after Injury, Illness, or Disability", Mathematica Policy Research Reports, https://EconPapers.repec.org/RePEc:mpr:mprres:8443f3e24e80421b965869ddba800ff3. [61]

Biasi, B. (2017), "Unions, Salaries, and the Market for Teachers: Evidence from Wisconsin", *SSRN Electronic Journal*, http://dx.doi.org/10.2139/ssrn.2942134. [72]

Bick, A., B. Brüggemann and N. Fuchs-Schündeln (2017), "Hours Worked in Europe and the US: New Data, New Answers", *American Economic Review* forthcoming. [41]

Blundell, R., A. Bozio and G. Laroque (2013), "Extensive and Intensive Margins of Labour Supply: Work and Working Hours in the US, the UK and France*", *Fiscal Studies*, Vol. 34/1, pp. 1-29, http://dx.doi.org/10.1111/j.1475-5890.2013.00175.x. [40]

Börsch-Supan, A. and M. Weiss (2016), "Productivity and age: Evidence from work teams at the assembly line", *The Journal of the Economics of Ageing*, Vol. 7, pp. 30-42, http://dx.doi.org/10.1016/J.JEOA.2015.12.001. [22]

Bucknor, C. and D. Baker (2016), "Still Working Hard: An Update on the Share of Older Workers in Physically Demanding Jobs", *CEPR Working Paper*, Center for Economic and Policy Research (CEPR), Washington DC, https://ideas.repec.org/p/epo/papers/2016-04.html. [30]

Burtless, G. (2016), "Labor force dynamics in the great recession and its aftermath: implications for older workers", *CRR WP*, No. 1, Center for Retirement Research at Boston College, http://crr.bc.edu. [6]

Carlsson, M. and S. Eriksson (2017), "The effect of age and gender on labor demand – evidence from a field experiment", *Working Paper 2017*, No. 8, IFAU, http://www.ifau.se/globalassets/pdf/se/2017/wp2017-08-the-effect-of-age-and-gender-on-labor-demand.pdf (accessed on 27 June 2017). [58]

CIPD (2016), *Creating longer, more fulfilling working lives: Employer practice in five European countries*, Chartered Institute of Personnel and Development, London, https://www.cipd.co.uk/Images/creating-longer-more-fulfilling-working-lives_2016-employer-practice-in-five-european-countries_tcm18-14265.pdf. [66]

Colvin, A. (2012), "American Workplace Dispute Resolution in the Individual Rights Era", Cornell University, ILR School, http://digitalcommons.ilr.cornell.edu/articles/833. [12]

Davey, J. (2014), "Age Discrimination in the Workplace", *Policy Quarterly*, Vol. 10/3, http://igps.victoria.ac.nz/publications/PQ/2014/PQ-Vol-10-No-3-2014.pdf. [56]

Davis, S. and J. Haltiwanger (2014), "Labor Market Fluidity and Economic Performance", *NBER WORKING PAPER SERIES*, http://www.nber.org/papers/w20479 (accessed on 19 September 2017). [2]

Desjardins, R. and A. Warnke (2012), "Ageing and Skills: A Review and Analysis of Skill Gain and Skill Loss Over the Lifespan and Over Time", *OECD Education Working Papers*, No. 72, OECD Publishing, Paris, http://dx.doi.org/10.1787/5k9csvw87ckh-en. [15]

Drydakis, N. et al. (2017), "Inclusive Recruitment? Hiring Discrimination against Older Workers", *IZA DP*, No. 10957, http://ftp.iza.org/dp10957.pdf. [57]

Duell, N. (2015), "Local economic strategies for ageing labour markets: Management practices for productivity gains of older workers", *OECD Employment Policy Papers*, No. 11, OECD Publishing, Paris, http://dx.doi.org/10.1787/5jrnwqkwpxjj-en. [64]

DWP (2017), *Fuller Working Lives A Partnership Approach*, Department for Work and Pensions, London, https://www.gov.uk/government/publications/fuller-working-lives-a-partnership-approach. [65]

Eurobarometer (2015), *Discrimination in the EU in 2015*, European Comission, Brussels. [55]

Eurofound and ILO (2017), *Working anytime, anywhere: The effects on the world of work*, Publications Office of the European Union, Luxembourg, and the International Labour Office, Geneva., http://dx.doi.org/10.2806/372726. [34]

European Commission (2012), *Special Eurobarometer 378 on Active Ageing*, https://ec.europa.eu/eip/ageing/library/special-eurobarometer-378-active-ageing_en. [73]

European Parliament (2013), *Combining the Entry of Young People in the Labour Market with the Retention of Older Workers*, IP/A/EMPL/ST/2012-04, April. [67]

Frimmel, W. et al. (2015), "Seniority Wages and the Role of Firms in Retirement", *IZA Discussion Paper*, No. 9192, http://ftp.iza.org/dp9192.pdf. [37]

Garthwaite, C., T. Gross and M. Notowidigdo (2014), "Public Health Insurance, Labor Supply, and Employment Lock", *The Quarterly Journal of Economics*, Vol. 129/2, pp. 653-696, http://dx.doi.org/10.1093/qje/qju005. [45]

Ghilarducci, T. et al. (2016), *Gender And Racial Disparities In Physical Job Demands Of Older Workers*, Schwartz Center for Economic Policy Analysis and Department of Economics, The New School for Social Research, Policy Note Series, http://www.economicpolicyresearch.org/images/docs/research/retirement_security/2016-4_Gender_Racial_Gaps_in_Older_Workers_Physical_Job_Demands.pdf. [29]

Goda, G., J. Shoven and S. Slavov (2011), "Implicit Taxes on Work from Social Security and Medicare", *Tax Policy and the Economy*, Vol. 25/1, pp. 69-88, http://dx.doi.org/10.1086/658381. [47]

Gruber, J. and B. Madrian (2004), "Health Insurance, Labor Supply, and Job Mobility", in McLaughlin, C. (ed.), *Health policy and the uninsured*, Urban Institute Press, Washington DC. [44]

Gruber, J. and K. Milligan (2010), "Do Elderly Workers Substitute for Younger Workers in the United States?", http://www.nber.org/chapters/c8262, pp. 345-360. [7]

H. Munnell, A. and A. Yanyuan Wu (2012), "Will Delayed Retirement by the Baby Boomers Lead to Higher Unemployment Among Younger Workers?", *CRR WP*, No. 22, Center for Retirement Research, http://crr.bc.edu/working-papers/will-delayed-retirement-by-the-baby-boomers-lead-to-higher-unemployment-among-younger-workers/. [8]

Hairault, J., F. Langot and T. Sopraseuth (2014), "Why is Old Workers' Labor Market More Volatile? Unemployment Fluctuations over the Life-Cycle", *Discussion Paper*, No. 8076, IZA, http://ftp.iza.org/dp8076.pdf (accessed on 20 September 2017). [5]

Hyatt, H. and J. Spletzer (2016), "The Shifting Job Tenure Distribution", *Discussion Paper*, No. 9776, IZA, http://ftp.iza.org/dp9776.pdf. [3]

Ipsos Reid (2012), *Three-Quarters (74%) of Canadians Think that Workplaces Discriminate Against Older Workers who are Looking for Jobs; Half (51%) Feel Similarly About Young Workers*, https://www.ipsos-na.com/download/pr.aspx?id=11807. [71]

Johnson, R. and J. Kawachi (2007), "Job changes at older ages: Effects on wages, benefits and other job attributes", *CRR*, No. WP 2007-4, Center for Retirement Research at Boston College, http://www.bc.edu/crr. [26]

Kaiser Family Foundation and Health Research & Educational Trust (2016), *Employer Health Benefits - 2016 Annual Report*, http://files.kff.org/attachment/Report-Employer-Health-Benefits-2016-Annual-Survey. [43]

Lee, S. and S. Lee (2016), "Comparing Employment Quota Systems for Disabled People Between Korea and Japan", *Asian Journal of Human Services*, Vol. 10, pp. 83-92. [10]

Lieberwitz, R. (2008), "Employment Discrimination Law in the United States: On the Road to Equality?", in Blanpain, R. (ed.), *New Developments in Employment Discrimination Law*, Bulletin of Comparative Labor Relations No. 68, The Hague: Kluwer. [74]

Mahlberg, B. et al. (2013), "Ageing, productivity and wages in Austria.", *Labour Economics*, Vol. 22/100, pp. 5-15, http://dx.doi.org/10.1016/j.labeco.2012.09.005. [19]

Monge-Naranjo, A. and F. Sohail (2015), *The Composition of Long-term Unemployment Is Changing toward Older Workers*, https://www.stlouisfed.org/~/media/Publications/Regional-Economist/2015/October/unemployment.pdf. [4]

Neumark, D. and J. Song (2013), "Do stronger age discrimination laws make Social Security reforms more effective?", *Journal of Public Economics*, Vol. 108, pp. 1-16, http://dx.doi.org/10.1016/j.jpubeco.2013.09.006. [53]

Neumark, D. and P. Button (2014), "Did Age Discrimination Protections Help Older Workers Weather the Great Recession?", *Journal of Policy Analysis and Management*, Vol. 33/3, pp. 566-601, http://dx.doi.org/10.1002/pam.21762. [54]

Neumark, D., I. Burn and P. Button (2015), "Is it harder for older workers to find jobs? New and improved evidence from a field experiment", *NBER Working Paper Series*, No. 21669, National Bureau of Economic Research, http://www.nber.org/papers/w21669. [59]

OECD (2005), *Ageing and Employment Policies/Vieillissement et politiques de l'emploi: United States 2005*, OECD Publishing, Paris, http://dx.doi.org/10.1787/9789264009608-en. [52]

OECD (2006), *Live Longer, Work Longer*, Ageing and Employment Policies, OECD Publishing, Paris, http://dx.doi.org/10.1787/9789264035881-en. [49]

OECD (2013), *OECD Employment Outlook 2013*, OECD Publishing, Paris, http://dx.doi.org/10.1787/empl_outlook-2013-en. [9]

OECD (2014), *Ageing and Employment Policies: France 2014: Working Better with Age*, Ageing and Employment Policies, OECD Publishing, Paris, http://dx.doi.org/10.1787/9789264207523-en. [68]

OECD (2015), *Ageing and Employment Policies: Denmark 2015: Working Better with Age*, Ageing and Employment Policies, OECD Publishing, Paris, http://dx.doi.org/10.1787/9789264235335-en. [60]

OECD (2016), *Back to Work: United States: Improving the Re-employment Prospects of Displaced Workers*, OECD Publishing, Paris, http://dx.doi.org/10.1787/9789264266513-en. [1]

OECD (2017), *Taxing Wages 2017*, OECD Publishing, Paris, http://dx.doi.org/10.1787/tax_wages-2017-en. [42]

OECD (2017), *Preventing Ageing Unequally*, OECD Publishing, Paris, http://dx.doi.org/10.1787/9789264279087-4-en. [11]

Olphert, W. and L. Damodaran (2013), "Older people and digital disengagement: a fourth digital divide?", *Gerontology*, Vol. 59/6, pp. 564-70, http://dx.doi.org/10.1159/000353630. [31]

Paccagnella, M. (2016), "Age, Ageing and Skills: Results from the Survey of Adult Skills", *OECD Education Working Papers*, No. 132, OECD Publishing, Paris, http://dx.doi.org/10.1787/5jm0q1n38lvc-en. [17]

Quintini, G. (2014), "Skills at Work: How Skills and their Use Matter in the Labour Market", *OECD Social, Employment and Migration Working Papers*, No. 158, OECD Publishing, Paris, http://dx.doi.org/10.1787/5jz44fdfjm7j-en. [16]

Rix, S. (2016), "Working late: policy relevance for older workers in the United States", *Australian Journal of Social Issues*, Vol. 51/2, Canberra, pp. 205-227, http://dx.doi.org/10.1002/j.1839-4655.2016.tb00374.x. [48]

Romeu Gordo, L. and V. Skirbekk (2013), "Skill demand and the comparative advantage of age: Jobs tasks and earnings from the 1980s to the 2000s in Germany", *Labour Economics*, Vol. 22, https://econpapers.repec.org/article/eeelabeco/v_3a22_3ay_3a2013_3ai_3ac_3ap_3a61-69.htm, pp. 61-69. [24]

Sanzenbacher, G., S. Sass and C. Gillis (2017), *How Job Changes Affect Retirement Timing by Socioeconomic Status*, Center for Retirement Research Brief 17-3, http://crr.bc.edu/briefs/how-job-changes-affect-retirement-timing-by-socioeconomic-status/. [21]

SHRM (2015), *2014 Older Workers Survey*, http://www.shrm.org/agingworkforce. [18]

SHRM (2016), *The New Talent Landscape - Recruiting Difficulty and Skills Shortages*, https://www.shrm.org/hr-today/trends-and-forecasting/research-and-surveys/pages/talent-landscape.aspx. [28]

Sonnega, A., B. Mcfall and R. Willis (2016), "Occupational Transitions at Older Ages: What Moves are People Making?", *WP 2016-352*, University of Michigan: Michigan Retirement Research Center , Ann Arbor, https://deepblue.lib.umich.edu/bitstream/handle/2027.42/135724/wp352.pdf?sequence=1&isAllowed=y. [25]

Sonnet, A., H. Olsen and T. Manfredi (2014), "Towards More Inclusive Ageing and Employment Policies: The Lessons from France, The Netherlands, Norway and Switzerland", *De Economist*, Vol. 162, pp. 315-339, http://dx.doi.org/10.1007/s10645-014-9240-x. [63]

Tavares, A. (2017), "Telework and health effects review", *International Journal of Healthcare*, Vol. 3/2, p. 30, http://dx.doi.org/10.5430/ijh.v3n2p30. [33]

The Sloane Center on Aging & Work (2013), *Business strategies for the age-diverse workforce*, Boston College, http://www.bc.edu/content/dam/files/research_sites/agingandwork/pdf/publications/FS33_BusinessStrategies.pdf. [62]

U.S. Department of Labor (2008), *Report of the Taskforce on the Aging of the American Workforce*, https://www.doleta.gov/reports/FINAL_Taskforce_Report_2_27_08.pdf. [69]

Van Giezen, R. (2013), "Paid Leave in Private Industry Over the Past 20 Years", *Beyond the Numbers*, No. Vol. 2, No. 18, Bureau of Labor Statistics, Washington DC, http://digitalcommons.ilr.cornell.edu/key_workplace/1160. [38]

Whitman, D. (2014), "The opportunities of an older workforce", in *OECD Year Book 2014*, OECD Publishing, Paris, http://www.oecd.org/forum/oecdyearbook/the-opportunities-of-an-older-workforce.htm. [32]

Annex 2.A. The labour market situation of older workers in the United States

About 20 key indicators illustrate features of and developments in the labour market situation of older workers in the United States over the past decade. These include not only employment and unemployment rates but also factors impacting employment prospects, such as gender differences, job quality, labour mobility and education and training. Annex Table 2.A.1 presents a summary of these indicators, placing the United States in an international context through comparison with OECD and highest and lowest five countries averages for each indicator. The United States performs above the OECD average in all the indicators, except in terms of employability of older workers where the United States ranks amongst the highest five OECD countries. The main findings for the United States follow:

- *Employment*: The employment rate for the age group 55-64 is slightly above the OECD average, but whereas the rate for the group 55-59 is now similar to the OECD average (it has remained steady for the past decade in the United States while it has increased significantly in the OECD), the employment rate of groups 60-64, 65-69 and 70-74 are still considerably above the OECD despite the noticeable improvement in the OECD on average, but the gap with the OECD average is considerably lower. While the gender gap in employment in the age group 55-64 has narrowed in the OECD area over the past decade, it remained stable in the United States but smaller than the OECD average.
- *Job quality*: The share of part-time work for the age group 55-64 is slightly lower than ten years ago, lower than the OECD average and three times lower than the highest five-OECD countries averages. Similarly, the incidence of self-employment is also below the OECD average. Besides, earnings for 55-64 year-olds are higher to the earnings of the 25-54 year-olds and similar to the OECD ratio in 2016.
- *Dynamics*: Both the retention and hiring rates were above the OECD averages both in 2006 and 2016, but whereas the retention rate has significantly increased in the past decade, the hiring rate has slightly declined for older workers. The effective labour force exit ages for both sexes are higher than the OECD average and have increased from 2006 but are still considerably below the highest five countries average.
- *Unemployment*: The unemployment rate for the labour force aged 55-64 and the incidence of long-term unemployment are significantly below the OECD average. A broad measure of joblessness among older workers – those either unemployed or marginally attached workers– shows a potential waste of resources that has slightly increased since 2006, but it is below the OECD average.
- *Employability*: Older workers have on average a relatively high education level (that has improved in the past decade) and participate more in training, much above the OECD and among the top five countries. In addition, the ratio measuring the age gap in training is very low in the United States, in contrast with the OECD average ratio.

Annex Table 2.A.1. Older workers scoreboard, 2006 and 2016, United States, OECD and High 5 and Low 5 countries

	United States		OECD[a]		High 5	High 5 countries	Low 5	Low 5 countries
	2006	2016	2006	2016	2016		2016	
Employment								
-- Employment rate, 50-74 (% of the age group)	56.1	53.9	47.0	50.8	72.3	AUS, ISL, JPN, KOR, NZL	31.7	BEL, GRC, SVN, ESP, TUR
of which 50-54	77.9	75.7	73.8	75.7	89.9	CZE, DEU, ISL, SWE, CHE	47.2	GRC, ITA, MEX, ESP, TUR
55-64	61.8	61.8	52.7	59.2	84.4	ISL, NZL, NOR, SWE, CHE	33.4	BEL, GRC, LUX, SVN, TUR
65-69	28.1	31.0	20.3	25.5	56.3	CHL, ISL, JPN, KOR, NZL	4.7	BEL, HUN, SVK, SVN, ESP
70-74	16.4	18.4	12.0	14.6	32.6	CHL, JPN, KOR, MEX, NZL	1.2	BEL, GRC, HUN, SVK, ESP
-- Gender gap in employment, 55-64 [(men-women)/men]	0.16	0.16	0.32	0.25	0.63	CHL, GRC, ITA, MEX, TUR	-0.05	EST, FIN, FRA, LVA, SWE
Job quality								
-- Incidence of part-time work, 55-64 (% of employees)	16.1	15.7	20.3	21.1	47.4	AUS, BEL, NLD, CHE, GBR	7.0	CZE, EST, GRC, HUN, SVK
-- Incidence of temporary work[c], 55-64 (% of employees)	3.3	-	8.9	7.9	32.7	CHL, KOR, POL, ESP, TUR	1.2	AUT, BEL, EST, LVA, NOR
-- Incidence of self-employment, 55-64 (% of total employment)	17.0	19.1	38.0	32.8	64.5	CHL, GRC, KOR, MEX, TUR	9.1	DNK, EST, HUN, NOR, SWE
-- Full-time[b] earnings, 55-64 relative to 25-54 (ratio)	1.08	1.11	1.09	1.10	1.40	AUT, BEL, FRA, GRC, PRT	0.91	CZE, KOR, NZL, SVK, GBR
Dynamics								
-- Retention rate[d], after 60 (% of employees t-4)	44.5	53.2	40.3	50.3	80.2	DEU, ISL, NLD, NOR, SWE	22.6	AUT, GRC, KOR, LUX, SVN
-- Hiring rate[e], 55-64 (% of employees)	11.4	10.2	9.2	9.1	33.9	CHL, JPN, KOR, MEX, TUR	2.2	BEL, FRA, ITA, NOR, SVN
-- Effective labour force exit age[f] (years) Men	64.8	66.8	63.6	65.1	72.0	CHL, ISL, JPN, KOR, MEX	60.0	BEL, FRA, GRC, LUX, SVK
Women	63.8	65.4	62.3	63.6	72.2	CHL, ISL, JPN, KOR, MEX	59.5	BEL, FRA, GRC, POL, SVK
Unemployment								
-- Unemployment rate, 55-64 (% of the labour force)	3.0	3.6	4.3	4.6	19.2	GRC, LVA, PRT, SVK, ESP	2.0	ISL, JPN, KOR, MEX, NOR
-- Incidence of long-term[g] unemployment, 55-64 (% of total unemployment)	16.3	18.2	26.3	44.3	88.9	BEL, GRC, IRL, LUX, SVN	4.2	CAN, ISR, KOR, MEX, USA
-- Marginally attached workers[h], 55-64 (% of the age group)	0.5	0.6	1.2	1.2	5.0	EST, FIN, LVA, PRT, ESP	0.2	CAN, CHL, CZE, SWE, USA
Employability								
-- Share of 55-64 with tertiary education (% of the age group)	37.7	41.9	20.0	26.2	47.6	CAN, ISR, JPN, GBR, USA	10.2	ITA, MEX, POL, PRT, TUR
-- Participation in training[i], 55-64								
Absolute (% of all employed in the age group)	-	56.8	-	41.2	59.7	DNK, FIN, NZL, SWE, USA	8.0	FRA, GRC, ISR, ITA, TUR
Relative to employed persons aged 25-54 (ratio)	-	0.94	-	0.78	0.94	CZE, EST, NZL, SVN, USA	0.26	AUT, FRA, GRC, JPN, KOR

Note: Higher values usually denote top performers, except for indicators on unemployment and on gender gap in employment. Top performers in job quality indicators are less obvious to assess.

a) Weighted averages for 35 OECD countries with the exception of earnings and education indicators which are unweighted.

b) Mean gross weekly earnings. The OECD average comprises only 27 countries.

c) Year 2006 refers to 2005.

d) All employees currently aged 60-64 with job tenure of five years or more as a percentage of all employees aged 55-59 4-years previously (years 2002-06 and 2012-16) and 5-year previously for the OECD and High 5 and Low 5 countries (years 2001-06 and 2011-16).

e) Employees aged 55-64 with job tenure of less than one year as a percentage of total employees.

f) Effective exit age over the five-year periods 2001-06 and 2011-16. The effective exit age (also called the effective age of retirement) is calculated as a weighted average of the exit ages of each five-year age cohort, starting with the cohort aged 40-44 at the first date, using absolute changes in the labour force participation rate of each cohort as weights.

g) Unemployed for more than one year.

h) Persons neither employed, nor actively looking for work, but willing to work and available for taking a job during the survey reference week. Additionally for the United States, persons having looked for work during the past 12 months.

i) Job-related training during year prior to the survey in 2012. The OECD average is an unweighted average of the 29 OECD countries/economies having participated in PIAAC and excludes Hungary, Iceland, Latvia, Luxembourg, Mexico, Portugal and Switzerland. Data correspond to 2015 for second-round countries Chile, Greece, Israel, New Zealand, Slovenia and Turkey. All remaining countries/economies correspond to the first round in 2012. .

Source: OECD estimations from the OECD Employment Database (www.oecd.org/employment/emp/onlineoecdemploymentdatabase.htm), the OECD Earnings Distribution Database (https://data.oecd.org/earnwage/average-wages.htm), the OECD Education Database (www.oecd.org/education/database.htm) and the OECD Survey of Adult Skills (PIAAC) (www.oecd.org/skills/piaac/).

Older workers most frequent occupations and industries

Future employment prospects for older persons will be influenced by the type of jobs they can attain and their workplace environment. In 2016, older workers in the United States represented around 23% of all employed persons (almost 6 percentage points more than a decade ago). Compared to prime-age workers, they are somewhat over-represented in self-employment, part-time and public sector jobs (Table 2.A.2), although the share of older workers in these categories has slightly declined since 2006. Nevertheless, 82% of all older workers are wage and salary workers. Not surprisingly, older workers are under-represented in manual occupations. However, a substantial proportion (mostly men) work in manual jobs, and contrary to prime-age workers, the share of older workers in these occupations has not decreased.

The top industries in terms of numbers of older workers are: educational and health services; wholesale and retail trade; business and professional services; and manufacturing, more than half of older workers are employed in one of these four industries. However, by far the most important industries for older workers (and also for prime-age workers) are education and health, employing almost one quarter of all older workers, especially women. Over the past decade, there has not been much change in the distribution of sectors employing older workers. Sectors where older workers are significantly under-represented are construction and professional and business services and older workers are greatly over-represented in agriculture, forestry, fishing and hunting sector, yet only 2.5% of all older workers are employed in this sector (Table 2.A.2).

Annex Table 2.A.2. Older workers (aged 55 and over) versus prime-age workers (aged 25-54) in the United States by selected job and workplace characteristics, 2016 and 2006

	2016						2006					
	Share of all older workers			Share of all prime-age workers			Share of all older workers			Share of all prime-age workers		
	Total	Men	Women	Total	Men	Women	Total	Men	Women	Total	Men	Women
% of all employed	**22.8**	**22.9**	**22.8**	**63.9**	**64.3**	**63.5**	**17.2**	**17.1**	**17.3**	**68.0**	**68.4**	**67.6**
Employment status												
Wage and salary worker	82.6	78.6	87.3	90.9	89.2	92.8	80.7	75.8	86.3	89.1	86.9	91.7
Self-employed	17.0	21.2	12.3	9.0	10.7	7.0	18.9	24.0	13.1	10.8	13.0	8.1
Family worker	0.3	0.2	0.5	0.1	0.1	0.2	0.4	0.2	0.6	0.1	0.1	0.2
Usual working time												
Full time	78.1	83.7	71.7	87.9	93.7	81.2	77.6	83.5	71.0	88.9	95.4	81.2
Part time	21.9	16.3	28.3	12.1	6.3	18.8	22.4	16.5	29.0	11.1	4.6	18.8
Occupation												
Non-manual occupations	65.6	57.4	75.0	62.4	52.3	74.0	65.9	58.1	74.9	60.8	49.7	70.1
Manual occupations	20.0	31.7	6.6	21.5	34.5	6.5	20.2	31.5	7.2	24.5	38.9	7.7
Service occupations	14.4	10.9	18.3	16.1	13.2	19.5	13.9	10.4	17.9	14.6	11.5	18.3
Sector												
Private	84.2	87.3	80.7	86.0	88.7	82.9	82.1	85.3	78.5	85.6	88.7	81.9
Public	15.8	12.7	19.3	14.0	11.3	17.1	17.9	14.7	21.5	14.4	11.3	18.1
Industry												
Agriculture, forestry, fishing and hunting	2.5	3.4	1.5	1.4	2.0	0.8	2.9	3.9	1.7	1.3	1.7	0.7
Mining	0.6	0.9	0.2	0.6	1.0	0.2	0.5	0.8	0.2	0.5	0.8	0.2
Construction	6.5	10.7	1.7	7.5	12.8	1.4	5.9	9.5	1.7	9.0	15.1	1.9
Manufacturing	10.8	14.4	6.7	10.6	14.0	6.7	11.0	14.4	7.0	12.4	16.0	8.1
Wholesale and retail trade	12.7	13.3	11.9	12.1	12.6	11.5	14.3	14.7	13.7	13.2	13.7	12.6
Transportation and utilities	5.9	8.6	2.9	5.5	7.7	2.8	5.5	7.9	2.9	5.6	7.8	3.0
Information	1.8	1.8	1.7	2.0	2.3	1.7	2.2	2.2	2.2	2.6	2.7	2.5
Financial activities	7.6	6.7	8.6	7.1	6.4	7.9	7.9	7.2	8.6	7.4	6.1	9.0
Professional and business services	11.8	13.2	10.3	13.0	14.2	11.7	10.4	11.9	8.7	10.9	11.4	10.4
Educational and health services	23.7	12.0	37.1	22.8	10.5	37.0	23.3	12.4	35.7	20.9	9.3	34.4
Leisure and hospitality	5.6	5.2	6.1	7.9	7.4	8.4	5.0	4.5	5.6	6.8	6.3	7.4
Other services	5.7	5.2	6.2	4.6	4.1	5.2	6.0	5.3	6.8	4.6	4.3	5.1
Public administration	4.9	4.7	5.0	4.8	5.0	4.6	5.2	5.2	5.1	4.8	4.8	4.7

Source: OECD calculations based on BLS/CPS.

Chapter 3.

Promoting the employability of United States workers throughout their working lives

In addition to strengthened economic incentives and age-friendly employer practices, employability and willingness to stay on are prerequisites for longer working lives. The employability of older workers depends importantly on three key factors: up-to-date skills, ready access to employment services, and good working conditions. This chapter assesses the situation in the United States in these areas. Older adults in the United States are relatively highly educated, skilled and among the most frequent participants in training in the OECD. However, the United States faces large disparities among older adults in education, access to training, and quality employment services as well as in working conditions.

Boosting the employability of older workers in the United States requires: First, the basic skills of workers throughout their working lives should be improved. Second, inequalities accumulated by those with poor basic skills need to be tackled. Finally, the access and quality of employment and training programmes for older jobseekers enhanced.

The statistical data for Israel are supplied by and under the responsibility of the relevant Israeli authorities. The use of such data by the OECD is without prejudice to the status of the Golan Heights, East Jerusalem and Israeli settlements in the West Bank under the terms of international law.

Introduction

Many barriers deter people from working longer. Some are related to employers' willingness to retain and hire older workers (Chapter 2) but other barriers affect older workers directly, which make it difficult for them to either stay in their existing job or find a new one. Problems include poor working conditions, limited training possibilities and interrupted careers earlier on in workers' lives as well as a lack of rewarding job opportunities at an older age.

Moreover, as a result of globalisation, digitalisation and rapid population ageing, people will not only be working longer but they will also be more likely to experience multiple jobs during their working lives. Lifelong learning and activation policies have a crucial role to play in fostering the employability of workers throughout their working lives and by doing so, reducing inequalities later in life.

This chapter first explores the impact of skill proficiency and training on the employability of older workers. It is likely to be harder for older adults with weak generic skills, such as literacy and numeracy skills but also Information and Communication Technology (ICT) skills, to find and keep a high-quality job. The chapter also reviews the main barriers that older adults face in obtaining training in the United States, notably the least educated among them.

Support by employment and training programmes for the older unemployed is the second area discussed in this chapter. Effective activation policies, in particular, are crucial to prevent workers cumulating disadvantages from experiencing poverty and long-term unemployment, and to avoid early exit from the labour force.

The final section of the chapter takes stock of measures that have been implemented in the United States to promote age-friendly working conditions. Drawing on good practices that can be found in other OECD countries, it puts forward areas where further actions could be taken. The extent to where firms award workers with job security, safe and healthy work conditions, and consultation with workers are also important determinants of older workers willingness to continue working. While many determinants of working conditions are primarily an issue for business, policies and institutions can provide employers with incentives and tools to improve them.

From old to new skills: the importance of training

US older workers are on average highly educated but with large inequalities

On average, older adults in the United States have high levels of educational attainment and basic skills proficiency, score high in problem solving and are among the most active users of ICT in comparison with their peers in other OECD countries. However, there are large disparities in skills, education and other socio-economic characteristics among Americans, which start at younger ages and are often further reinforced with age.

Low education dividend in the future

Contrary to other OECD countries, educational levels are not increasing in the United States, removing a potential source of productivity growth. Over 41% of the population aged 55-64 in the United States had tertiary-level education in 2015; this is well above the OECD average of 26% (Figure 3.1). In the future older workers will generally be better educated, but in the United States the size of this "education dividend" is much lower compared with other OECD countries. Whereas in the United States there will be little increase in the proportion of older workers who have completed tertiary education over the next 30 years, especially amongst men, this proportion will rise considerably in many OECD countries. Thus, in the future, older adults in the United States will lose some of their competitive advantage as the level of education of older workers in other OECD countries rises to similar levels as their own.

Figure 3.1. Older workers of tomorrow will be better educated, except for men in Germany and the United States

OECD, EU28 and selected OECD countries by gender, 2015 and 2045
Percentage share of population aged 55-64 by educational attainment

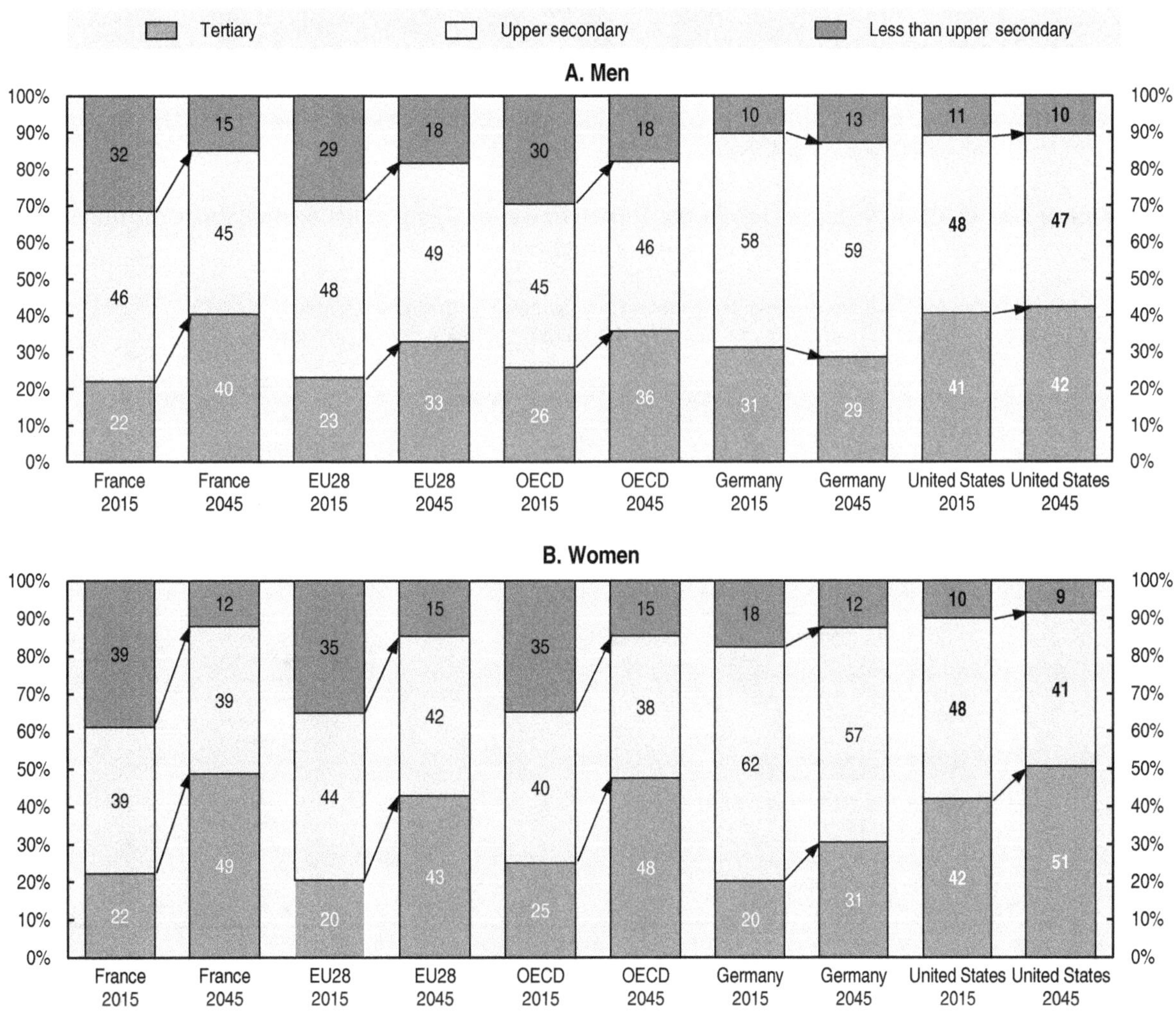

Note: These projections of the education level of older people (55-64) in 2045 are calculated taking the education attainment of people aged 25-34 in 2015 and assuming that that they acquire no further education during the next 30 years and that mortality rates do not vary significantly by education levels between 25-34 and 55-64.

Source: OECD calculations based on *OECD Education at a Glance, Educational attainment and labour-force status dataset* (http://stats.oecd.org/Index.aspx?DataSetCode=EAG_NEAC) and Eurostat (http://ec.europa.eu/eurostat/web/education-and-training/data/database).

StatLink http://dx.doi.org/10.1787/888933644338

Poor prospects of future US older workers relative to other OECD countries

US older workers have high levels of proficiency on average both in numeracy and literacy compared with their peers in other countries; but this is largely because of their higher educational attainment. Once education is taken into account by comparing individuals with the same level of education and language background (excluding foreign-born adults), the basic skills of older adults in the United States are relatively weak by international standards based on the Survey of Adult Skills (PIAAC) (Figure 3.2, Panel A). Besides, unlike many other OECD countries, there has been little sign of improvement in recent decades. Currently, young adults in the United States have similar or weaker literacy skills than their counterparts in the mid-90s (OECD, 2013[1]), and their average basic skills are not very different from those of older persons (Figure 3.2, Panel B). Finally, adult skills are closely linked to the performance of the initial schooling system. The US results from the Programme for International Student Assessment (PISA) (2016[2]) on the basic skills of 15 year-olds are below the OECD average in both reading and mathematics. Thus, not surprisingly, US young adults also score well below the average in the Survey of Adult Skills (Figure 3.2).

Figure 3.2. Small skills gap by age in the United States but poor skills performance of future older workers

Progress in literacy skills between two age groups, selected OECD countries, 2012
Score on the literacy scale

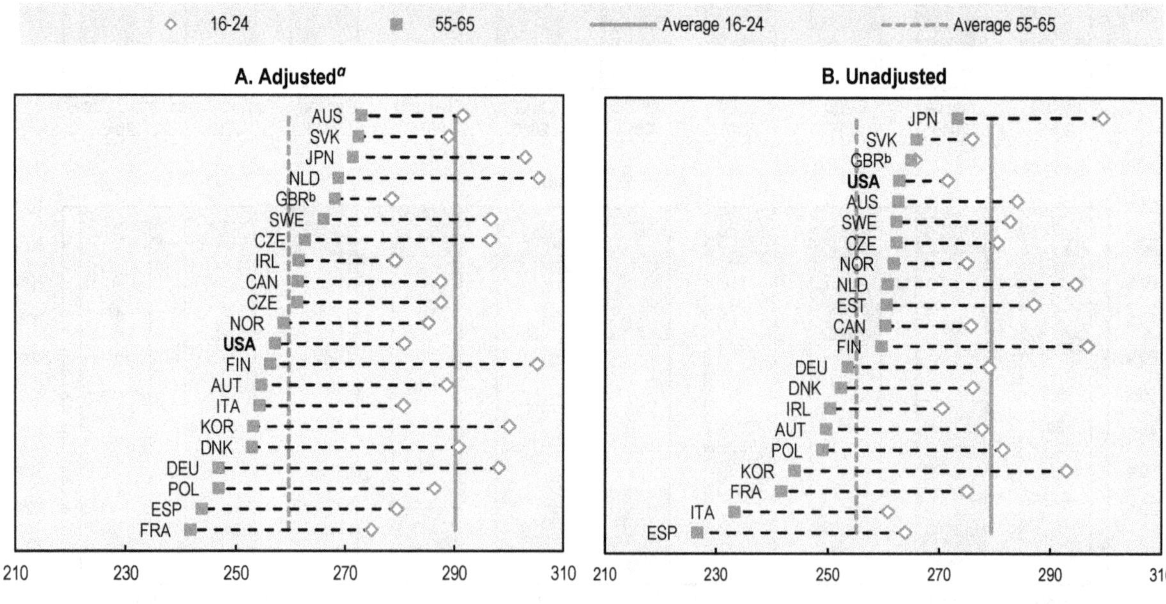

a) Comparing individuals with the same level of education and language background (excluding foreign born adults).
b) England and Northern Ireland
Source: OECD (2013), *OECD Skills Outlook 2013: First Results from the Survey of Adult Skills*, OECD Publishing, Paris.

StatLink http://dx.doi.org/10.1787/888933644357

Basic skills such as numeracy and literacy are important as they are the basis for employability and the ability to update and learn new skills. However, in an increasingly complex and digitalised society other cognitive skills, particularly problem solving and the use of ICT skills, are even more relevant for the employability of individuals. The OECD has developed in PIAAC a new domain of competency designed to assess problem solving in technology-rich environments that represents the intersection of what are sometimes described as "computer literacy" skills (i.e. the capacity to use ICT tools and applications) and the cognitive skills required to solve problems. In this new domain, older Americans outperform their counterparts in other OECD countries: the share of older persons with high levels of proficiency in the United States is one of the highest among all OECD participant countries in PIAAC. However, the share of young people aged 20-24 with high levels of proficiency is one of the lowest among OECD countries (Figure 3.3). All in all, the future prospects of older Americans *vis-à-vis* their peers in other OECD countries must be a matter of concern, as young cohorts replace older ones and the basic skills of other developed countries workforces will progressively outpace those of the United States, taking the edge of the competitive advantage of the US workforce.

Figure 3.3. US older adults are among the most proficient in the use of ICT but US young adults among the least

Proficiency (levels 2 or 3) in technology-rich environments of two age groups, 2012 or 2015[a]

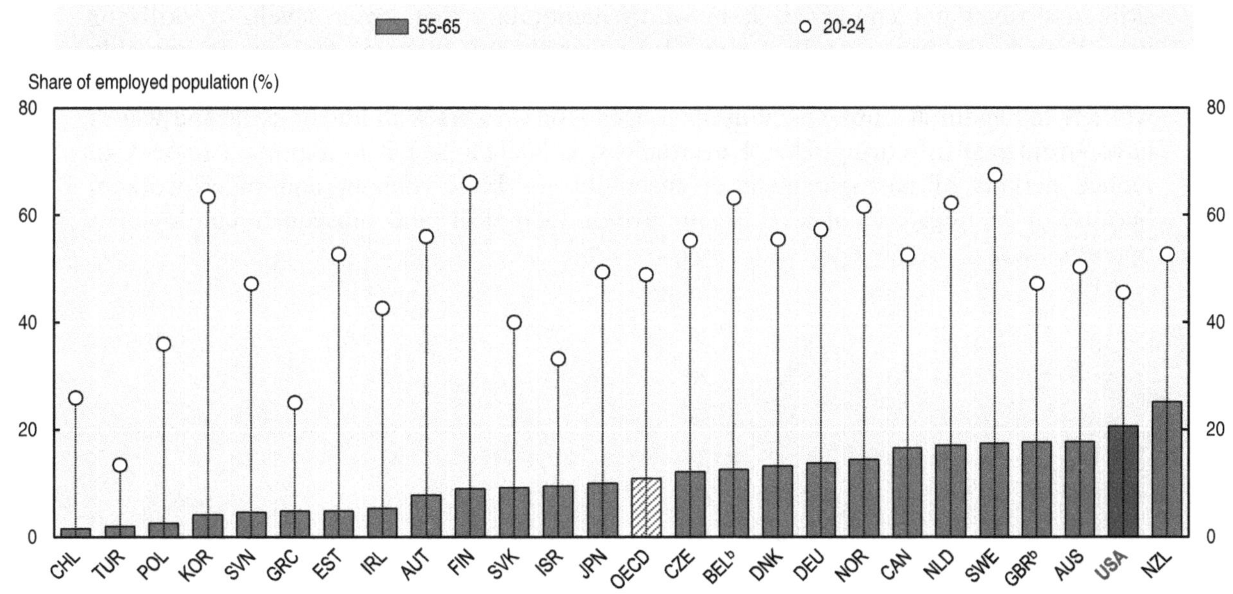

Note: The OECD is a weighted average of the countries shown in the figure.
a) For Chile, Greece, Israel, New Zealand, Slovenia and Turkey the year of reference is 2015.
b) Data for Belgium refer only to Flanders and data for the United Kingdom refer to England and Northern Ireland jointly.
Source: OECD calculations based on the Survey of Adult Skills (PIAAC) (2012, 2015), www.oecd.org/skills/piaac/.

StatLink http://dx.doi.org/10.1787/888933644376

Large skills discrepancies among adults

A further source of concern is the large skills discrepancies among adults within the United States, which is higher than in most other OECD countries (OECD, 2013[3]). There is also evidence that socio-economic background has a stronger influence on adult basic skills in the United States than in most countries (OECD, 2013[1]), mainly because migration status and ethnicity remain important predictors of skills proficiency. Finally, the US population is becoming more racially and ethnically diverse (Pew Research Center, 2015[4]). This diversity is still concentrated in the youngest age groups, but the older population will gradually become more diverse (Mather, Jacobsen and Pollard, 2015[5]), potentially leading to even more inequalities among older Americans in the future if current disparities in skills proficiency continue.

Labour market status is another important source of skills inequality. As expected, employed workers have higher levels of education and skills than unemployed workers in the same age group. However, on average for the same age group, early retirees in the United States have somewhat higher skill levels than unemployed and inactive older adults, although lower than employed workers (Table 3.1). This highlights the potential for firms to hire retired workers in case workforce requirements increase. However, the observed gap in skills amongst the unemployed and early retirees relative to employed workers raises the question whether periods out of the labour force for older workers lead to skill loss.

Exclusion from the labour market may negatively impact older workers' chances of being re-hired if certain skills are lost more quickly when not practiced. Mazzonna and Peracchi (2017[6]) use repeated observations on older workers who retire and find that retirement reduces both physical and mental capacities. However, in addition to the possibility of skill loss when not employed, it is worth mentioning that lower levels of skills of unemployed and retired workers may also be partly driven by a selection of less able workers into retirement and unemployment. For example, firms may incite more able workers to remain in employment at older ages – or workers with higher skills and wages have an interest in retiring later. Nevertheless, it is clear that it is important to seek to reduce periods of unemployment or inactivity for both younger and older workers because of the negative impact this can have on their skills and subsequent employment opportunities.

Table 3.1. Retirees have higher skills than the older unemployed but lower skills than the older employed

Characteristics of individuals aged 50-65

Status	Education (years)	Literacy (scores)	Numeracy (scores)
United States			
Employed	12.3	270	258
Unemployed	11.9	258	241
Retired	11.8	269	250
Inactive	10.2	242	222
France			
Employed	10.6	250	244
Unemployed	10.3	247	234
Retired	9.5	245	240
Inactive	9.0	231	219
Germany			
Employed	14.0	261	266
Unemployed	13.6	260	260
Retired	13.3	243	247
Inactive	12.9	244	237
Japan			
Employed	12.8	283	281
Unemployed	12.9	302	275
Retired	13.0	269	281
Inactive	12.1	274	272
United Kingdom			
Employed	11.2	269	261
Unemployed	10.9	257	248
Retired	10.9	272	263
Inactive	9.7	254	240
EU average			
Employed	12.4	260	258
Unemployed	11.3	249	242
Retired	11.5	250	248
Inactive	10.7	238	230
OECD average			
Employed	12.4	260	258
Unemployed	11.3	249	242
Retired	11.5	250	248
Inactive	10.7	238	230

Note: The OECD an unweighted average and excludes Hungary, Iceland, Latvia, Luxembourg, Mexico, Portugal and Switzerland. The EU is an unweighted average of the following 20 countries: Austria, Belgium (Flanders), Cyprus, the Czech Republic, Denmark, Estonia, Finland, France, Germany, Greece, Ireland, Italy, Lithuania, Netherlands, Poland, Slovakia, Slovenia, Spain, Sweden and the United Kingdom (England and Northern Ireland).

Source: OECD calculations based on the Survey of Adult Skills (PIAAC) (2012, 2015), www.oecd.org/skills/piaac/.

StatLink http://dx.doi.org/10.1787/888933644471

Adult education and training (AET) in the United States

In addition to preventing skill depreciation as a result of unemployment or inactivity, workers should have good opportunities and incentives to upgrade their skills and acquire new ones. A very good way to develop skills is to use existing skills, since skills use and skills development are mutually reinforcing processes that can help to slow or reverse age-related declines in skills (OECD, 2013[3]). In this respect, US workers, including older workers, use their skills at work (Chapter 2) and participate in AET more than in most OECD countries (Figure 3.4).

Combined private and public investments make the United States the top country spending on post-secondary education per student (OECD, 2017[7]) and among the countries that spend most on AET. American post-secondary institutions, government agencies and employers spend USD 1.1 trillion (over 6% of GDP) annually on formal and informal higher education and training (Carnevale, Strohl and Gulish, 2015[8]). However, in the United States there are large barriers to AET that prevent a part of the US workforce benefiting from further education and training. In the United States, most AET is provided by employers that primarily invest in college-educated prime-aged workers. Alternatively, individuals themselves have to invest in increasingly costly private post-secondary education. Consequently, a large share of Americans faces notable barriers to access additional education and training. Among them are older adults, who have less access to both employer-sponsored and publicly funded training programmes than younger workers. This implies that their skills remain weak and may face a vicious cycle in which poor proficiency leads to fewer opportunities to further develop proficiency and vice versa. Thus, far from correcting the inequalities that exist at the time of leaving school, which in the United States are already large (OECD, 2017[9]), AET reinforces inequalities accumulated over the life course.

One explanation for this tendency is that employers may be reluctant to make investments in training older workers out of concern that they may not recoup their training costs before older employees retire (Eyster, Johnson and Toder, 2008[10]). In addition, older workers themselves may be afraid of pursuing training, either because they fear their managers will not support them or they doubt their own abilities (U.S. Department of Labor, 2008[11]). Moreover, many older jobseekers are not well informed about the skills they will need to obtain a job or the best and most cost-effective way to obtain them (Van Horn, Krepcio and Heidkamp, 2015[12]). Thus, according to Jenkins (2016[13]), it is important to disrupt ageing to break down the barriers and create new opportunities to learn as people get older.

Public policies and initiatives (both private and public) have a role to play in addressing these challenges. First, policy makers should insist on maximum transparency of training providers and require them to report on costs, duration, completion rates, and employment and earnings outcomes of their courses so adult learners can make informed decisions. Second, the public sector should support the access to post-secondary education for those with fewer resources. Third, access to employment and training programmes for older jobseekers and the quality of services received should be enhanced. Finally, promoting positive attitudes from both employers and older adults may pay off. Awareness and information campaigns might help reduce both employers' reluctance to make investments in training older workers and older workers' willingness to participate in training. All these actions will lead to a more skilled workforce with lower gaps in access to AET.

Vocational Education and Training (VET)[1] *in the United States*

Many of the basic features of the US system are strong. For instance, its extensive decentralisation leads to diverse and flexible forms of provision meeting the needs of many groups of learners and to a rich field of policy development and innovation, involving state governments and many non-government organisations. A significant proportion of VET is provided by companies to their employees independent of government or educational connections. Private employers spent USD 177 billion in formal training and USD 413 billion in informal training in 2013 whereas the federal job training accounts only USD 18 million.

However, the system includes substantial barriers to post-secondary attainment (Kuczera and Field, 2013[14]). First, as shown in the previous section, basic skills of US teenagers and high school graduates are relatively weak compared with many other OECD countries. Second, decentralization means that the choices faced by any individual are more difficult and more uncertain, with many routes to a target career or occupation. Third, since costs and returns are highly variable, the financial risks of investing in post-secondary education can be higher in the United States. As a result, investing in post-secondary education is often more confusing and risky than in many other OECD countries.

US workers are among the most active participants in AET but with large inequalities

In terms of further education and training, US adults, including older adults, are some of the most engaged participants among OECD countries (Figure 3.5). According to PIAAC (2012), around 62% of prime-age adults participated in some form of education or training in the last 12 months, well above the OECD average of 52% (Table 3.2). However, these averages mask significant differences in the access to AET. First, labour market status affects the probability of being engaged in AET even more than in other countries. In the United States, the majority of employees (60%) participate and even many of the unemployed (36%) are also involved in job-related training, although the gap between these two groups is quite substantial (Figure 3.4, Panel A). Moreover, as in many OECD countries, the US participation rate in job-related training for those who are not in the labour force is low (17%). There are also some differences by gender, firm size and sector which also affect the probability of receiving training (Table 3.2). Finally and above all, access of workers to continued training is closely linked to the level of initial education. Workers with only high school education or less are much less likely to have participated in job-related training than those with tertiary education (Table 3.2).

Figure 3.4. US adults participate in education and training more than most OECD countries, but large discrepancies exist by employment status

Share of job-related adult participation in education and training by employment status, 2012 or 2015[a]

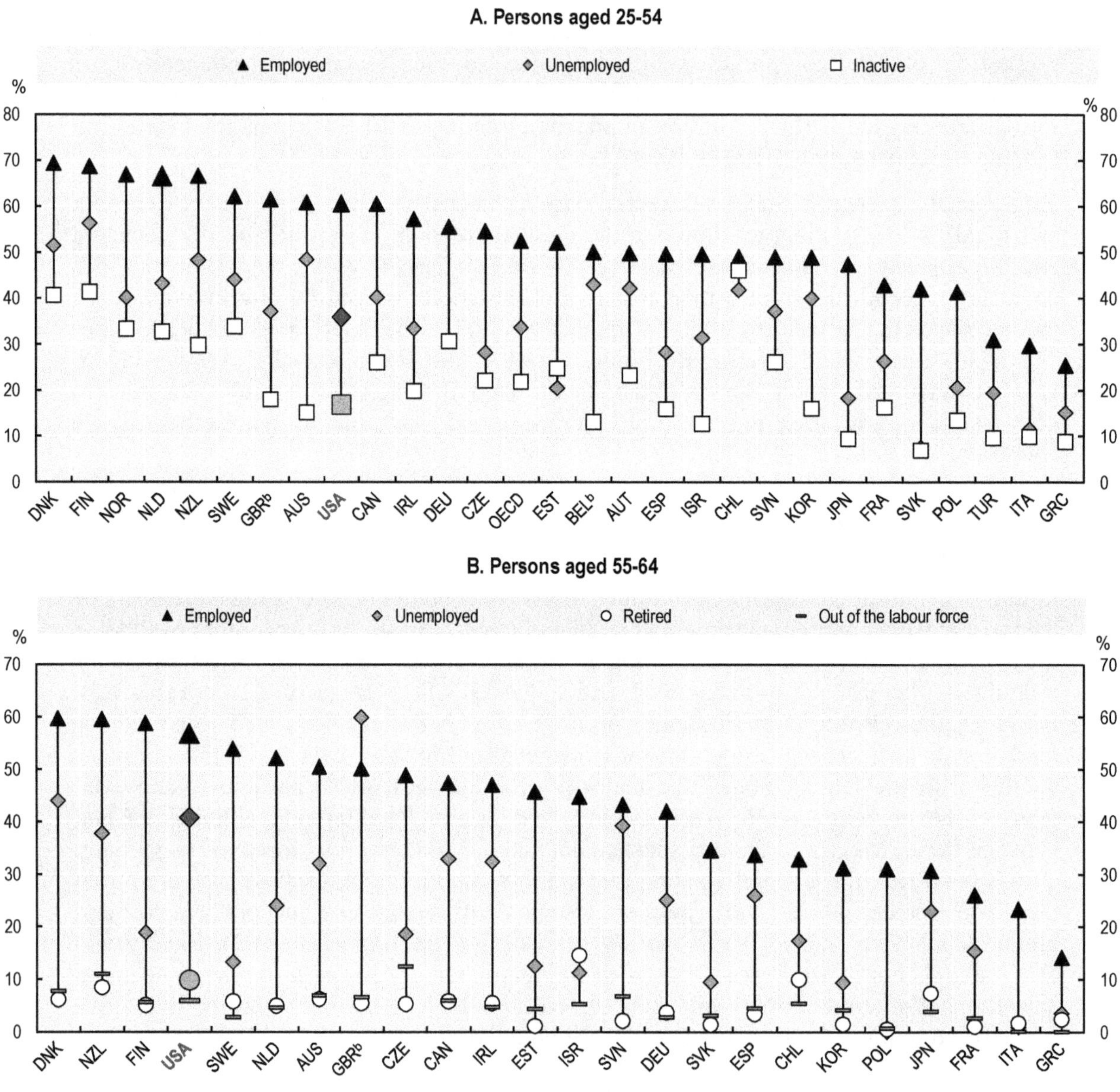

a) For Chile, Greece, Israel, New Zealand, Slovenia and Turkey the year of reference is 2015.

b) Data for Belgium refer only to Flanders and data for the United Kingdom refer to England and Northern Ireland jointly.

Source: OECD calculations based on the Survey of Adult Skills ((PIAAC) (2012, 2015), www.oecd.org/skills/piaac/.

StatLink http://dx.doi.org/10.1787/888933644395

Older workers and AET

As in other countries, older workers in the United States participate less in AET than prime-age workers, but the gap between the two age groups in the United States is smaller than in the OECD on average (Table 3.2). While 50% of older workers are engaged in some

AET, this rises to 62% for prime-age workers (in comparison, the OECD averages for the two groups are 34% and 52%, respectively). A gap in AET by age is expected, but the quality and quantity of job-related training provided by employers to older workers over the past decades might be a cause of concern: only 11% of employers' spending on formal training was devoted toward workers aged 55 or more (Carnevale, Strohl and Gulish, 2015[8]) whereas the share of employees who are older than 55 is around 23%[2]. Moreover, according to PIAAC data, in the United States employees over 55 received 81 hours per year of job-related training compared with 139 hours for employees between the ages of 25 and 34; and the gap is even larger when considering all types of training.

Table 3.2. Participation in adult education and training by age group, United States and OECD, 2012

	United States		OECD average	
	Older workers (55-65)	Prime-age workers (25-54)	Older workers (55-65)	Prime-age workers (25-54)
Gender				
Men	49.7	62.1	35.7	54.0
Women	51.4	61.7	33.1	49.8
Education				
Lower seconday or less	18.4	30.6	13.8	24.7
Upper secondary	42.4	52.7	32.0	46.9
Tertiary	71.0	80.5	60.4	71.7
Firm size				
Small	59.7	61.9	42.9	51.6
Medium	68.3	73.9	60.6	68.4
Large	85.2	84.1	72.7	78.4
Industrial sector				
Construction	43.8	60.1	34.7	49.1
Education	78.9	80.0	69.2	74.0
Mining and quarry	50.2	61.7	40.1	52.1
Public administration and defense	77.0	87.9	69.6	79.3
Total	50.6	61.9	34.3	51.9

Note: The OECD average excludes Hungary, Iceland, Latvia, Luxembourg, Mexico, Portugal and Switzerland.

Source: OECD calculations based on the Survey of Adult Skills (PIAAC) (2012, 2015), www.oecd.org/skills/piaac/.

StatLink http://dx.doi.org/10.1787/888933644490/

Among older workers there are also significant discrepancies in access to AET. In the United States, there is already a small gap in favour of older women (Table 3.2) which will likely be reinforced by the larger increase in educational attainment of women compared to men in the next decades (Figure 3.1). By firm and sector there are also significant differences, over 85% of older workers employed in large firms receive training compared with less than 60% in small firms, and, in sectors that employ more older workers, around 79% of them in the education sector received training compared with less than 50% in the construction or mining sectors. Finally, educational attainment is also the main driver of inequality in access to AET among older workers. Thus, even though a decline in participation for older workers relative to prime-age workers can be observed across all levels of education, older workers (aged 50-64) with at least some education at the college level record significantly higher rates of participation on average than prime-age workers with only high school education or less (Table 3.2).

Inequalities in access to employer-based programmes

Access to employer-based programmes as well as to post-secondary VET is increasingly difficult for a significant part of the workforce. First, the cost of post-secondary education has skyrocketed in recent years[3], while government support has eroded significantly.[4] Second, there is some evidence that over the past two decades employer-based training programmes have been on the decline (Advisers, 2016[15]). This was particularly noticeable for apprenticeships in the United States, which decreased by 40% from 2003 to 2013. However, since 2013 the trend has reversed and by the end of 2016 the number of apprentices was slightly higher than in 2003[5]. In part due to the Workforce Innovation and Opportunity Act (WIOA) that has better aligned and integrated apprenticeship programmes into the public workforce system. Further, there are very promising local programmes[6] and the current US government has announced that it will expand apprenticeship programmes[7].

Programmes designed along the lines of an apprenticeship concept – combining short classroom sessions with a firm-based approach – are more effective for older workers, as is informal, self-determined training with a clear focus on practical, relevant work issues (OECD, 2017[16]). However, apprenticeships have been traditionally focused on younger adults and only recently have countries started to promote the access of adults to apprenticeship schemes. One example is New Zealand Apprenticeships, a programme introduced in 2014 which gives all apprentices the same level of government support, regardless of age[8].

Employment programmes and older jobseekers

The Great Recession pushed many older workers in the United States into long-term unemployment, with the share of those unemployed for one year or longer reaching a historical high of 42% in 2011 amongst older adults. Although long-term unemployment among the older labour force is gradually decreasing, its incidence remained higher in 2016 than a decade ago (Table 2.A.1 in Annex 2.A). Thus, providing effective employment and training assistance is crucial to prevent vulnerable workers from becoming long-term unemployed, and ultimately, to avoid their exit from the labour force.

Public Employment Services for jobseekers in the United States

Unemployment compensation

Unemployment insurance (UI) is the major tool in the United States to provide income support to the unemployed (severance pay plays a minor role). The UI programme provides eligible unemployed individuals temporary benefits that partially replace their lost wages. The UI programme is a federal-state programme that is generally funded through taxes on employers and, in some states, employee contributions. UI benefits are generally available to eligible unemployed workers for up to 26 weeks[9], although recently many states have opted to reduce payment duration and the extent of UI eligibility. However, income support provided by UI benefits is not sufficient to prevent poverty and exclusion. Around one-quarter of all displaced workers exhaust their unemployment benefit entitlement before finding a job and they have poorer employment outcomes in the long run and face bigger income losses when they do find a new job. As a result they face a higher risk of poverty and strongly rely on means-tested social benefits for considerable periods (OECD, 2016[17]).

Active labour market policies programmes (ALMPs)

In addition to UI, there are, at the broadest level, three key sets of ALMPs in the United States to help the unemployed: employment services and job search assistance; job training programmes; and employment subsidies. Employment services and job search assistance seek to help workers find work quickly and to improve the quality of matches between workers and vacancies by helping workers with a given set of skills match to appropriate employment opportunities. Typical services include the provision of labour market information, job search workshops and labour exchange services, which collect and refer workers directly to openings. By contrast, job training programmes seek to improve individuals' labour market outcomes by helping them develop skills. Finally, employment subsidies seek to support targeted groups directly by subsidising their employment.

The US workforce system (Box 3.1) is a network of federal and state-funded employment and training programmes largely administered at the federal level by the US Departments of Labor, Education, and Health and Human Services. It provides employment and training services to jobseekers and connects employers to qualified workers through a nationwide network of over 2 400 American Job Centers (AJCs known also as One-Stop Centers) (U.S. Government Accountability Office, 2011[18]). Despite the objective of the Workforce Innovation and Opportunity Act (WIOA) that in 2015 replaced the Workforce Investment Act (WIA) of 1998 (Box 3.2) to reduce the number of programmes, the US system remains fragmented, consisting of several large programmes accessible to any American and many smaller programmes that provide services to narrow groups. Each programme includes one or a combination of the three ALMPs mentioned. The Employment Service and WIOA programmes account for about 80% of worker-assistance participants. The remaining workers receive assistance through one of nearly four dozen narrowly tailored programmes.

Box 3.1. The US federal worker-assistance system

Most Americans are eligible for employment assistance through one of two laws: the Wagner-Peyser Act of 1933 or the Workforce Innovation and Opportunity Act (WIOA) that in 2014 replaced the Workforce Investment Act (WIA) of 1998.

The Wagner-Peyser Act and WIOA form the backbone of the federal worker-assistance system. The Wagner-Peyser Act was a Great Depression era law that matched individuals seeking work with New Deal public-works programmes through a nationwide network of public employment offices known as the Employment Service. Today, the original Wagner-Peyser Employment Service still exists and provides job-search assistance and counselling for any worker seeking new employment.

WIA, which amended the Wagner-Peyser Act of 1933, was aimed at better serving the needs of employers and employment-ready individuals through local career employment and training services. When the bill passed in 1998, the economy was growing strongly and unemployment was low, around 4% of the labour force, and dropping. There were many job openings and relatively few jobseekers, so the primary focus of the One-Stop Centers was matching unemployed workers with available jobs rather than providing training or other skill development. Congress re-authorised WIA in 2003, but did not make any substantive updates until WIOA, which amended again the Wagner-Peyser Act.

Box 3.2. Highlights of the Workforce Innovation and Opportunity Act (WIOA)

WIOA, which more strongly integrates employment and training programmes and provides for more opportunities for work-based learning, represents the first major reform of federal job training programmes in nearly 20 years. WIOA is not an older worker bill, although a number of its provisions are of particular relevance to older workers and could make the Act more responsive to their needs. The goals of WIOA include improving the provision of services, especially for individuals with barriers to employment (notably, individuals over the age of 55 are among the groups singled out); streamlining services and connections between different programmes, the UI system and sector partners; and allowing for flexible transfers of funds between WIA programmes.

WIOA eliminates 15 small programmes, but preserves the existing adult, displaced worker and youth programme models, as well as the Employment Service. It also eliminates the core and intensive service sequence, which it combines into a single career services category, and allows workers to bypass these services and enrol directly in training. WIOA will be more oriented toward economic regions within states and local areas have flexibility to serve jobseekers with the greatest need by transferring up to 100% of funds between Adult and Dislocated Worker programmes. Additionally, WIOA puts an increased emphasis on partnerships with business and on-the-job training, reimbursing eligible employers for up to 75% of the costs to train workers.

WIOA also strengthens evaluation and data reporting requirements by standardising them across programmes. For example, job training programmes will be evaluated by independent third parties at least every four years, with a minimum of one multistate random control trial study to be conducted by September 2019. It also requires that the data published in state and local performance reports of core employment and training services be open to the public and disaggregated by subgroups, including age, sex and ethnicity. An impediment to serving older workers in the past was the lack of data on just how they fared compared to other groups: the new requirements should be an improvement.

According to the Council on Foreign Relations (2016[19]) WIOA has been a positive development, but it largely leaves the existing system intact. WIOA did not address several major issues with the US worker assistance system, such as eliminating the inequities between the Trade Adjustment Assistance programme launched in 1962 to link job loss to trade and other programmes, providing enough funding to guarantee adequate assistance for every worker, or insulating financing from the politics of the congressional appropriations process. Nevertheless, the extent to which outcomes for older jobseekers will improve under WIOA is likely to depend as much on federal regulations, state and local implementation, economic conditions, funding levels and other policy considerations as the specific reforms embodied in the law.

Source: WIOA (2014), HR 803, www.congress.gov; Council on Foreign Relations (2016), *No Helping Hand: Federal Worker-Retraining Policy*; and Wandner, S., D. Balducchi and C. O 'leary (2014), *Selected Public Workforce Development Programs in the United States: Lessons Learned for Older Workers*, AARP, Washington, DC.

ALMPs effectiveness and evaluation

In general

There is evidence that ALMPs can help funnel workers into jobs, which reduces unemployment even during downturns. A recent meta-analysis of impact estimates from over 200 recent econometric evaluations of ALMPs from around the world from Card et al. (2015[20]) shows that on average, ALMPs show positive impacts in the medium and long term and that training programmes are overall effective in helping the unemployed find employment. Lechner et al. (2013[21]) confirm that training measures tend to have a positive impact on employment outcomes in the medium and long term, especially if training leads to the acquisition of formal vocational qualifications and if it is workplace-based.

However, ALMPs are more effective for some groups and in some contexts than others but as Immervoll and Scarpetta (2012[22]) stress, there is very limited information on the distributional effects of different policies, and even less systematic evaluation of possible equity-efficiency trade-offs. This makes it difficult to draw general lessons of what works for whom. On average, ALMPs have larger effects for females and long-term unemployed and smaller effects for older workers, and programmes have larger impacts in periods of slow growth and higher unemployment (Card, Kluve and Weber, 2015[20]). In addition, certain types of programmes work better for specific subgroups of participants. Young people entering the labour force for the first time can benefit from programmes that combine classroom and vocational instruction, as well as programmes that offer on-the-job training. However, youth training programmes in the United States vary in design, which leads to discrepancies in their effectiveness.

For older jobseekers

US unemployed older adults are more likely to stop searching for a job if they are: in fair or poor health or if they have a work-limiting health condition; female; or married with a non-working spouse. They are also more likely to stop searching if they are wealthy or covered by a pension system. Instead, the local unemployment rate seemed to have a surprisingly small effect (Rutledge, 2014[23]). Besides, opportunities to change occupation decline for workers changing jobs after age 50 (Rutledge, Sass and Ramos-Mercado, 2016[24]).

Merkurieva (2016[25]) shows that involuntary job loss results in an average worker retiring 15 months earlier. Using data of the Health and Retirement Study, a nationally representative panel of individuals over age 50 in the United States, she finds that one quarter of older laid-off workers retire after displacement. About 80% of these layoff-induced retirements happen right after displacement while the other 20% stay and keep searching for a new job, eventually retiring after an average unemployment spell of 27 months. The share of immediate retirements rises rapidly with age at job loss, from only 3% at age 50 to more than 50% by age 70.

Re-employment rates are lower for older displaced workers aged 55 and over, those with long job tenure and those with low levels of education. Many of these workers actually withdraw from the labour market altogether. But the picture is not necessarily rosy either for all those who find a new job, as many of them face considerable and often persistent wage losses, especially older workers (OECD, 2016[17]). According to the 2008 Panel of the Survey of Income and Program Participation (SIPP), average hourly wages for re-employed displaced workers aged 55 years and over are as much as 40% lower on the new job, compared with the old job.

Employment measures may help older displaced workers who have the most difficulty finding work again (OECD, 2016[17]). These workers have often spent their entire careers developing skills for one type of job; if that job is permanently lost to international competition or new technologies, then they need to develop new skills or face a significant loss of income.

The evidence is mixed however on whether programmes targeted at older workers can help them find employment or secure higher wages. For instance, although the evidence on the effectiveness of age-targeted wage subsidies to increase the employment of older workers is scarce, it shows, at best, limited overall effectiveness. In general, subsidised work appears simply to displace unsubsidised work, with little net gain in employment of older workers. A closer look shows differences in effectiveness by gender, with some net gains for women and only in some regions. Albanese and Cokx (2015[26]), for example, find in Belgium small positive short-run impacts on reduced working time and larger ones on the employment rate, but only for employees at high risk of leaving to early retirement with no effect on wages. Bookman et al. (2012[27]) using a natural experiment in Germany only found employment effects for women in East Germany.

Similarly, impact assessments do not show significant increases in income for these workers after completing retraining programmes. This is because many of these workers were at the height of their experience and lifetime earnings before losing their jobs and are unlikely to see higher wages in any new career. Nonetheless, ALMPs can help these workers identify new positions and prevent further wage erosion (Council on Foreign Relations, 2016[19]). For instance, in a recent study, Dauth and Toomet (2016[28]) find that subsidised training programmes in Germany improved the probability to remain in paid employment, particularly for workers over 55. The results suggest that the main driver of these outcomes is postponed retirement, potentially because of improved job satisfaction. Although as a study of U.S. trade adjustment assistance programmes suggests, dislocated worker fare the best when they find employment in their training field and when they receive a degree or certificate through training, particularly women who receive training in health care professional fields (Heinrich, 2013[29]).

Employment and training programmes for older jobseekers in the United States

In the United States there are three main federal employment and training programmes that are potentially available to older workers, as well as two small programmes specifically targeted to them (Box 3.3). As outlined above, older workers also benefit from UI and have access to general public employment services that provide basic job search assistance.

Box 3.3. Key employment and training programmes for older workers in the United States

There are three main federal employment and training programmes that older workers have access to:

1. **The Employment Service (ES)** is part of the One-Stop delivery system and provides public employment services, including registering and matching vacancies with jobseekers, employability assessment, re-employment services and job search workshops.

2. **Adult and Dislocated Worker programmes.** Under WIA, there were three tiers of services that were provided: core, intensive and training. Core services included basic job search and placement activities and were available to the general public without any eligibility requirements. Intensive assistance was available to customers who face employment barriers and they may subsequently receive more intensive job search assistance. Finally, training services were available to enable workers to retain new positions or become qualified for higher-skill, better-paid positions. WIOA eliminates the core and intensive service sequence enabling workers to bypass these services and enrol directly in training (see Box 3.2). The Adult programme provides employment and training services for adults aged 18 or older. The Dislocated Workers programme targets laid-off workers and displaced "homemakers" aged 18 and over.

3. **Trade Adjustment Assistance (TAA) for Workers programme**. The TAA Program's mission is to transition workers who have lost or may lose their jobs as a result of foreign trade, to in-demand careers. The TAA Program's benefits and services include: up to two years paid training, employment and case management services, job search allowances, relocation allowances, wage supplements for reemployed workers age 50 and older, and a health coverage tax credit.

There are also two small programmes specifically targeted to older workers

4. **The Senior Community Service Employment Programme (SCSEP)** is funded and operates under the Older American Act (OAA) but is run by the US Department of Labor (DOL). OAA in 2016 re-authorised among other programmes the SCSEP for three years (FYs 2017-2019). It offers part-time community service employment opportunities for low-income unemployed individuals aged 55 or over at non-profits or government agencies, with a view to prepare them to enter or re-enter the workforce. SCSEP uses a combination of measures to track performance outcomes, the most critical of which include: Six Months' Average Earnings, Entered Employment rates, and Employment Retention rates. Under SCSEP reauthorisation, these performance outcome measures will be changed to align with WIOA relevant performance indicators: Employment Rate (2nd Quarter and 4th Quarter after exit) and Median Earnings (2nd Quarter after exit).

Box 3.3. Key employment and training programmes for older workers in the United States *(Cont.)*

5. **The Reemployment Trade Adjustment Assistance (RTAA) programme.** The RTAA programme is a benefit available to workers who lost their jobs as a result of international trade, aimed at workers over the age of 50. The benefit provides a wage supplement to older workers once eligible participants accept new employment at a lower wage. RTAA participants are also entitled to receive employment and case management services and are eligible to apply for the Health Coverage Tax Credit and TAA-approved training.

ES and the WIOA Dislocated Worker programmes are the public workforce programmes that serve the greatest number of older workers.

Source: Wandner, S., D. Balducchi and C. O 'leary (2014), *Selected Public Workforce Development Programs in the United States: Lessons Learned for Older Workers*, AARP, Washington, DC.

Compared with other OECD countries, very little is spent in the United States on ALMPs

Despite the large potential of ALMPs to help US workers, the current level of public investment of the United States is low by both international and historical standards (Figure 3.5, Panel A). The United States spent just 0.1% of GDP on ALMPs in 2015 compared to 0.5% spent on average by OECD countries.[10] The breakdown by age is not available.

In fact, the United States spent in the 2010s less than half of what it did on such employment programmes 30 years ago (Dunn, 2013[30]). Besides, the total number of participants of all ages in employment programmes is relatively small in relation to the total number of jobseekers (Table 3.3). However, the small percentage of eligible older workers served under WIOA is particularly noticeable; funds are not sufficient to serve all who are potentially eligible and very few – far fewer than in younger age groups – receive training under WIOA (Table 3.4)

Figure 3.5. Compared with other OECD countries, very little is spent on active labour market programmes and training

Expenditure on ALMPs by main category, selected OECD countries, 2015 or latest year available, percentage of GDP

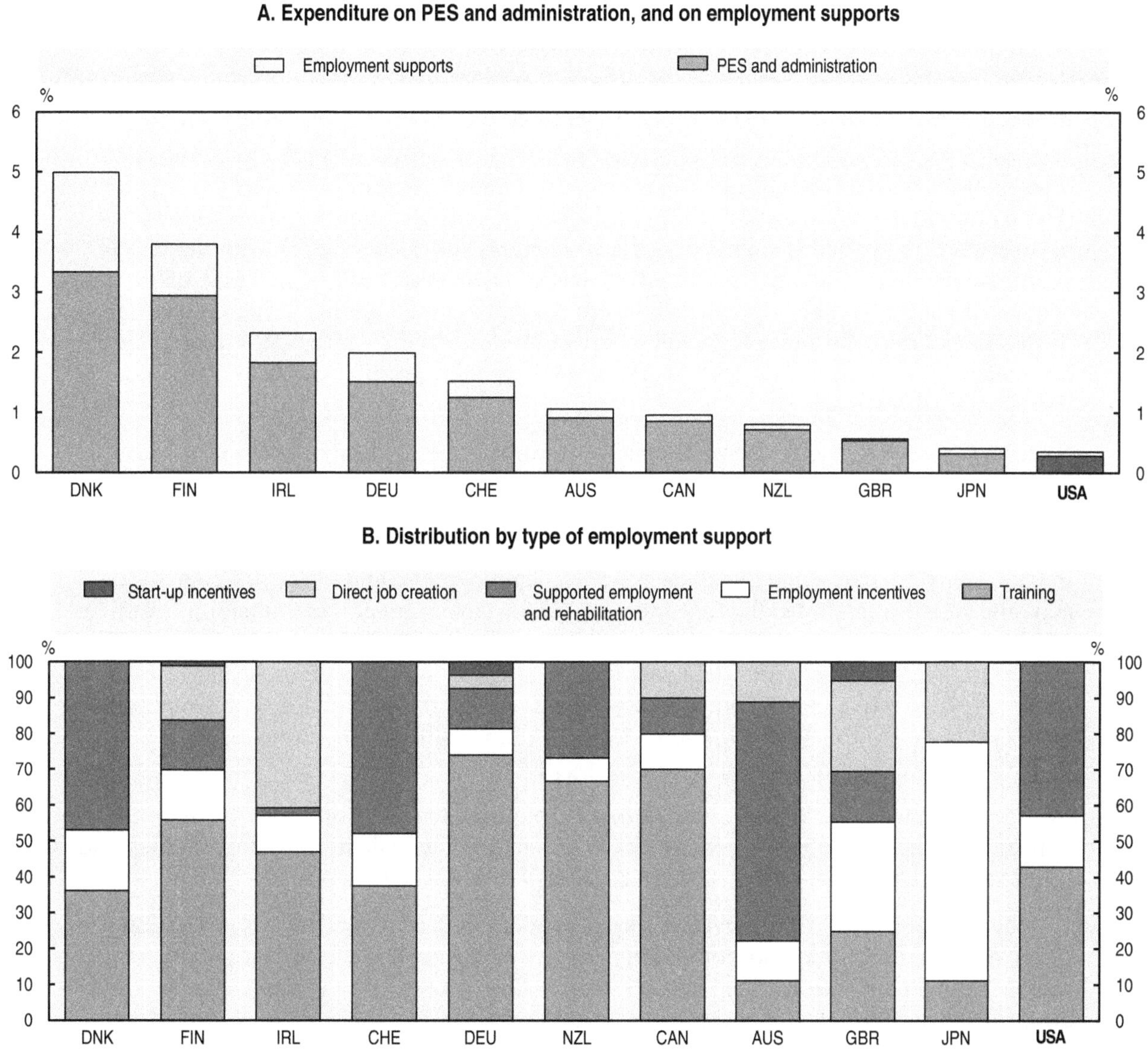

GDP: Gross domestic product.

Note: Countries are ranked in decreasing order of expenditure in each respective panel. Data refer to 2014 for New Zealand and to 2010 for the United Kingdom.

Source: OECD calculations based on *OECD/Eurostat Labour Market Programme Database*, http://dx.doi.org/10.1787/data-00312-en.

StatLink http://dx.doi.org/10.1787/888933644414

Towards better employment policies to assist older jobseekers

Improving the evaluation and effectiveness of employment programmes in the United States

The performance evaluation system under WIA served as a disincentive for staff to offer programmes to older workers. One-Stop Centers serving jobseekers were evaluated on the basis of placements and post-programme earnings compared to previous earnings. Because older re-employed workers' earnings often fell short of their former earnings and because many older workers could only find part-time work, post-WIA earnings were often lower, thus adversely affecting the performance measures of service providers (Heidkamp, Mabe and Degraaf, 2012[31]). However, introduction of a more sophisticated performance evaluation system has not lead to improved outcomes. During the last few years, states have evaluated programmes based on a statistical model that takes into account participants' age. Nonetheless, there has not been a significant increase either in the number or in the percentage of older workers served (Table 3.3). Other possible disincentives to cater for older workers include the priority to serve low-income individuals and veterans.

Nevertheless, performance measurement is scarce among all programmes in the United States. Most programmes track outcome measures such as the number of participants who found jobs after some months, retained employment, or saw a wage gain. However, only five of the 47 US programmes between 2004 and 2011 had undergone a comprehensive impact study to determine whether workers' employment and wage outcomes could actually be attributed to the programme (U.S. Government Accountability Office, 2011[18]). Furthermore, the U.S. Government Accountability Office reported that half of the programmes had not received a performance review in the previous seven years. The absence of effective programme measurement limits the ability of policymakers to compare programmes and determine which ones are worthwhile investments.

Fortunately, this seems to be changing; in 2012 DOL conducted a process evaluation of SCSEP (Kogan et al., 2012[32]) and the new requirements of information imposed by WIOA (Box 3.2) could prove very useful in improving the evaluation of programmes that provide employment services to older jobseekers in the United States.

The evaluation of SCSEP provided recommendations that included: (1) arranging for skills training in addition to community service assignments; (2) providing direct job search training and assistance; and (3) increasing access to AJC services by either co-locating staff members at AJCs or specifically arranging for participants to use core services. Since the evaluation, DOL has offered technical assistance to grantees to address these recommendations and also held a competition among some SCSEP grantees for grants to expand training options for participants. A continuation of these efforts is to be encouraged.

Table 3.3. Few older workers served by WIA services

Number and percentage of individuals exiting WIA services, 2006-15

Year	18-54	55+	Participants 55+	Labour force 18-54	Labour force 55+	Unemployed 18-54	Unemployed 55+
	Number		Percentage				
2006	720 923	81 829	10.2	..	0.3	..	10.6
2007	934 778	121 419	11.5	..	0.4	..	14.6
2008	1 033 265	138 536	11.8	0.83	0.5	12.5	10.2
2009	1 399 200	201 406	12.6	1.15	0.7	11.7	9.7
2010	1 514 128	219 448	12.7	1.25	0.7	13.3	10.3
2011	1 490 458	228 026	13.3	1.24	0.7	14.4	11.2
2012	1 319 601	229 931	14.8	1.10	0.7	14.2	11.9
2013	1 272 209	239 771	15.9	1.06	0.7	15.5	13.9
2014	1 107 505	202 691	15.5	0.92	0.6	16.4	14.2
2015	996 179	192 648	16.2	0.83	0.5	16.4	15.8

Note: Numbers for each year are from April that year to March next year.
Source: OECD calculations based on WIASRD Data Books (www.doleta.gov/performance/results/) and Bureau of Labor Statistics (BLS) Current Population Survey (CPS).

StatLink http://dx.doi.org/10.1787/888933644509

Table 3.4. Far fewer older workers than in younger age groups receive training provided by WIA programmes

Percentage of jobseekers who received training, by age

	18 to 21	22 to 29	30 to 44	45 to 54	55 and over
2006	25.6	25.6	22.2	17.1	11.2
2007	18.7	18.0	14.9	10.8	7.0
2008	13.6	14.1	12.1	9.3	6.3
2009	11.8	13.1	12.0	9.7	6.5
2010	13.4	14.6	13.6	11.5	7.6
2011	11.0	12.1	11.7	9.9	6.3
2012	12.3	12.5	11.3	8.9	5.5
2013	12.2	11.6	10.1	8.0	4.9
2014	15.7	13.7	11.6	8.7	5.2
2015	16.3	14.9	12.0	8.8	5.2

Note: Numbers for each year are from April that year to March next year.
Source: OECD calculations based on WIA State Annual Reports and Summaries (WIASRD) Data Books (www.doleta.gov/performance/results/) and Bureau of Labor Statistics (BLS) Current Population Survey (CPS).

StatLink http://dx.doi.org/10.1787/888933644528

Good practices in OECD countries

Personalised action plans together with targeted group activities are recommended as the best means of getting the older unemployed back to work (PES-to-PES, 2012[33]).

- The older unemployed is far from constituting a homogeneous group, and personalised action plans, if they are to be effective, must be based on individual profiling. As an example, a greater emphasis has been placed on intensive counselling for the older unemployed under the German *Perspektive 50plus*, Employment Pacts for older workers in the regions running from 2005-15, although it was primarily the younger seniors who benefit from such programmes (see Box 3.4).
- Identifying problems and making arrangements for marketing the skills of older workers is important. This sometimes requires not only offering job counsellors further training, but also raising awareness among staff of job centres about this objective. Moreover, the creation of specific teams with lower counsellor-to-client ratios can help to tackle some of the additional challenges facing many older workers. In addition, counsellors should be better equipped to address the real problems encountered by older jobseekers and to establish, early on, a solid profiling of their chances of finding a job quickly. The UK Government introduced Older Claimant Champions in all Jobcentre Plus regions, to increase awareness of the barriers faced by older claimants and how to address them (DWP, 2017[34]).
- A number of ALMPs have achieved good outcomes using group activities targeted at the older unemployed. For example, in the Netherlands, organising counselling sessions in self-help groups has been found useful in tackling social isolation and the lack of networking opportunities while enhancing job search skills (OECD, 2014[35]). Job clubs, whether they are age-centered or not, can also help to identify "hidden" vacancies. Because of the stereotypes that employers tend to entertain regarding older workers, it may also be more important for this target group to benefit from measures that bring jobseekers directly into contact with employers, such as job fairs, speed dating and work trials.

Furthermore, the potential for empowering the resources that people have should not be underestimated. The Senior Network in Denmark (Box 3.5) is an example of an innovative practice that engages the older unemployed themselves in job search: unemployed older workers are reaching out to employers directly through participation in teams to find jobs for themselves or to promote other older workers as a resource. Participating in local independent networks receives financing from the public budget; in relying on the efforts of members, they ensure a dynamic and enthusiastic approach to job search.

Box 3.4. Germany's *Perspektive 50 Plus* programme (2005-15)

In 2005, the Federal Ministry of Labour and Social Affairs launched and financed the *Perspektive 50 Plus* - Employment Pacts for Older Workers in the Regions. All former programmes and centralised measures were financed by the Federal Employment Agency. This programme ran from 2005 to 2015. It aimed to re-activate and integrate older workers (50+), predominantly those who are low- or semi-skilled and long-term unemployed, into employment. Furthermore, the programme worked to change the attitudes of employers as well as to identify and share best practices and innovative tools.

Local impact. About 77 regional employment pacts were set up with nearly all Jobcentres as partners as well as with a wide range of local stakeholders such as companies, chambers and various associations, trade-unions, municipalities, training institutions, churches, and social service providers (Duell and Vogler-Ludwig, 2012[36]). Regional partners were able to adapt the programme to fit their regional and local needs, which is made possible through the rigorous simplification of administrative rules. The budget was free-to-use and Jobcentre counsellors had a great deal of discretion.

Services provided. Coaching, profiling, training in communication skills and job application training, job training, internships, and wage subsidies.

Evaluation. Evaluation of the first phase conducted in 2007 showed that the success of the programme rested on the combination of individualised counselling and coaching as well as on proactive outreach towards employers. The most recent evaluation showed that placement results were better than in the case of more traditional approaches (Knuth, Stegmann and Zink, 2014[37]).

Limitations. i) The average age of the effectively activated and placed unemployed is relatively young (about 54 years with a peak at 51 years) and the share of people aged 60 and more represented only 3% of all participants placed in the regular labour market; and ii) The programme does not sufficiently raise awareness about more effectively coping with ageing (Büttner et al., 2008[38]).

The new programmes launched in 2016 were targeted towards the (very) long-term unemployed, among whom many are older workers.

Source: Duell, N. and K. Vogler-Ludwig (2012), *European Employment Observatory EEO Review: Employment policies to promote active ageing. Germany*, European Employment Observatory, Brussels; Knuth, M., T. Stegmann and L. Zink (2014), "Die Wirkungen des Bundesprogramms Perspektive 50plus;. Chancen für ältere Langzeitarbeitslose, (Impact of the Federal Programme 50+. Results for the older long-term unemployed)", *IAQ-Report*, No. 2014-01, Universität Duisburg-Essen, http://www.iaq.uni-due.de/iaq-report/2014/report2014-01.pdf; and Büttner, R. et al. (2008), "Perspektiven auf dem Arbeitsmarkt auch mit 50plus. Ausgewählte Ergebnisse aus der Evaluation des Bundesprogramms Perspektive 50plus für ältere Langzeitarbeitslose, (Perspectives in the labour market also for people aged 50+. Selected results of the evaluation of the Federal Programme 50+)", *IAQ-Report*, No. 2008-3, http://www.iaq.uni-due.de/iaq-report/2008/report2008-03.pdf.

Box 3.5. Senior networks in Denmark

The "senior networks" consist of local, independent networks for seniors who are looking for jobs and other activities (OECD, 2015[39]). The local networks are based on voluntary and active contributions from their members, and receive public financing. The Danish Government has allocated DKK 6.3 million per year for the period 2014-17. To be eligible for public support, the local network must have a co-operation agreement with at least one jobcentre, and at least 25 unemployed members over the age of 50. In some of the local networks a small fee is paid by the members to cover local social activities.

The primary aim is to find jobs for seniors. Members are unemployed, above the age of 50, and are searching for jobs. Early retired persons and pensioners are also included. "Help to self-help" is the basic concept of the network. Outreach activities to promote older workers are also among the priorities.

Source: OECD (2015), *Ageing and Employment Policies: Denmark 2015: Working Better with Age*, OECD Publishing, Paris.

Finally, going local might help to boost opportunities for vulnerable groups among older people. As the examples in Denmark (Box 3.5), Germany (Box 3.4) and Canada (Box 3.6) show, the employment chances of older persons can be improved by involving all local actors: industry, trade unions, joint agencies and local authority agencies. What makes these programmes particularly successful are:

- *Flexibility*: Local authorities have the flexibility to customise and tailor projects according to their local labour market situations and client needs.
- Projects include a *mix of services and activities*: Group-based employment assistance services and job search assistance and employability improvement activities.
- *Engagement of local employers*: Establish and maintain links with local employers in a variety of ways to motivate and encourage employers to hire older workers. Improving awareness among local employers of the valuable role older workers can play in helping them to address their challenges in recruitment and retention.

Box 3.6. The Targeted Initiative for Older Workers (TIOW) programme in Canada

TIOW was launched in 2007 as a temporary, two-year pilot initiative to support unemployed older workers (typically between the ages of 55-64) living in small, vulnerable communities of 250 000 or less to re-integrate into the labour market and to improve their employability (Hicks, 2015[40]). Unemployed older workers between the ages of 50-54 and over the age of 64 may also be eligible for TIOW provided that their participation is not at the exclusion of those in the core age group. TIOW is an initiative between the Government of Canada and each participating province and territory and normally implemented via community-based organisations. TIOW projects include a mix of group-based employment assistance services such as résumé writing, counselling, interview techniques, and job search assistance and employability improvement activities such as skills upgrading and training, work placements, and self-employment assistance.

TIOW's group-based project model places significant emphasis on peer mentoring and support. Project participants are encouraged to learn from and support one another during the training. The initiative has been very successful and has been renewed three times to-date in Budgets 2008, 2011, and 2014 (until 2017) respectively. Initially limited to vulnerable communities experiencing high unemployment or significant downsizing, Budget 2014 broadened TIOW eligibility criteria so that communities experiencing skills mismatch or unfulfilled employer demand can now participate. As of March 2015, more than 35 280 unemployed older workers have been targeted by provinces and territories for TIOW participation in small, vulnerable communities across the country.

Evidence shows that the programme supports local community adjustment, and most employers indicate that they would participate in TIOW again. The evaluation report (2014[41]) shows that 30% of TIOW participants did not have high school diplomas; half were unemployed for more than 12 months prior to participation, and more than half lived in communities with unemployment rates of 10% or more. Findings from various phases of programme evaluations indicate consistently positive results.

Given that provinces and territories have the flexibility to customise and tailor TIOW projects according to their local labour market situations and client needs, there have been numerous examples of innovative and successful practices across Canada. The Government of Canada, in collaboration with provinces and territories, produced in 2014 a "Best Practices Compendium" with a compilation of best practices that can be shared widely so that the model can be replicated within other jurisdictions.

All in all, TIOW is an innovative project presented as a good practice in local employment and skills strategies in G20 countries. TIOW has much to contribute to the design and management of active labour market policies and programmes in Canada and internationally for years to come.

Source: Hicks, P. (2015), "Local economic strategies for ageing labour markets: The Canadian Targeted Initiative for Older Workers in Fort St. James, British Columbia", *OECD Local Economic and Employment Development (LEED) Working Papers*, No. 2015/3, OECD Publishing, Paris, http://dx.doi.org/10.1787/5jrnwqk5d4f7-en; and Employment and Social Development Canada (2014), *Summative Evaluation of the Targeted Initiative for Older Workers*, Ottawa, http://www.esdc.gc.ca/eng/publications/evaluations/skills_and_employment/2014/tiow.shtml.

Working conditions

Improving the employability of older adults via better education and skills and an effective employment support system for jobseekers is important to enable older adults remain in the labour force at later ages. However, that is not enough; there is one underlying requirement to effectively reach that goal: older adults should be willing and able to work; and working conditions are one of the decisive factors affecting both.

Towards better job quality throughout worker's career

There is evidence that working conditions can have a profound impact on workers' physical and mental health (OECD, 2015[42]) and recent studies (Böckerman and Ilmakunnas, 2017[43]) and surveys indicate that for many people, working conditions are one of the decisive factors in the choice between work and retirement. In the United States, Angrisani et al. (2013[44]) find that job quality indicators are strongly predictive of labour force transitions. Their analysis shows that a higher wage is associated with a higher probability of remaining in full-time employment and a lower probability of moving to part-time or out of the labour force. Interestingly, individuals with higher wages are also more likely to retire. Physical effort, age discrimination and stress are all non-monetary factors that decrease the chances of remaining in full-time employment while increasing the chances of retiring early. Thus, to ensure that workers are willing and able to continue working for longer, policies and institutions should provide employers with incentives and tools to improve working conditions in their companies.

Improving working conditions not only benefits workers by providing them better, healthier and longer working lives, but also benefits employers, since job satisfaction and productivity at the firm level are also positively related (Böckerman and Ilmakunnas, 2017[43]; Arends, Prinz and Abma, 2017[45]). Thus, in a context of rapidly ageing population, not only governments, but also employers, trade-unions and civil societies, should not miss this opportunity. In addition, in this context, work organisations should also make the most of a diverse workforce. Therefore, complementarities between generations of workers should adequately be reflected in an age-friendly work organisation and good working conditions at all ages. A broad-based strategy to enhance job quality should be implemented not only by strong and effective actions by governments but also by employers, trade unions and non-governmental organisations.

Even if younger workers may be considered as more able to carry out physically and mentally demanding work than older workers, enhancing job quality is crucial to reduce their exposure to strenuous work. Working conditions should be adapted and modified to facilitate career mobility so that people can move out of arduous occupations. In particular, assistance such as retraining and offers of alternative job opportunities would need to be provided throughout the career to ensure that workers do not get sick and disabled on the job. Currently, too many policies relating to strenuous work are still confined to making provision for early retirement or disability benefits.

Working conditions and job quality in the United States

A recent study (Maestas et al., 2017[46]) provides some insights on working conditions in the United States. According to the study, the US workplace overall is "very physically and emotionally taxing". However, the analysis found that for workers over 50, conditions improve: Older workers report having more flexible work schedules, more predictable hours, fewer scheduling changes, less stress, and greater ease in arranging time off to take care of personal matters. Besides, the vast majority of workers aged 50-59 predict they will have the physical and mental ability to continue in their jobs for another ten years. Nevertheless, larger shares of older workers than younger workers feel under-employed or have unsupportive bosses and there are large discrepancies by level of education.

To measure and assess the quality of jobs in an international perspective, the OECD has developed a framework with three objective and measurable dimensions that can be observed for all OECD countries (OECD, 2014).[11]

- A first dimension, the quality of the working environment, captures non-economic aspects of jobs including the nature and content of the work performed, working-time arrangements and workplace relationships. These are measured as the incidence of job strain characterised as high job demands with low job resources.
- The second dimension, labour market security, captures those aspects of economic security related to the risks of job loss and its economic cost for workers, and is defined by the unemployment risks and benefits received in case of unemployment.
- The third dimension, earnings quality, captures the extent to which earnings contribute to workers' well-being in terms of average earnings and their distribution across the workforce.

The United States performs better than the OECD average in the three indicators of job quality for older workers. However, in the earnings quality indicator, the average earnings mask a combination of a more unequal distribution and higher average earnings across the workforce than the OECD average (Figure 3.6, Panel A). Besides, the United States is far from reaching job quality levels reached by top OECD performers in all three indicators.

When comparing the job quality in the United States by age group (Figure 3.6, Panel B), the situation is somewhat better for US older workers as compared with their younger counterparts in all three indicators, thanks to a lower unemployment risk and a better coverage in terms of benefits (labour market insecurity indicator) and also older workers are less likely to be confronted with high job demands and low job resources (job strain indicator).

Finally, there are also large inequalities in job quality among American workers (Figure 3.6, Panel C). Not only there are large differences in working conditions by level of education, but these differences are larger than in the OECD on average. One of the major reasons to encourage people to remain in the labour force at later ages is the idea that working longer might provide much-needed income to older workers who could not otherwise afford to retire. However, to the extent that inequalities in health and wealth go hand-in-hand (McNamara and Williamson, 2013[47]), those most in need of additional income are in higher risk of not being able to work. Thus, certain sectors and industries with high outflows to disability pension and early retirement should be a special focus of attention to enhance access to job quality.

Figure 3.6. Above-average working conditions among older workers in the United States but far from reaching job quality levels in top OECD countries

Job quality indicators of older workers, of different age groups and education levels, United States and OECD

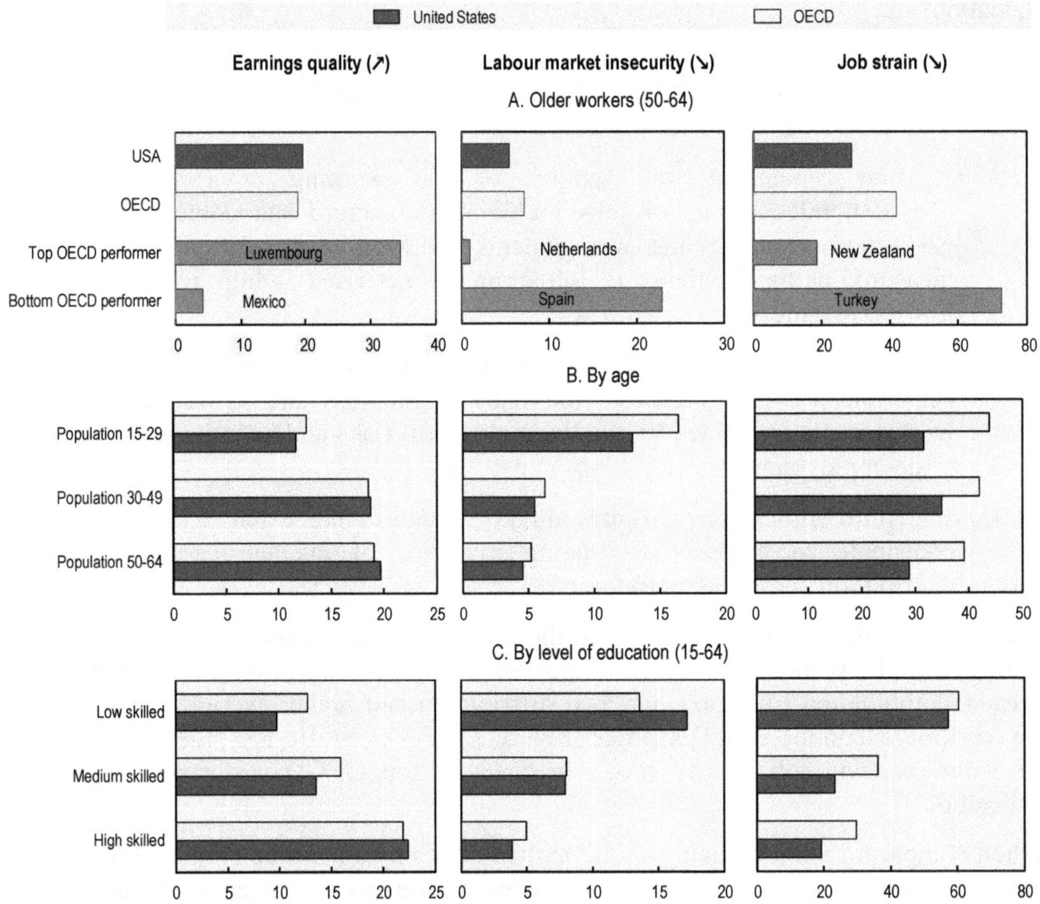

Note: An upward ↗ (downward ↘) pointing arrow for an indicator means that higher (lower) values reflect better performance. *Earnings quality*: Gross hourly earnings in USD adjusted for inequality. *Labour market insecurity*: Expected monetary loss associated with becoming unemployed as a share of previous earnings. *Job strain*: Percentage of workers in jobs characterised by a combination of high job demands and few job resources to meet those demands. Data on earnings quality and labour market security refer to 2013 or latest available. Data for job strain refer to 2015 or latest available.

Source: OECD calculations based on *OECD Job Quality database* (https://stats.oecd.org/Index.aspx?DataSetCode=JOBQ).

StatLink http://dx.doi.org/10.1787/888933644433

Actions to address the safety and health of older workers in the workplace

Studies have so far found that occupational safety regulations have had only a minimal effect on workplace safety performance. One of the main alternative measures discussed in the literature is the use of experience-rated workers compensation premiums. The premise of experience rating is that employers who maintain safer workplaces are rewarded with lower premiums, while those with more workplace accidents face higher premiums. This approach is used in Australia, Canada and New Zealand. In the United States it has been widely adopted as well, although small firms are usually excluded from its mandatory application. However, the use of experience rating in workers' compensation is controversial and the evidence from the literature is mixed (Liz et al., 2012[48]). Insurers may pay little attention to the safety justification of experience rating and rely on it almost exclusively as an underwriting tool. Thus, it is paramount that policymakers design and implement experience rating in such a way that can be used as an effective tool for improving safety. Although more research is needed (Liz et al., 2012[48]), recent studies show positive results (Tompa, Cullen and McLeod, 2012[49]). Moreover, Neuhauser, Seabury and Mendeloff (2013[50]) find that lowering the threshold to subject more employers (mostly small firms) to experience rating would improve safety of workers at these smaller firms.

The US Occupational Safety and Health Administration (OSHA) has taken a number of actions since 2005 that address the safety and health of workers in the workplace. For instance, the 2011 campaign was conducted to prevent heat illness in outdoor workers and the distracted driving campaign. OSHA continues to seek and study feedback on this issue. For example, OSHA's Office of Small Business Assistance hosted a Small Business Forum in 2009 on "Safety and Health Issues in an Aging Workforce". The broader European healthy workplaces campaigns (Box 3.7) and some initiatives like the Initiative New Quality of Work (INQA) in Germany (Box 3.8) could provide useful information to US stakeholders to implement innovative campaigns and initiatives to improve competiveness, health and working conditions.

As it has been mentioned, workers with low socio-economic backgrounds have a higher chance of being in bad health, one common reason among older workers for permanent withdrawing from the labour market and definitive loss of human capital for society. Yet a considerable proportion of them would like to return to work. Occupational Safety and Health (OSH) services and disability policies have a crucial role to play in this respect. Early intervention is often the best way of preventing long-term dependence on benefits, particularly among older workers. In the first place, it is important to mitigate the effects of bad working conditions in a preventative way through toolkits and guidance material for companies with a focus on older workers. The European Agency for Safety and Health at Work (EU-OSHA) E-guide "Health and safety at work is everybody's business" prepared by EU-OSHA Europe is a practical tool to help employers and workers manage OSH in the context of an ageing workforce.[12] The E-guide offers simple explanations of the issues, along with practical examples of how to deal with risks relating to ageing and how to make sure that all workers stay safe and healthy in the long term, as well as links to further resources.

Box 3.7. The European Healthy Workplaces campaigns

The European Agency for Safety and Health at Work (EU-OSHA) runs since 2000 Healthy Workplaces Campaigns, backed by the EU institutions and the European social partners, and co-ordinated at the national level by the Agency's network of focal points. In 2007, the duration of each campaign increased from one year to two years, responding to the increasing need to raise awareness of safety and health issues at different levels by providing accessible data, information and tools over a more sustained period of time.

The key objectives are:

- Promote sustainable work and healthy ageing from the beginning of working life
- Highlight the importance of prevention throughout working life
- Assist employers and workers (including in small companies) by providing information and tools for managing OSH in the context of an ageing workforce
- Facilitate information exchange and good practice

The campaigns have grown from strength to strength, in particular with a wider network of stakeholders and media partners committed to the campaign, and more campaign materials being produced and distributed or accessed online.

The success of the Healthy Workplaces campaigns, their capacity to permeate organisations at different levels and the positive cascade effect from policy-makers to shop floors are largely due to the commitment and effort of the broad range of network of partners, which encompasses all professional profiles in different sectors across Europe.

The central issue varied in each campaign, the present 2016-2017 Healthy Workplaces for All Ages campaign, for instance, promotes sustainable work and healthy ageing. The campaign promotes the importance of risk prevention through the whole working life, and raises awareness of tailoring work to individual abilities, assists employers and workers by providing information and tools for managing occupational safety and health in the context of an ageing workforce, and facilitates the exchange of good practice in this area.

The Healthy Workplaces Good Practice Awards are an important component of each campaign. The competition is organised by EU-OSHA in co-operation with Member States and the Council presidencies of the EU, to recognise outstanding and innovative contributions to workplace safety and health. The Good Practice Awards also serve as a platform for sharing and promoting good practice across Europe.

The campaigns are now the largest of their kind in the world and they can be used as a reference to guide stakeholders in other regions and countries to implement similar campaigns.

Source: https://osha.europa.eu/en/healthy-workplaces-campaigns

Box 3.8. Initiative New Quality of Work (INQA) in Germany

Aim: Improving the quality of work in ways which benefit companies and employees. Launched in 2002 by the German Federal Ministry of Labour and Social Affairs and leading social partners, today INQA brings various actors together which includes Federal and State-level government, business associations, trade unions, the Federal Employment Agency, companies, social insurance providers and foundations.

Tools: collecting good practice examples on job quality at company level; monitoring collective bargaining agreements on shaping quality of work; and increasing the attractiveness of jobs, especially in small companies in rural areas. Furthermore, the initiative is responsible for conducting research and elaborating guidelines and has led to the establishment of local networks for the promotion of age management throughout Germany.

Expert task forces have prepared different INQA memorandum putting forward strong messages, in particular:

- *Prevention is necessary for a longer healthy working life* in the 2012 memorandum entitled "Securing the future through prevention –Strategies for a world of work aligned to demographic change".
- *Skills promotion contributes to improving workplace conditions and boosting a company's capacity for innovation and competitiveness* in the 2016 memorandum entitled "Competence, health and good working conditions – for the future of work".

After more than ten years, the results are proving positive. Many businesses are committed to sound practical solutions and ensuring competitiveness in the context of demographic change, and are making use of the various INQA campaigns and the resources offered by the Initiative for those purposes.

Source: http://www.inqa.de/EN/Home/home.html.

Flexible retirement

Some older workers are not able or willing to continue full-time work at older ages. Inflexible working patterns mean that many of them face a stark choice between full-time work and full-time retirement. Entry into "phased" or "partial retirement may be an option to facilitate a smooth transition into retirement, thereby preventing older workers from quitting work abruptly. This requires modifying inflexible arrangements of pension as indicated in Chapter 1 as well as both employers and employees to become more flexible in terms of retirement and working patterns. According to Graham (2014[51]), flexible approaches to retirement and to part-time work are linked to higher levels of well-being, at least in labour markets where flexible work is a choice. In particular, voluntary part-time workers have more life satisfaction, less stress and are more satisfied with their jobs than full-time workers.

A solution that might benefit both older workers and employers

Given the potential negative effects of job switches among older adults (Chapter 2), extending on-going employee-employer relationships might benefit both employers and employees. However, some older adults might want to continue working for their current employer on different terms than standard full-time jobs. According to surveys in the United States (Collision, 2014[52]), a significant proportion of workers envision a phased transition into retirement during which they will continue working, reduce hours with more leisure time to enjoy life and work in a different capacity that is less demanding and bringing greater personal satisfaction.

A nationally representative survey conducted in 2012 by AARP and the Society for Human Resource Management (SHRM), covering 1 000 adults aged 50 and more who were working or looking for work, illustrated that about one third of older workers consider it very important that their employer offers flexible working time (AARP, 2012[53]). About one fourth also attached great importance to a compressed work schedule, telecommuting and a formal phased retirement programme. The importance of such flexible work arrangements declined somewhat with age: 37% of workers aged 50-59 considered flex time very important, compared with only 27% of workers aged 70 and more. However, these findings may be related to a positive selection bias of more healthier and motivated workers who continue working beyond age 70. Another AARP survey, covering 1 500 adults aged 45-74 who were working or looking for work in 2013, illustrated that 91% of them selected a friendly working environment as an essential part of their ideal job (AARP, 2014[54]).

All in all, in a context of increasing participation of older workers, particularly over age 65, where older workers seem to consider flexible working options very important and employers recognise the need to mitigate potential knowledge loss as older workers retire, phased or partial retirement options seem to be the answer to align both employers and employees' needs. These options refer to a broad range of flexible retirement arrangements, both informal practices and formal workplace policies, which allow employees approaching normal retirement age to reduce the hours worked or work for their employers in a different capacity after retirement. Employers can use phased retirement as a human resource tool not only to retain workers with essential skills or knowledge, but also to tackle skill shortages issues. For instance, in the United States the Manufacturing Institute (MI) is concerned that there is a major shortage of high quality manufacturing educators and an emerging best practice is for older workers to serve as adjunct faculty while continuing to work in a part-time basis. This helps to introduce the future workforce to the most in-demand skills while creating a talent pipeline for the company and the community.

An option still uncommon in many OECD countries

Several countries and sectors have facilitated flexible retirement over the past few years. Good examples are found in Australia where the Transition-To-Retirement Pensions (TRIPs) let workers move from full-time to part-time work and complement their income with the pension. About 20% of Australian workers over 55 have participated in this programme since it was introduced in 2005. EU countries have also implemented flexible retirement schemes but their prevalence varies largely by country (Eurofound, 2016[55]). It was most common in 2012 for people aged 55–69 who are in employment or retired to report having at some point reduced their working hours in a move towards full retirement in the Netherlands (21%), Finland (18%), Belgium and Sweden (both 17%)

while less than 1% do so in Latvia or the Slovak Republic. Flexible retirement may be easier to implement in countries, such as the Netherlands, where a voluntary part-time culture is common.

Low and unequal prevalence of phased retirement in the United States

Phased retirement could be harder to implement in countries where the voluntary part-time culture is less common. In the United States, despite many employers report that they enable employees to reduce their work hours[13], part-time work is less widespread than in many OECD countries (Figure 3.7). In the United States, in 2016, 16% of workers aged 55-64 and 39% of those aged 65 and more worked less than 35 hours per week in their main job. An incidence below the OECD average, despite the definition of part-time employment is less strict in many other countries.

Figure 3.7. Low prevalence of part-time work among older workers in the United States, 2016

Part-time employment of older workers (55-64) as a share of total employment, by age groups

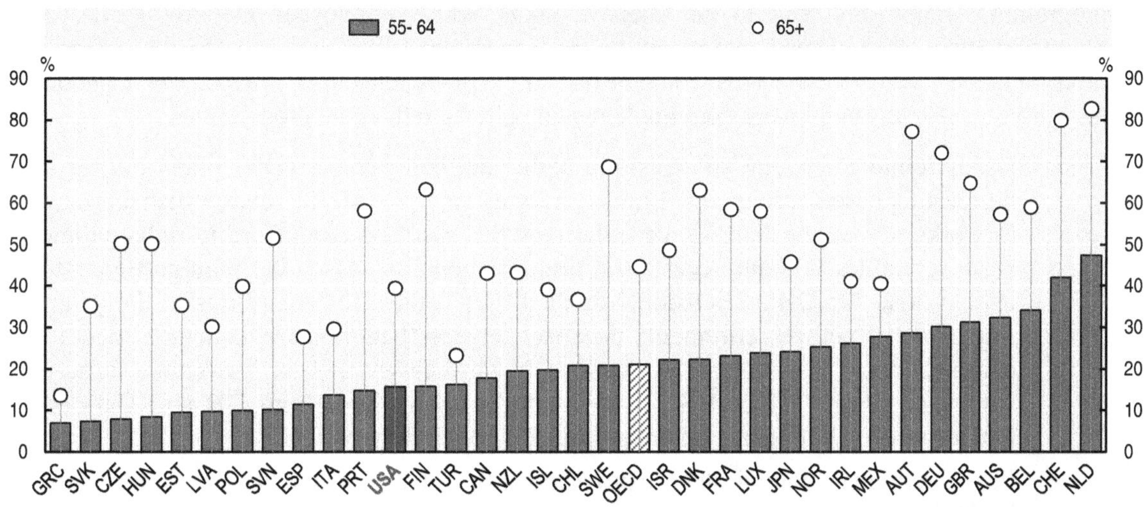

Note: Part-time employment is based on national definitions which is less than 35 hours per week in the United States. The OECD is a weighted average and excludes Korea. For definitions for other countries, see www.oecd.org/els/employmentpoliciesanddata/LFSNOTES_SOURCES.pdf.

Source: OECD dataset on Incidence of full-time part-time employment - national definition, http://stats.oecd.org//Index.aspx?QueryId=9582.

StatLink http://dx.doi.org/10.1787/888933644452

In the United States, very few older workers benefit from phased retirement options and few employers offer them (particularly formal phased retirement programmes). Besides, there is little indication that the prevalence of phased retirement has changed much in recent years, and if nothing changes, these programmes may be unlikely to increase in the near future.

Box 3.9. Main barriers to phased retirement in the United States

From worker's side, while there may be unobserved barriers to a gradual reduction in hours, there are reasons, mainly financial, that explain why more workers may plan to retire gradually than actually do.

- Gradually retiring may have consequences for employer-provided health and pension benefits. For example, in the private sector part-time workers are less likely to be eligible to participate in workplace retirement plans than full-time employees and employers are not required to provide benefits to part-time employees.
- Americans' low savings approaching retirement and a desire to maximise earnings prior to retiring fully.
- Further, many workers retire sooner than they thought they would and therefore may not be able to carry out their plan to reduce work hours leading into retirement.

From the side of the employers, the main barriers come from the potential challenges in complying with various laws and regulations when designing a phased retirement programme. Employers tend to be selective about which employees they offer phased retirement, and those denied enrolment in the programme may sue on grounds of age discrimination. Even if these claims would be difficult to prove, the threat of expensive litigation may discourage many employers from implementing phased retirement programmes.

- Issues relate to receipt of pensions under defined benefit (DB) plans during a period of phased retirement. Employers may not provide in-service distributions to workers younger than 62, yet relatively few workers can afford to reduce their work schedules without access to retirement benefits. Also, DB plan participants usually lose substantial pension wealth if they reduce their earnings in the years immediately before retirement, because pension benefits are generally tied to earnings near the end of the career. Nevertheless, this is becoming largely irrelevant since 11% of US private sector workers have both DB and Defined Contribution (DC) plans and only about 2% rely solely on DB.[14]
- Phased retirement complicates the provision of other types of benefits as well, including health insurance, life insurance, and disability. For example, many employers do not provide benefits to part-time workers, and antidiscrimination rules make it difficult to provide exceptions for older workers. Federal law requires that benefits provided through tax-qualified plans be fairly evenly distributed between highly compensated and lower-paid employees. For formal phased retirement programmes is difficult to meet these standards because most employers gear them toward well-paid workers, who tend to have the specialised skills and knowledge that employers value and who can generally afford to reduce their work schedules. Federal law also prohibits employment discrimination against workers age 40 and older (see Chapter 2).
- There are also logistics barriers. Only some of the industries, due to how their work is structured, are more likely to offer phased retirement. For example, in education it is logistically easier to reduce working hours than in manufacturing.

Source: U.S. Government Accountability Office (2017), *Older Workers: Phased Retirement Programs, Although Uncommon, Provide Flexibility for Workers and Employers*, Washington DC, http://www.gao.gov/products/GAO-17-536; U.S. Department of Labor (2016), *Labor Market and DOL-Funded Employment Assistance for Older Workers Literature Review Report*, IMPAQ International, Washington, DC; and Johnson, R. (2011), "Phased Retirement and Workplace Flexibility for Older Adults", *The ANNALS of the American Academy of Political and Social Science*, Vol. 638/1, pp. 68-85, http://dx.doi.org/10.1177/0002716211413542.

Although there is no nationally representative data on the prevalence of phased retirement in the United States, a 2008 report[15], a more recent report from the U.S. Government Accountability Office (2017[56]) and surveys like the last Employee Benefits Survey of the Society for Human Resource Management (SHRM)[16], indicate that formal phased retirement programmes are relatively uncommon. It is far more common for employers to implement other informal programmes that take the form of reduced work schedules or rehiring retired workers. Why flexible retirement options are not more widespread seems to be related to several barriers from both employers and workers that make difficult the expansion of formal, and even informal, phased retirement programmes (see Box 3.9).

Even in the public sector, these types of programmes have proved to be difficult to implement. In 2014, the Office of Personnel Management (OPM) issued the final regulations on Phased Retirement to permit US federal employees to phase into retirement by shifting from full-time to part-time work and receive partial retirement benefits while continuing to accrue prorated future retirement benefits. In order to take advantage of the phased retirement programme, workers must spend at least 10% of their time mentoring younger workers, thereby ensuring critical knowledge transfer. While the plan is seen as a best practice in encouraging phased retirement, and has the potential to reach 2.5 million government employees, to date very few government agencies have chosen to make it available to their employees resulting in very few workers have signed up for phased retirement.[17]

It is not only the case that few workers gradually retire from their career jobs, but there are also inequalities in access to flexible retirement options on top of all the inequalities that workers experience throughout their working lives. Workers with higher-paying jobs and at the top of the occupational hierarchy have the most access to flexible work options (Golden, 2009[57]). Further, the more secure the worker's status is within an organisation, the more likely they are to use the flexible programmes that are available (McNamara and Williamson, 2013[47]). Finally, large firms offer phased retirement more than small firms as well as employers in certain industries, particularly in industries with technical and professional workforces such as education, government, utilities, consulting, and high-tech companies (U.S. Government Accountability Office, 2017[56]).

Directions for Policy

Older adults in the United States are relatively highly educated, highly skilled and among the most active participants in training in the OECD area. In addition, job quality and working conditions in the United States are above the OECD average and the situation for older workers is better compared with their younger counterparts. However, the United States faces several issues. First, contrary to many OECD countries, educational levels and skills proficiency are not increasing among younger generations in the United States. This might lead to poorer skills proficiency prospects of future generations of older workers relative to other OECD countries. Second, there are large inequalities in access to education and training among older US adults. Finally, there is much room for improvement regarding job quality and working conditions. The United States is far from being among the top OECD performers, flexible work arrangements, in particular to implement phased retirement, are scarce and there are also large inequalities in access to good working conditions among US workers.

Public policies and institutions have an important role to play in helping jobseekers, particularly older adults most in need, by providing income support, assisting with job search or ensuring access to skills development. However, in the United States, income support provided by unemployment benefits is not sufficient to prevent poverty and exclusion, and, despite the large potential of employment and training programmes to help the unemployed, the current level of public investment is low by both international and historical standards, in particular for older jobseekers. Finally, WIOA has been a positive development. It strengthens evaluation and data reporting requirements of programmes and might benefit older workers since now there is data on how they fared compared to other groups. However, it largely leaves the existing system intact.

The following measures can improve the employability of older workers:

- *Take concerted action to boost basic skills of workers throughout their working lives and tackle inequalities accumulated by those with poor basic skills.* Two compelling arguments underline the priority which needs to be attached to action on basic skills – skills matter, and without action, the United States will fall further behind other countries which could harm the prospects of future generations of older workers as well as reinforce the persistence of inequalities at an older age (OECD, 2013[1]).
- *Improve access to employment and training programmes for older jobseekers and the quality of services received.* It is not clear how successfully the federally-funded employment programmes (WIOA) in the United States are meeting the challenge of helping growing cohorts of older jobseekers to find jobs. Despite the improvement in the performance evaluation system under WIOA that might help to increase the number of older workers served, there is a need for a careful evaluation of the impact of employment and training programmes on employment outcomes of older jobseekers, in particular those at risk of long-term unemployment. The evaluation of SCSEP programmes was a first step but it should be expanded to other programmes.
- *Enhance opportunities for phased retirement.* Phased retirement is more common in other OECD countries than in the United States. In the United States, low-paid workers planning to phase into retirement confront financial obstacles. In addition, there are barriers stemming from the difficulty in complying with various laws and regulations that may discourage many employers from implementing phased retirement programmes. More research is needed to help guide policy choices. A first step should be to monitor and analyse the reasons of the very slow deployment of the federal phased retirement programme. Moreover, the United States could learn from existing flexible retirement options in other OECD countries.
- *Encourage and assist employers to enhance working conditions throughout working lives.* In order to foster sustainable work and healthy ageing, the U.S. Department of Labor, in collaboration with OSHA, should seek to promote best practices among employers in terms of preventing poor working conditions. Employer groups themselves should be encouraged to set up websites with information on best practices and tools for employers to assess their own performance as an age-friendly employer. The European Healthy Workplaces campaigns and the Healthy Workplaces Good Practice Awards can serve as an example.
- *Design and implement experience rating programmes* that effectively motivate employers to improve safety and expand the experience rating of workers' compensation insurance to smaller firms. In the absence of such an expansion, OSHA should target its enforcement efforts toward smaller firms.

Notes

1. In the United States, VET is commonly known as Career and Technical Education, or CTE.
2. U.S. Bureau of Labor Statistics (BLS).
3. CollegeBoard, "Trends in College Pricing 2012" (2012).
4. CollegeBoard, "Student Aid 2012 Source Data," available at http://trends.collegeboard.org/sites/default/files/student-aid-2012-source-data_01122013.xls
5. https://doleta.gov/oa/data_statistics.cfm.
6. http://www.npr.org/2014/11/06/361136336/in-south-carolina-a-program-that-makes-apprenticeships-work
7. https://www.dol.gov/newsroom/releases/osec/osec20170811
8. New Zealand Apprenticeships replaced the Modern Apprenticeships programme, which had been designed for 16-21 year-olds.
9. Extended UI benefits are sometimes made available to those who exhaust these UI benefits, as has occurred during the recent recession.
10. This may be an underestimate since some state-funded programmes outside of the federally-funded ones may not be included.
11. http://www.oecd.org/statistics/job-quality.htm
12. https://healthy-workplaces.eu/en/healthy-workplaces-all-ages-e-guide.
13. Transamerica 15th Annual Retirement Survey (2014)
14. https://www.ebri.org/publications/benfaq/index.cfm?fa=retfaq14.
15. See in https://www.transamericacenter.org/retirement-research/global-retirement-survey/the-new-flexible-retirement
16. https://www.shrm.org/hr-today/trends-and-forecasting/research-and-surveys/pages/2017-employee-benefits.aspx.
17. As of August 2016, less than 100 federal employees had signed up for phased retirement. http://federalnewsradio.com/retirement/2016/08/less-100-federal-employees-signed-phased-retirement/

References

AARP (2012), *What Are Older Workers Seeking?: An AARP/SHRM Survey of 50+ Workers*, Washington DC, https://www.aarp.org/content/dam/aarp/research/surveys_statistics/econ/2012/What-Are-Older-Workers-Seeking-An-AARP-SHRM-Survey-of-50-Plus-Workers-AARP.pdf. [53]

AARP (2014), *Staying Ahead of the Curve 2013: the AARP work and career study: older workers in an uneasy job market*, Washington DC, http://www.aarp.org/content/dam/aarp/research/surveys_statistics/general/2014/Staying-Ahead-of-the-Curve-2013-The-Work-and-Career-Study-AARP-res-gen.pdf. [54]

Advisers, C. (2016), *Active Labor Market Policies: Theory and evidence for what works*, https://obamawhitehouse.archives.gov/sites/default/files/page/files/20161220_active_labor_market_policies_issue_brief_cea.pdf. [15]

Albanese, A. and B. Cockx (2015), "Permanent Wage Cost Subsidies for Older Workers. An Effective Tool for Increasing Working Time and Postponing Early Retirement?", *CESifo Working Paper Series*, No. 5301, https://papers.ssrn.com/sol3/papers.cfm?abstract_id=2598003. [26]

Angrisani, M. et al. (2013), "Labor Force Transitions at Older Ages: The Roles of Work Environment and Personality", No. 295, University of Michigan: Michigan Retirement Research Center , Ann Arbor, http://www.mrrc.isr.umich.edu/publications/papers/pdf/wp295.pdf. [44]

Arends, I., C. Prinz and F. Abma (2017), "Job quality, health and at-work productivity", *OECD Social, Employment and Migration Working Papers*, No. 195, OECD Publishing, Paris, http://dx.doi.org/10.1787/43ff6bdc-en. [45]

Böckerman, P. and P. Ilmakunnas (2017), "Do Good Working Conditions Make You Work Longer? Evidence on Retirement Decisions Using Linked Survey and Register Data", *Discussion paper series*, No. 10964, IZA, Bonn, http://ftp.iza.org/dp10964.pdf. [43]

Boockmann, B. et al. (2012), "Do hiring subsidies reduce unemployment among older workers? evidence from natural experiments", *Journal of the European Economic Association*, Vol. 10/4, pp. 735-764, http://dx.doi.org/10.1111/j.1542-4774.2012.01070.x. [27]

Büttner, R. et al. (2008), "Perspektiven auf dem Arbeitsmarkt auch mit 50plus. Ausgewählte Ergebnisse aus der Evaluation des Bundesprogramms Perspektive 50plus für ältere Langzeitarbeitslose, (Perspectives in the labour market also for people aged 50+. Selected results of the evaluation of the Federal Programme 50+)", *IAQ-Report*, No. 2008-3, http://www.iaq.uni-due.de/iaq-report/2008/report2008-03.pdf. [38]

Card, D., J. Kluve and A. Weber (2015), "What Works? A Meta Analysis of Recent Active Labor Market Program Evaluations", *Discussion Paper*, No. 9236, IZA, Bonn, http://ftp.iza.org/dp9236.pdf. [20]

Carnevale, A., J. Strohl and A. Gulish (2015), *Employers' Role in the $1.1 Trillion Postsecondary Education and Training System*. [8]

Collision, C. (2014), *The retirement readiness of three unique generations: Baby boomers, generation X, and millennials*, US: Transamerica Center for Retirement Studies, http://www.transamericacenter.org/docs/defaultsource/resources/center-research/tcrs2014_sr_three_unique_generations.pdf. [52]

Council on Foreign Relations (2016), *No Helping Hand: Federal Worker-Retraining Policy*, http://www.cfr.org/report/no-helping-hand-federal-worker-retraining-policy. [19]

Dauth, C. and O. Toomet (2016), "On Government-Subsidized Training Programs for Older Workers", *LABOUR*, Vol. 30/4, pp. 371-392, http://dx.doi.org/10.1111/labr.12082. [28]

Duell, N. and K. Vogler-Ludwig (2012), *European Employment Observatory EEO Review: Employment policies to promote active ageing. Germany*, European Employment Observatory, Brussels, http://www.economix.org/pdf/EEO%20Review%20Germany-Older%20Workers.pdf. [36]

Dunn, W. (2013), *The US Labour Market Recovery Following the Great Recession*, http://dx.doi.org/10.1787/5k4ddxp3xlvf-en. [30]

DWP (2017), *Fuller Working Lives A Partnership Approach*, Department for Work and Pensions, London, https://www.gov.uk/government/publications/fuller-working-lives-a-partnership-approach. [34]

Employment and Social Development Canada (2014), *Summative Evaluation of the Targeted Initiative for Older Workers*, Ottawa, http://www.esdc.gc.ca/eng/publications/evaluations/skills_and_employment/2014/tiow.shtml. [41]

Eurofound (2016), *Extending working lives through flexible retirement schemes: Partial retirement*, Publications Office of the European Union, Luxembourg, http://dx.doi.org/10.2806/004233. [55]

Eyster, L., R. Johnson and E. Toder (2008), *Current strategies to employ and retain older workers*, The Urban Institute, Washington DC, https://www.urban.org/sites/default/files/publication/31531/411626-Current-Strategies-to-Employ-and-Retain-Older-Workers.PDF. [10]

Golden, L. (2009), "Flexible Daily Work Schedules in U.S. Jobs: Formal Introductions Needed?", *Industrial Relations: A Journal of Economy and Society*, Vol. 48/1, pp. 27-54, http://dx.doi.org/10.1111/j.1468-232X.2008.00544.x. [57]

Graham, C. (2014), "Late-life work and well-being", *IZA World of Labor*, IZA, Bonn, http://dx.doi.org/10.15185/izawol.107. [51]

Heidkamp, M., W. Mabe and B. Degraaf (2012), *The Public Workforce System: Serving Older Job Seekers and the Disability Implications of an Aging Workforce*, The NTAR Leadership Center, https://www.dol.gov/odep/pdf/NTAR_Public_Workforce_System_Report_Final.pdf. [31]

Heinrich, C. (2013), *Targeting Workforce Development Programs: Who Should Receive What Services? And How Much?*, http://umdcipe.org/conferences/WorkforceDevelopment/Papers/Workforce%20Development_Heinrich_Targeting%20Workforce%20Development%20Programs.pdf. [29]

Hicks, P. (2015), "Local economic strategies for ageing labour markets: The Canadian Targeted Initiative for Older Workers in Fort St. James, British Columbia", *OECD Local Economic and Employment Development (LEED) Working Papers*, No. 2015/3, OECD Publishing, Paris, http://dx.doi.org/10.1787/5jrnwqk5d4f7-en. [40]

Immervoll, H. and S. Scarpetta (2012), "Activation and employment support policies in OECD countries. An overview of current approaches", *IZA Journal of Labor Policy*, Vol. 1/1, pp. 9, Bonn, http://dx.doi.org/10.1186/2193-9004-1-9. [22]

Jenkins, J. (2016), *Disrupt Aging: A Bold New Path to Living Your Best Life at Every Age*, NYC-based Public Affairs, Washington DC. [13]

Knuth, M., T. Stegmann and L. Zink (2014), “Die Wirkungen des Bundesprogramms Perspektive 50plus;. Chancen für ältere Langzeitarbeitslose, (Impact of the Federal Programme 50+. Results for the older long-term unemployed)”, *IAQ-Report*, No. 2014-01, Universität Duisburg-Essen, http://www.iaq.uni-due.de/iaq-report/2014/report2014-01.pdf. [37]

Kogan, D. et al. (2012), *Evaluation of the Senior Community Service Employment Program (SCSEP). Process and Outcomes Study: Final Report,*. [32]

Kuczera, M. and S. Field (2013), *A Skills beyond School Review of the United States*, OECD Reviews of Vocational Education and Training, OECD Publishing, Paris, http://dx.doi.org/10.1787/9789264202153-en. [14]

Lechner, M., C. Wunsch and P. Scioch (2013), “Do Firms Benefit from Active Labour Market Policies?”, *IZA DP*, No. 7614, Bonn, http://ftp.iza.org/dp7614.pdf. [21]

Liz, M. et al. (2012), “A Critical Review of Literature on Experience Rating in Workers’ Compensation Systems”, *Policy and Practice in Health and Safety*, Vol. 10/1, pp. 3-25, http://dx.doi.org/10.1080/14774003.2012.11667766. [48]

Maestas, N. et al. (2017), *Working Conditions in the United States: Results of the 2015 American Working Conditions Survey*, RAND Corporation, Santa Monica, CA, http://dx.doi.org/10.7249/RR2014. [46]

Mather, M., L. Jacobsen and K. Pollard (2015), “Aging in the United States”, *Population Bulletin*, No. 2, Population Reference Bureau, http://www.prb.org.. [5]

Mazzonna, F. and F. Peracchi (2017), “Unhealthy Retirement?”, *Journal of Human Resources*, Vol. 52/1, pp. 128-151, http://dx.doi.org/10.3368/jhr.52.1.0914-6627R1. [6]

McNamara, T. and J. Williamson (2013), *Unequal prospects : is working longer the answer?*, Routledge. [47]

Merkurieva, I. (2016), “Late Career Job Loss and the Decision to Retire”, *Discussion Paper Series, Department of Economics*, https://ideas.repec.org/p/san/wpecon/1606.html#cites. [25]

Neuhauser, F., S. Seabury and J. Mendeloff (2013), “Increasing Experience Rating for Small Employers: Would Lowering the Threshold for Experience Rating Improve Safety?”, No. 955, RAND: Center for Health and Safety in the Workplace, https://www.rand.org/content/dam/rand/pubs/working_papers/WR900/WR955/RAND_WR955.pdf. [50]

OECD (2013), *Time for the U.S. to Reskill?: What the Survey of Adult Skills Says*, OECD Skills Studies, OECD Publishing, Paris, http://dx.doi.org/10.1787/9789264204904-en. [1]

OECD (2013), *OECD Skills Outlook 2013 : First Results from the Survey of Adult Skills.*, OECD Publishing, Paris, http://dx.doi.org/10.1787/9789264204256-en. [3]

OECD (2014), *Ageing and Employment Policies: Netherlands 2014: Working Better with Age*, OECD Publishing, Paris, http://dx.doi.org/10.1787/9789264208155-en. [35]

OECD (2015), *OECD Employment Outlook 2015*, OECD Publishing, Paris, http://dx.doi.org/10.1787/empl_outlook-2015-en. [42]

OECD (2015), *Ageing and Employment Policies: Denmark 2015: Working Better with Age*, OECD Publishing, Paris, http://dx.doi.org/10.1787/9789264235335-en. [39]

OECD (2016), “PISA 2015 Results in Focus”, *PISA in Focus*, No. 67, OECD Publishing, Paris, http://dx.doi.org/10.1787/aa9237e6-en. [2]

OECD (2016), *Back to Work, United States : Improving the Re-employment Prospects of dIsplaced Workers*, OECD publishing, Paris, http://dx.doi.org/10.1787/9789264266513-en. [17]

OECD (2017), "United States", in *Education at a Glance 2017: OECD Indicators*, OECD Publishing, Paris, http://dx.doi.org/10.1787/eag-2017-72-en. [7]

OECD (2017), "Preventing Ageing Unequally", in *Preventing Ageing Unequally*, OECD Publishing, Paris, http://dx.doi.org/10.1787/9789264279087-4-en. [16]

OECD (2017), *Educational Opportunity for All: Overcoming Inequality throughout the Life Course*, Educational Research and Innovation, OECD Publishing, Paris, http://dx.doi.org/10.1787/9789264287457-en. [9]

PES-to-PES (2012), *Peer Review on Public Employment Services and Older Workers*, European Commission, Brussels. [33]

Pew Research Center (2015), *Modern Immigration Wave Brings 59 Million to U.S., Driving Population Growth and Change Through 2065: Views of Immigration's Impact on U.S. Society Mixed*, Washington DC, http://www.pewresearch.org. [4]

Rutledge, M. (2014), *How long do unemployed older workers search for a job?*, http://crr.bc.edu/wp-content/uploads/2014/02/IB_14-3-508.pdf, pp. 14-3. [23]

Rutledge, M., S. Sass and J. Ramos-Mercado (2016), *How job options narrow for older workers by socioeconomic status*, Center for Retirement Research at Boston College, http://dlib.bc.edu/islandora/object/bc-ir:107028. [24]

Tompa, E., K. Cullen and C. McLeod (2012), "Update on a systematic literature review on the effectiveness of experience rating", *Policy and Practice in Health and Safety*, Vol. 10/2, pp. 47-65, http://dx.doi.org/10.1080/14774003.2012.11667776. [49]

U.S. Department of Labor (2008), *Report of the taskforce on the aging of the American workforce*, https://www.doleta.gov/reports/FINAL_Taskforce_Report_2_27_08.pdf. [11]

U.S. Government Accountability Office (2011), *Multiple Employment and Training Programs: Providing Information on Colocating Services and Consolidating Administrative Structures Could Promote Efficiencies*, Washington DC, http://www.gao.gov/products/GAO-11-92. [18]

U.S. Government Accountability Office (2017), *Older Workers: Phased Retirement Programs, Although Uncommon, Provide Flexibility for Workers and Employers*, Washington DC, http://www.gao.gov/products/GAO-17-536. [56]

Van Horn, C., K. Krepcio and M. Heidkamp (2015), *Improving Education and Training for Older Workers*, AARP, Washington, DC, https://www.aarp.org/content/dam/aarp/ppi/2015/improving-education-training-older-workers-AARP-ppi.pdf. [12]

ORGANISATION FOR ECONOMIC CO-OPERATION AND DEVELOPMENT

The OECD is a unique forum where governments work together to address the economic, social and environmental challenges of globalisation. The OECD is also at the forefront of efforts to understand and to help governments respond to new developments and concerns, such as corporate governance, the information economy and the challenges of an ageing population. The Organisation provides a setting where governments can compare policy experiences, seek answers to common problems, identify good practice and work to co-ordinate domestic and international policies.

The OECD member countries are: Australia, Austria, Belgium, Canada, Chile, the Czech Republic, Denmark, Estonia, Finland, France, Germany, Greece, Hungary, Iceland, Ireland, Israel, Italy, Japan, Korea, Latvia, Luxembourg, Mexico, the Netherlands, New Zealand, Norway, Poland, Portugal, the Slovak Republic, Slovenia, Spain, Sweden, Switzerland, Turkey, the United Kingdom and the United States. The European Union takes part in the work of the OECD.

OECD Publishing disseminates widely the results of the Organisation's statistics gathering and research on economic, social and environmental issues, as well as the conventions, guidelines and standards agreed by its members.

OECD PUBLISHING, 2, rue André-Pascal, 75775 PARIS CEDEX 16
(81 2016 30 1 P) ISBN 978-92-64-19009-2 – 2018

www.ingramcontent.com/pod-product-compliance
Lightning Source LLC
Chambersburg PA
CBHW061217240926
51846CB00006B/1261